Timothy Paziuk

Professional
CORPORATIONS
The Secret to Success

Blue Beetle
BOOKS

Professional Corporations: The Secret to Success 2nd Edition
Copyright © 2004, 2011 Tim Paziuk

First published in 2004
This edition published 2011
Trade paperback ISBN 978-0-9733307-1-7
Blue Beetle Books Inc.
Box 8120
Victoria, BC, V8W 3R8
www.bluebeetlebooks.com
Tel: 250.704.6686

Inquires regarding requests to reprint all or part of Professional Corporations: The Secret to Success should be addressed to Tim Paziuk at the address below.

TPC Financial Group Limited
760 Hillside Ave.
Victoria, BC, V8T 1Z6
Tel: 250.385.0058
Toll Free: 888.315.0058
Email: info@tpcfinancial.com
www.tpcfinancial.com

It is recommended that legal, accounting and other professional advice is sought before acting on any information contained in this book as each individual's financial circumstances are unique.

The authors, publishers and all others directly or indirectly involved with this book assume no responsibility or liability, direct or indirect, to any party for any loss or damage by errors or omission, regardless of cause, as a consequence of using this book, nor accept any contractual, or other form of liability for such use. The personal services of dedicated professional financial and legal advisors should be sought.

ISBN 978-0-9733307-1-7

Written in collaboration with Mike Wicks
Edited by Karla Dolinsky
Cover design and book layout by Tom Spetter
Custom publishing services provided by Blue Beetle Books Inc.

Printed and bound in Canada by Friesens

For Patti
(more)

Since the first edition of Tim Paziuk's book on the "business of business" for physicians and dentists, he has become a highly sought after speaker at medical conferences across Canada.

This new, and completely revised edition for 2011 includes updated rules, regulations and tax tables for every province and territory in Canada.

Entrepreneurs have to think like business people in order to survive. For professionals, being businesslike may not be vital to survival but it will, without question, help them keep more of what they earn.

Professional Corporations - The Secret to Success explains in simple terms why every professional should probably incorporate, and shows them how they can use their corporation to keep a larger percentage of every dollar they make. This comprehensive, easy-to-read book is an invaluable guide to setting up, buying, running and selling professional corporations.

In this new edition, follow Sven (a doctor from Kamloops) and Lange's (a dentist from Richmond, B.C.) email conversations with Tim as they discuss many of the tax and regulatory issues facing them as they run their practices.

Timothy (Tim) Paziuk is a financial coordinator from Victoria; British Columbia. He is a Chartered Financial Planner, a Certified Financial Planner, a Chartered Life Underwriter and a Chartered Financial Consultant.

Tim has over 30 years' experience working with professional corporations in Canada. He moved to Victoria from Edmonton in 1991 and established TPC The Planning Centre Inc. to provide integrated financial planning to professionals. In 2001 TPC Financial Group Ltd. was founded and in 2003 the two companies merged. TPC Financial Group Ltd. currently operates in Alberta, British Columbia, Ontario, and the Yukon Territory.

Mike Wicks (president of Blue Beetle Books Inc.) is a ghostwriter and authors' guide. He works with experts to help conceptualize and structure their publications, and tune their words.

Table of Contents

Acknowledgements

I set a goal in my life to write a book – this is it. When I think back to how I got here, I'm reminded of all the people who helped me along the way, some knowingly, some unwittingly. I would like to acknowledge those people.

First to Patti, my wife, who believed I could do it and gave me the time and encouragement to persevere in writing Professional Corporations and then to write this revised and expanded edition. I have always wanted to give a talk entitled "Home Field Advantage," based on my belief that it's infinitely easier to accomplish great things when the important people in your life are backing you. Not once did I hear Patti utter a discouraging word. She kept me focused on the task at hand, evenings, weekends, even on holidays. Writing wasn't all consuming but it did divert my attention, albeit temporarily, away from our relationship. Thank you for your belief and patience and know that I'll always love you for it.

To my father who taught me that what you do is more important than what you have. Life at home, when I was growing up was a little different; my father worked during the day (and often at night) and then on weekends he was heavily involved in the military or Knights of Columbus. I never really appreciated what he did until I was old enough to go with him. At thirteen I joined the army cadets to be with him. At eighteen I joined his service club. During our time together I discovered that regardless of your socio-economic lot in life, in the end you are judged by what you do. If I could give my dad an award, it would be for lifetime achievement as a father, grandfather and for community service. Thanks, Dad.

To my mother who taught me it's not how smart you are but how you treat others. My mom was a classic stay-at-home mom. With Dad absent a lot of the time, Mom and I spent most of our time alone together. She is the wisest person I've ever known. Mom's philosophy is simple: treat others with compassion, believe the best of everyone, and always have an extra setting at the table. I always do, Mom. Thank you.

To Fiona Hunter for the inspiration. Fiona is the best trust and wills lawyer I've ever had the pleasure of working with. Because of her I had the idea of writing this book. In my conference room I have three reference books; Fiona has written two of them. When asked by clients for a referral I always point to those books and say, "You should use Fiona Hunter; she's the best there is. She's the one who wrote the book."

To Stewart Johnston for his input. Stewart is sincere and straightforward and another lawyer who I call upon frequently for a variety of things. He's quick to respond and has always been helpful. Stewart, thank you for allowing me to call on you with my "quick questions."

To my big brother Brian who taught me that dedication and hard work can take you to the top; I've enjoyed watching him excel in his career. He had many jobs as a young man before starting with the City of Edmonton Fire Department and for the last twenty-five years has been a keen student in his field. He never stops learning. In my opinion, there are few, if any, more dedicated and committed to excellence. Thank you, Brian, for being such an incredible role model.

To Dr. David Christie for his endless support and insight. I owe so many things to Dave and his wife, Sue. The most important thing I have to thank them for is for introducing me to Patti. Professionally, Dave was my first client in Victoria. He wasn't incorporated at the time and was frustrated about how things were going. He listened to what I was doing and asked me to take charge of making things work for him. I did. Dave, Sue, you often thank me for taking care of you, but it is I who thank you for your belief and trust in me.

To Grant McNeill for his input and belief in the project. I'm a financial planner, not an accountant. Grant is a chartered accountant and a great friend. When I mentioned to him that I was planning on writing a book on the subject, Grant's response was "Great idea. I don't know anyone who knows more about it than you." With those words I started this project. Grant gave up numerous Wednesday nights and often met me over breakfast to discuss various topics and tax issues. Thank you, Grant, for your help and friendship. Without you I wouldn't have had the confidence to write this book.

To Dr. Wayne MacNicol and Dr. Judith Hooker for agreeing to be on the cover. I didn't want to use actors or models; I wanted a real physician and a real dentist. Wayne practices medicine in Whitehorse and Judith practices dentistry in Victoria. I should thank their spouses, too, Arlene for Wayne's appearance and Bob for Judith's appearance. I know both of you encouraged their participation. Thanks, Wayne and Judith, for supporting the book and the author.

To Mike Wicks and his team at Blue Beetle Books. Without Mike there would be no book. I had an idea, Mike had the tools to take my vision and make it a reality. Your professionalism, dedication and patience are greatly appreciated. Thank you, Mike, Tom and Karla.

To Bill Dyer and Glen Humaniuk, my mentors. I met them both in 1979 when I began my career. Bill introduced himself the first day and offered his guidance. Glen became a friend over the years and pushed me to excel. Bill, Glen, thank you for the great examples you set.

To Ken Aberg, my creator, not in the biblical sense but in a career sense. He took a chance and hired me. Ken, thank you for the opportunity.

I would like to thank Bill Scott for his help with the technical aspects of this book and for being brave enough to leave accounting and come and work with me.

Thanks to Adam Neal for helping me update Internet information in the book.

To my sister Gail for her help over the last 20 years. You helped me raise two great kids and allowed me the time to develop my career. Thanks for all your love and support.

To Justin and Brittany, my children. I hope this proves I was doing my homework when I told you I was! Thank you for sticking with me and being patient. I gave up time with you to work on this book and I'll always be proud of the way you handled my lack of presence. I love you both.

Tim Paziuk
Revised January 2011

FOREWORD

It's been seven years since Tim Paziuk wrote Professional Corporations and it has changed his life as a financial advisor forever. He has become known nationally for his insight and unique approach to the financial well being of doctors and dentists in Canada, especially those who are new graduates, or recent immigrants.

As the new guru in this field Tim is constantly asked to speak at conferences and to associations across Canada.

Over the last seven years he has spoken at the Pacific Dental and International Dental Conferences more than once. He's addressed the faculties of dentistry at University of British Columbia, University of Saskatchewan and Dalhousie University, as well as at the Continuing Education University of British Columbia, McMaster University, St. Joseph Hospital, the Canadian Ophthalmology Society, Advocis of Vancouver, and the Ontario Anesthesiology Association

Tim has delivered seminars and consulted in cities across Canada including: Toronto, Vancouver, Victoria, Burlington, Halifax, Edmonton, Whitehorse, Saskatoon, Whistler and Hamilton and has also spoken to numerous medical and dental study groups. He was the subject of a feature article in the National Post by Jonathan Chevreau, and was interviewed on video for the Wealthy Boomer (Chevreau's Financial Post blog). He has also been recognized twice by Advisors Edge magazine as one of Canada's best financial planners.

His newfound fame has resulted in an onslaught of e-mails from physicians and dentists who have been either misinformed, or not informed at all, about their financial situation, and he enjoys the challenging questions they pose to him.

The British Columbia Securities Commission has authorized Tim to offer fee-for-service financial planning, allowing him to provide the holistic approach to planning that is the foundation of his philosophy. Working as a professional coordinator, he now helps dozens of clients across Canada (mostly medical practitioners) keep more of what they earn.

It has been my pleasure to work with him on this book; he is a true professional.

Michael Wicks
January 2011

What is a Professional Coordinator?

A professional coordinator is an individual who coordinates the many professionals on your team. A parallel position in a major corporation would be the chief operating officer. When you set up your professional corporation you hired a lawyer, accountant and banker and you probably now work with an insurance broker, investment advisor and maybe a financial planner and bookkeeper. To liaise effectively with all these people you have to understand what each should know and whether they actually know what they're doing. A professional coordinator will fill that role for you and make sure that everything, and everybody is working in your best interests.

Why I Wrote This Book

The following story is typical of how a professional medical practitioner, even while receiving advice from a professional financial advisor, can end up paying hundreds of thousands of dollars more to the Canada Revenue Agency (CRA) than is necessary. It's the reason I decided to write this book and the reason you should read it.

Dr. Durrant was 58 years old when I first met him. He had moved to British Columbia from Alberta 10 years before. Over the years he and his wife had become close friends with both their lawyer and their accountant in Alberta, and out of loyalty continued to use them when they transplanted themselves to B.C.

The Durrant's enjoyed an extremely good income and were helping four children with post-secondary education whilst supporting Mrs. Durrant's father and disabled sister.

They paid a great deal of tax and were frustrated that they never seemed to get ahead financially. They believed their situation was hopeless and that no one could help them.

This assessment would have been reasonable had they still been in Alberta. However, at the time of their move, their Alberta advisors had overlooked the jurisdictional differences between that province and their new home province of B.C. In reality, there was a great deal they could do to improve their financial situation. The first step, however, was to accept that they might not have been given the best advice by their well-meaning advisors in Alberta.

I met Dr. Durrant after a client of mine introduced us. It had taken him many years to persuade his friend that someone else just might be able to help with his financial situation. During our first meeting I told him that all I could do was assess his current situation and determine whether he had indeed been given the best advice possible, or whether there was something more that could be done to ease the financial pressures he and his wife were facing.

After our initial discussion a follow up meeting was arranged where we discussed financial planning and the need to look at their legal and financial situation as a whole. Finally, enough trust was established that the doctor and his wife felt comfortable allowing me to prepare a comprehensive report on the couple's financial situation. This would determine whether or not the current strategy was the most effective one.

The report showed that the couple owned three properties and had total assets of $1,250,000, of which $600,000 was in registered retirement savings plans (RRSPs). Their debt amounted to $675,000, giving them a net worth of $575,000.

Their objectives were well defined but difficult for them to realize. Dr. Durrant ran his practice as a professional corporation and felt he was going through life on a treadmill. He worked long hours to maintain his standard of living and was finding it very stressful. Retirement seemed a long way off and he was starting to doubt that he would ever be in a position to stop working. Because they were supporting so many family members, the couple needed $240,000, after taxes, annually. Their annual retirement income goal was $72,000, once their children had completed their schooling and their other family responsibilities had diminished.

Our discussions centered on a few key objectives and then gradually widened to include many other aspects of their lives. The bottom line was that Dr. Durrant wanted to be able to retire debt free at age sixty-five. However, his present stress levels were a concern for both him and his wife and neither felt that he could continue at his present pace until retirement. Mrs. Durrant also worried how the family would manage if her husband became ill, disabled or died.

I discovered that the couple supported four adult children in one form or another. The financial support of Mrs. Durrant's father and disabled sister amounted to $5,000 a month, which was taken from Dr. Durrant's professional corporation and taxed in his hands. Paying taxes was a big problem for the couple. In the previous year, the Professional Corporation was stripped of all cash to pay approximately $165,000 in personal income tax, and they were concerned that this might become a standard rather than a one-off occurrence.

At this point I helped the couple establish their priorities. First, they wanted to regularize their tax situation. Second, they wanted to help family members who required assistance while at the same time maintaining their current lifestyle.

They jointly owned two properties with family members and wanted to be assured that they would not lose money as a result of unforeseen circumstances. They also wanted to minimize their future tax liability on these properties. One property was a cottage owned with Dr. Durrant's sister. They wanted to ensure that this cottage stayed in the family even after their deaths. The second property was Dr. Durrant's mother's principal residence over which there were some concerns regarding ownership and tax liabilities.

Finally, the couple wanted to maximize their after-tax cash flow and felt their current bankers were not assisting them with this goal.

We divided their objectives into four categories:

- risk management
- legal issues
- cash flow and investments
- taxation.

I worked through each issue with their accountant, lawyer, banker, investment advisor, and insurance agent. It became apparent that by not changing their corporate structure when they moved to a new jurisdiction they were overpaying the CRA by approximately $50,000 a year.

As I helped them move toward their financial objectives I began to wonder how they came to be in such a complicated situation. Why hadn't their lawyer or accountant advised them to change their corporate structure when they moved to British Columbia? Would the situation have been any different if they had moved to Ontario? I concluded that the reason they were not given better advice was simply because lawyers and accountants are not always aware of these important jurisdictional differences.

As a professional, you are dependent on the advice of others. You've studied long and hard to be able to practice your profession. You're probably not well versed in law, accounting, tax, risk management, or investing. You could be, but you're probably more interested in having a life away from your practice. You hire others for these jobs, but do they really know what's in your best interests? The Durrant's story made me realize that all advisors are not created equally.

This brings me back to why I wrote this book; it's designed to give you information about professional corporations, how they are set up, managed and maximized. Not everything mentioned in this book is applicable to everyone; however, it will give you enough information to ask the right questions of your existing advisors.

I begin with the initial incorporation of a practice and follow through to selling the practice, estate planning, and discuss planning for retirement. If you have questions feel free to e-mail me at tim@tpcfinancial.com. I'll try to respond to all questions and will post answers on my web site at www. tpcfinancial.com.

Tim Paziuk

Introduction

After working with professional people for over 30 years I have come to the conclusion that they fall into two basic categories: those who are simply in business by default and those who are business people. I can assure you that most professionals are just in business by default. If you have trouble differentiating between the two, it reinforces my conclusion that the majority of professionals are in business by default.

Think back, there you were, on graduation day, ready to start practicing your craft. Regardless of which faculty you were in, your training ensured that you could competently earn a living dealing with the public. In most cases the first step wasn't to go out and incorporate a business, but rather to begin building your practice. Over time you may have been introduced to the idea of incorporating your practice, and regardless of whether you did or not, you were making money by practicing what you were taught. You were, de facto, running a business.

The thing is, if you don't incorporate you are deemed a "sole proprietor." You have employees, loans, taxes, and responsibilities, and your life centres on treating patients. You're running a business, it's just not an incorporated business.

Does incorporating your business automatically make you a businessperson? Probably not. Why? Because your primary focus will continue to be earning money through practicing your profession, treating patients, and (usually for tax purposes) you just happen to be incorporated.

Here's a test. When someone asks you what you do for a living, how do you respond? Do you tell them, "I'm a dentist," or "I'm a physician"? Or, do you tell them that you are a businessperson who happens to be a dentist or physician?

Think about the most financially successful people you know. Chances are they are business people. The reason is simple. Our free enterprise system is designed to encourage economic growth. The drivers behind economic growth are businesses, incorporated businesses.

Owners of companies have to think, and act, like business people in order to survive. Professionals don't have to think like business people in order to survive; however, they do have to act like business people in order to maximize their efforts and income.

Professional Corporations will help you understand the benefits and applications of an incorporated business. Remember, a professional corporation is an incorporated business. Understanding how to use it properly and making it work for you is the key to a secure financial future.

If you were working for a large company you'd have a big safety net. Most large corporations have management teams, personnel departments, payroll departments, lawyers, accountants, purchasing agents, computer technicians, and boards of directors. They have employee benefits including pensions, medical coverage, dental plans, life insurance, and disability insurance, and maybe stock option plans, share purchase plans, and employee profit-sharing plans.

Now let's look at your situation, as a professional you've decided to go it alone, forgoing the corporate safety net. As an incorporated professional you've assumed the responsibility of practitioner and business owner. In order to ensure success during your business lifetime you should strive to maximize your corporate ability by retaining the best possible advisors to act as your corporate departments. But, you must never assume that everyone you're working with now or in the future knows everything that can help you.

The various sections of this book are designed to make you aware of things you may be able to do to save you money, maximize your financial opportunities, and ensure a financially secure and safe retirement. Being informed about the choices open to you will enable you to ask your advisors the right questions. Regardless of the profession, whether it is law, banking, insurance, or investment management there are exceptional practitioners and merely good ones. You deserve to work with the exceptional ones. This book will give you the power to know the difference.

————◆◆◆————

It is quite amazing how we suddenly become aware of things that we pay attention to; for instance, after making the decision to purchase a specific new vehicle we start to see that make and model everywhere. Of course, they were always there we just didn't notice them. It's the same when someone mentions our name. No matter how crowded or noisy it is, nor how engrossed we are in a conversation, we immediately take notice.

So, it was a few years ago when I was stuck at Heathrow Airport. The fog had socked in the airport; looking out at the runways was an exercise in frustration and futility, the yellowish glare reflecting back into the terminal had a sickly feel to it. The departure boards were flashing the word 'delayed' on every line and the terminal was getting increasingly full as people arrived, but nobody left. Schedules across Europe were in turmoil and no one was going anywhere fast.

For my part, I'd found a small haven in the form of a booth at Caffè Italia where I was lingering over my breakfast and drinking my third cup of coffee, reluctant to give up my sanctuary. I was trying to get home to Victoria from a conference in London and was starting to fear that I may never see home again. It was then that a conversation between a young Asian woman and a young family caught my attention. It was the words and phrases; doctor, dentist, setting up practice, and incorporating as a business that called to me just as if I was overhearing my name being spoken at a party. I don't often eavesdrop, but I'm a financial coordinator and over the last seven years I have devoted myself almost exclusively to helping doctors and dentists keep more of what they earn. Looking back, the serendipity of the situation amazes me; my successful book Professional Corporations: The Secret to Success, was due for a complete overhaul and I was just about to start writing the new edition, and here were two professionals discussing exactly the kind of concerns my book addresses.

Over the time it took for me to slowly drink my fourth cup of coffee I learned that the family were South African and heading to Canada where the husband was to set up practice in Dawson Creek, northern BC, under the Family Physicians for B.C. program. They were returning from visiting family in England before commencing their new life. The young woman was also returning to Canada, from a year travelling. She had graduated as a dentist from the University of Toronto, where she received her Doctor of Dental Surgery after writing and passing her National Dental Examination Board examination. She had also completed the dental residency program at Mount Sinai hospital in Toronto and was ready to start practicing as a dentist in Canada. As such, she had a lot in common with her new physician friend; they were both starting new careers and were concerned about setting up their practices, both in terms of medical practices and as businesses.

By this time I was itching to enter the conversation.

⸺•◆•⸺

The young Asian woman looked across at me in a somewhat challenging manner; so there I was caught red-handed, or at least red-eared, eavesdropping. I smiled and said, "Excuse me, but I couldn't help overhearing that you are health professionals and discussing the pro's and con's of incorporating your practices. It's just that that's my profession, and I'm the author of a book about just that subject." Once they realized that I was not some creep being nosy they smiled and invited me to join them. The doctor's name was Sven, and he introduced me to his wife Yolanda, and their children Peter and Henrik; the young woman then reached across the table and announced, "I'm Lange", which sounded like to me like 'Lornjay'.

The table I had deserted was quickly filled with four long-suffering travelers; it felt like I had jumped ship and was now hanging on for dear life to someone else's life raft. I insisted on buying everyone beverages and added several pastries to the order, so that we wouldn't be encouraged to vacate our prime piece of real estate.

Over the course of the next hour or so I learned that Lange was setting up her dental practice in the city of Richmond, B.C., just outside Vancouver and Sven and Yolanda were filled with doubts about whether they had made the right decision to come to Canada. Chief amongst their concerns was their lack of knowledge of how to run a practice and the mass of jurisdictional, provincial and federal rules and regulations they were going to have to navigate.

I told them a little about my history, how I got to where I was in my career, the fact that I specialize in working with health professionals and the very different approach to financial planning I advocated. It was a pleasure to see young people in the early stages of their careers so keen to start out correctly, to do things the right way from the outset. I saw them as blank canvasses. By this time the children were getting bored and fidgety and the server was hovering, waiting to seat the ever-growing lineup of people waiting for tables. I gave my new friends my business card and told them that I would be happy to carry on our conversations online and answer any questions they had about setting up a professional corporation.

We left the restaurant and re-entered the chaos of terminal three, for the interminable wait for our flights.

***

Now, years later, they are valued clients and friends. During the writing of the new edition of this book I realized that many of the questions they had emailed me over the ensuing years are worth sharing. The value lies in the fact that this communication offers an insight into real concerns faced by professionals as they go about running their businesses.

Please note that the messages that are featured throughout this book are not in chronological order; I have placed them in the chapters according to the subject matter they discuss. Having said that, here is the very first message I received from Sven.

Re: Heathrow Chance Meeting

From: Sven Hansen

To: tim@tpcfinancial.com

Hi Tim

It was so great to meet you at Heathrow airport the day that the 'Jack the Ripper' fog closed it down. What a journey that was, it took us two days to get to Toronto to begin the first stage of our Canadian adventure. I'm now in Dawson Creek and setting up my practice. I hope you don't mind me taking you up on your kind offer of answering a few questions.

By the way, Yolanda and the boys say hi; you were a big hit with Peter and Henrik as soon as those cinnamon buns arrived!

Anyway, my question is: can you tell me what the benefits are to incorporating my practice? I thought it was a good idea but my accountant says I shouldn't even think about it until I am earning enough to be able to leave money in the company.

Best wishes

Sven

Re: Re: Heathrow Chance Meeting

From: tim@tpcfinancial.com

To: Sven Hansen

Hi Sven

It's good to hear from you; I'm glad you made it to Canada and more specifically to Dawson Creek. How's northern BC treating you?

Of course, I'm more than happy to answer any questions you have. I'm really glad you came to me with this specific question, as this is a very common misconception held by many accountants.

He or she is correct in that leaving money in a company is a major benefit of having a corporation, but it's by no means the only benefit.

Some of the other benefits of incorporating a practice are access to the small business tax rates, access to the enhanced capital gains deduction, the option to drop out of the Canada Pension Plan, among others. But for you, potentially the most beneficial reason to consider incorporation is income splitting.

If Yolanda has little or no income, especially while she is staying at home to look after Peter and Henrik, you can use your professional corporation to income split even if you take all the money out of your company. Income splitting reduces your overall household tax payable, leaving you personally with more money.

So, bottom line, go ahead and incorporate! And, feel free to ask more questions. You have a wonderful family and I would very much like to help you succeed in Canada. Give Yolanda and the boys my very best wishes.

Tim

P.S. Have you heard from Lange lately?

CHAPTER ONE

The Professional Corporation

This book is primarily for dentists and physicians because of their unique situation; however, the majority of the information is applicable to many other professions. Because each individual's circumstances are different, legal and accounting experts in your particular jurisdiction should confirm all recommendations in this book, prior to implementation. Although every effort has been made to ensure accuracy, changing laws and rules make it impossible to be completely current in all cases.

Please note that each province and territory has its own rules and regulations, both in terms of governments and professional associations. Throughout this book I use various provinces as examples – if you are practicing in a different jurisdiction to those mentioned it is very important that you check the rules and regulations pertaining to your specific locality.

What Is It?

A professional corporation is a separate legal entity and differs from a normal corporation, in that it is obliged to follow a very rigid set of rules as defined by various medical and dental colleges and associations across Canada. It is also different in that it does not provide the shareholder(s) and director(s) protection from creditors. It can, however, enter into contracts and own property in its own name, separately and distinctly from its owner. Because it is a separate legal entity it is required to file its own tax return.

Who Should Incorporate?

When I moved to Vancouver Island in 1991, I met a dentist in Victoria. He had been working for about 12 years and had established a thriving practice. I asked him if he was incorporated and he told me that he wasn't because his accountant had said that until he could afford to leave some money in the company there was no benefit to incorporating.

After reviewing his situation I began to wonder if the reason he didn't have any money left was because he was spending it all, or whether it was because he was paying too much tax. I spoke to his accountant and was told that their firm had a policy of not incorporating professionals, period. Individual circumstances were never considered.

This odd policy was confirmed some time later when I had cause to represent another dentist who was using the same accounting firm. Although he was with a different accountant in the firm, the same rule of thumb was used.

This was one of my first run-ins with "rules of thumb," which I like to call ROT. These so-called rules are akin to old wives' tales but they are relayed through the financial world rather than around a kitchen table. They may contain a grain of truth but that grain is lacking content. Throughout this book you will find these rules of thumb discussed, and subsequently "busted."

After reviewing these dentists' individual circumstances with another accountant, it was clear that both would benefit from incorporation. They have since moved on to more proactive accountants and have incorporated their practices.

All professionals should probably incorporate at some point, in order to reduce their overall tax burden and maximize the financial potential of their practices. Very few are ineligible to incorporate. An example of someone who can't incorporate is a physician who is a salaried employee of a laboratory. If you have an employee-employer relationship at your place of employment you probably can't incorporate.

Why Incorporate?

In simple terms, it's the difference between an 85-cent dollar and a 55-cent dollar. It's the difference between being able to choose which government programs you want to access and which ones you want to establish yourself. It's about being able to legally split income. It's about choices.

Individuals in Canada are taxed on their worldwide income, and tax rates federally are applied to all provinces and territories. The current federal tax rates range from 15 to 29 per cent depending on the amount of taxable income. Provincial and territorial rates range from about 4.0 to 17.5 per cent. On a combined basis the tax payable by individuals ranges from 19.0 to 46.5 per cent.

Compare this to corporate tax rates; on the first $500,000 of "active business income" the tax rates range, on a combined federal and provincial/territorial basis, from about 12 to 19 per cent.

If you earn $150,000 and pay tax as an individual you would pay about $54,000 in income tax. That would leave you $96,000 for paying personal bills and for investment. Let's now assume that you're incorporated and earn $150,000; if you left it all in the corporation you would pay about $27,000 in income tax leaving $123,000. Now, obviously you can't keep all $123,000 in the professional corporation because you need the money personally to pay bills. But don't worry, in chapter 7 we'll look at how you move money in and out of a professional corporation, but until then just bear in mind that there is more money available because you initially paid less tax.

The *Income Tax Act* of Canada is highly complex. It basically tells us what we can and can't do. The majority of it deals with corporations and you, as the owner of a corporation, can make many of the Canada Revenue Agency's (CRA) rules work in your favour, if you know what you are doing. The thing to remember is that companies have more opportunities to be creative within the CRA's rules than individuals.

The government continually introduces laws and regulations that affect the economy of the country. The majority of the fiscal laws relate to corporations. As a professional corporation you can benefit from many of these laws. An example of this is the capital gains deduction.

The taxation of capital gains came into law on January 1, 1972. So until that time, capital gains (the increase in value of capital assets such as land, building, stocks) were tax-free. In 1985 the federal government further introduced into the *Income Tax Act* the capital gains deduction. In an attempt to stimulate investment in the capital markets in 1985, it was decided that every Canadian would be allowed $20,000 of capital gains tax-free, increasing to $50,000 in 1986, and then $100,000 in 1987. This deduction was supposed to increase to $500,000 in 1990, but as you will see its popularity was its downfall.

This deduction extended to every man, woman and child. Immediately people began moving assets around in order to trigger the sale (and ultimately the capital gain) and apply the deduction against existing assets; for example a husband would transfer some of the shares in his company to his spouse and elect to move them at Fair Market Value (FMV).

This maneuver would increase the cost base of the wife's shares and eliminate the current tax liability. Only future increases in value would have tax implications. This applied to any asset that had a capital gain. Suppose you purchased a rental property for $100,000 in 1980 and it increased in value to $120,000 by 1985. If you sold it you would have a capital gain of $20,000. When the capital gains deduction came in, if you transferred it to your spouse at FMV they would have a cost base of $120,000. The amount of the capital gain would be the difference between the cost base and FMV. If after you transferred the property to your spouse they sold it immediately for $120,000, the gain would be zero resulting in no tax payable.

In 1987, in an effort to curb this activity, the government changed the law and froze the limit of capital gains to $100,000. They also divided capital gains into two categories: the sale of personal assets and the sale of shares of certain privately held businesses and farms. Certain private business owners and farmers were allowed to maintain the $500,000 limit while most individuals were limited to $100,000. Individuals continued to apply the $100,000 to their cottages and rental property, by transferring ownership, or sale, until 1992 when the government changed the law and disallowed the capital gains deduction on "real property."

Seeing this gift disappear on real property caused even more people to rearrange their affairs, by transfer or sale, to capture this deduction. This again changed in 1994, when a federal law was passed removing the capital gains deduction from everything except shares of a qualifying privately held Canadian corporation, and qualifying farm property.

The current limit now stands at $750,000 and is applicable on the shares of a properly designed professional corporation. (As a side note, it's interesting that the government came up with an idea to try to stimulate the economy and discovered that people simply moved their existing assets around without making any new investments at all.)

So what do we learn from this history lesson? As tax laws are introduced, you should be positioned in such a way as to take advantage of new opportunities. As you read further, this book will help you recognize these opportunities.

There are few professionals who shouldn't incorporate, but in some cases it isn't the best course of action. For instance, I recently met a physician who was thinking about incorporating. When I asked her what her plans were, she told me that she was probably going back to school within a year and wasn't sure where she would be after that. It didn't make sense for her to incorporate until she knew what she was going to do because if she incurred the costs of incorporation now, not only would she have to maintain the corporation while she was in school, but she could find herself having to dissolve it if she moved to a new jurisdiction with different rules, including the United States.

If you are an American citizen practicing in Canada, you probably shouldn't incorporate because of the extensive filing requirements for US citizens controlling foreign corporations. Although the US Internal Revenue Code does not require the inclusion, in US personal tax returns, of amounts earned by a corporation engaged in an active business, or personal services business, wholly within a foreign country (such as Canada), if the Canadian corporation earns passive income through rents, dividends or interest, and through services rendered outside of Canada, the US citizen must include annually the pro-rated share of the distributable income earned by the controlled foreign corporation.

Most corporations protect their shareholders by limiting the liability to the assets of the company. In the event of bankruptcy or litigation, creditors are usually limited to the company's value. Most professional corporations do not provide the same protection. In order to set up a professional corporation you must first get approval from your association that requires you to sign a waiver which states you will not be limited to corporate assets in the event of liability. This means that all assets are exposed. The fact is, whether you are incorporated or not, you are in the same position – exposed. It does, however, give rise to another situation.

I have a number of married clients who are both in the same profession, such as a couple who are both emergency physicians. They were wondering if they could both be in the same professional corporation. The short answer is yes, but the bigger question is whether the benefits outweigh the risks.

Having both of them in the same professional corporation would reduce the annual costs related to running two corporations; however, what additional exposure is created? Like most couples they have acquired their assets in joint names. This means that their assets are combined. If they are both in the same professional corporation, all their corporate and personal assets are on the line. By having two separate professional corporations, if one of them is sued (and assuming there is not adequate liability coverage) the assets of the other professional corporation are protected.

The other significant advantage of maintaining two professional corporations is the ability to take advantage of the small business tax rate. By maintaining two separate professional corporations, each professional would be allowed $500,000[1] of small business income in 2010. This effectively means they could each leave a total of up to $500,000 of earned income in their professional corporations and have it taxed at the low corporate rate.

A quick review of the following table will give you an idea of the pros and cons of setting up a professional corporation.

Pro	Con
Access to Capital Gains Deduction (if qualifying)	Capital gains deduction not available to all professional corporations[2]
Access to small business tax rates	Additional cost
Can opt out of the Canada Pension Plan	Can be difficult to value
Easier to split income	Must follow stricter rules
Tax deferral	Losses can be trapped inside the corporation[3]
Continued existence	Potential for double taxation

---

1 Except in Manitoba, Nova Scotia and the Yukon, which are still at $400,000.
2 The capital gains deduction does not provide any benefit if the practice can't be sold (e.g. shares of a medical practice; there just isn't a market).
3 Any business that is not operating at a break-even point should not incorporate from a tax point of view. A loss earned in a corporation cannot be transferred to its shareholders. Losses that arise in a corporation can only be offset against earnings in that corporation.

What Are "Associated Companies"?

There are many things to be concerned about in relation to incorporating. When you're working in a group situation make sure you don't run into a problem with the associated company rules.

Definition: Companies can be associated, for tax purposes, where the same person, or group of individuals controls two or more companies directly, or indirectly.

When one Canadian-controlled private corporation is associated with other Canadian-controlled private corporations, these corporations must be treated as a group when applying the small business deduction on active business income.

For example, if you have a professional corporation and are the only shareholder, (as in diagram one on page 56) and you have an interest in another incorporated business in which you are a 50 per cent shareholder with your spouse, the professional corporation and the other company are associated for tax purposes and the two companies will only be able to claim the lower corporate tax rate on $500,000 between them. This situation can arise when there are two professionals in the same family. Each may have separate professional corporations, which are both eligible for the entire small business deduction if they are not associated.

However, companies can be associated in less obvious ways. One little-known tax trap can be found in a family trust. For example, if two members of a family are both incorporated professionals, and one of them decides to set up a family trust, and one of the beneficiaries of that trust happens to be a minor child of theirs, their professional corporations are associated on a de facto basis because parents of minor children are deemed to be 100 per cent owners of the trust property. If the trust assets are the shares of a professional corporation, then each parent is deemed to own 100 per cent of those shares. In the case above, even though each parent had their own professional corporation, they became associated for tax purposes by way of the family trust. Since it is the small business deduction along with the small business abatement that reduces tax rates to about 18 per cent on the first $500,000 of active business income, sharing it with other corporations can seriously diminish its tax efficiency.

In order to provide tax support to small businesses, a small business deduction is provided to Canadian-controlled private corporations on their active business income (up to specific income thresholds). For federal tax purposes, the small business deduction reduces the basic federal corporate income tax rate to approximately 13 per cent for the first $500,000 of active business income of Canadian-controlled private corporations. For provincial purposes most provinces and territories have increased their small business income limits over the past few years to provide further tax breaks for small businesses. The federal tax abatement is equal to 10 per cent of taxable income earned in the year in a Canadian province or territory, less exempt income.

Being married is not the only way that companies can be associated. If you have more than one professional working in the same place and sharing staff, and other practice-related costs, you could find yourself associated. This is because the CRA can argue you are carrying on a business as a professional partnership. It's very important that you understand the potential danger of this situation. Don't assume that your accountant or lawyer can give you a definitive answer. Ask them to check on your behalf and then write you a letter stating that they have reviewed the structure and are advising you that you do not have an "associated" companies issue.

By way of example, a few years ago I was working with a physician who worked in a clinic with three other doctors. All four were incorporated. Each had their own practice but they shared the same staff and office. They drew up an agreement amongst themselves, which detailed the responsibility of each partner, and each month they put an equal amount of money into the clinic to pay the bills. When I reviewed the agreement with a tax accountant he discovered the professional corporations were in fact associated, not because the doctors owned shares in each other's professional corporations but because they had set up what amounted to a common business and were, in essence, carrying on as a professional partnership.

CHAPTER TWO

Incorporating Your Practice

Before I send you into the arms of the paid professionals who guide you through the process of incorporation, let me provide you with an insight into some of the key considerations you will need to deal with at this early stage. First, we'll look at four basic corporate structures before moving onto things like the minute book, and then we'll pull it all together.

One of the most confusing issues facing most professionals is when to incorporate. There are so many differing opinions that it's hard to tell if the benefits outweigh the costs. The bottom line is that the decision should not be based on opinion; it should be based on the facts. This chapter will help you review the facts and make a qualified decision.

When Do I Incorporate?

There is no predetermined point at which you should incorporate. Your personal circumstances will determine the best course of action in your particular case. I have already mentioned the commonly held belief that you should wait until you have enough surplus cash to leave some in the company. I have also heard it said that unless your income is at least $125,000 pre-tax it doesn't make sense, or if you are single it doesn't make sense. I'm sure that if you ask around you can find a few more "Rules of Thumb." But do any of these rules of thumb make sense?

I'm a great believer in keeping things simple. If I could, I would hand out incorporated companies at the same time students receive their degree. If students started to develop the habits of running a business right from the outset I believe they would find the transition from student to business owner a lot less overwhelming.

Although there are expenses related to setting up and maintaining a professional corporation, these costs are relatively minimal. You can set up a professional corporation for less than $2,500 using a lawyer, and less than $1,000 if you do it yourself. Bookkeeping costs should be the same whether you are incorporated or not. With professional corporations you will incur annual maintenance fees of about $500 using a lawyer and about $150 if you file the annual return yourself. Accounting fees will be higher because you have to file a personal and a corporate tax return along with an annual corporate financial statement. These amounts range from $1,500 to about $3,500 annually. Filing your personal tax return (without the professional corporation) will probably be about $800 to $1,500.

The estimated additional annual cost of having a professional corporation, using a lawyer and accountant, versus being a "sole proprietor" is about $1,500.

I have met hundreds of professionals who have waited to incorporate. In most cases the cost of incorporating was significantly higher than it would have been had the incorporation taken place shortly after grad school. For instance, depending on your particular profession and circumstances, you may have already started to accumulate assets and debt. When you incorporate it is normally beneficial to have your business assets inside your professional corporation along with all business debt. The more assets and debt you accumulate prior to incorporating, the more complicated the process of incorporation becomes.

Sometimes the cost of moving assets and debts into the company is so costly that the effectiveness of having the professional corporation is undermined. For these reasons, in most cases, the sooner you incorporate the better. If you already have assets and debt you should carefully analyze the costs and benefits of incorporating. Do not assume that you shouldn't, or that it's too late; have an accountant or financial planner run at least two models for you to illustrate the effects of incorporating versus not incorporating.

I recently reviewed the affairs of a physician who was 62 years old and not incorporated. He had accumulated significant personal assets while running a very successful practice. After completing my review it was apparent that he could save a significant amount of taxes by setting up a professional corporation and transferring into it only specific assets. The cost of incorporating and transferring the assets was about $12,000, but the tax savings were about $125,000! The high cost of incorporating in this example is not typical; it was due to the value of the assets of the practice. But even with such a high initial outlay, the return on investment made it worthwhile.

Who Should I Contact First?

Many myths and biases surround the incorporation of professional practices. I've learned over the last 30 years, that every situation is different and each professional has the right to have his or her circumstances analyzed individually. Even as I was writing this book I came upon an article in a national newspaper on professional corporations. The so-called expert from Ontario stated that he worked with many physicians and dentists and none was incorporated. He just didn't incorporate professionals - so much for analyzing personal circumstances.

Before you purchase or set up a practice, or incorporate your existing practice, you should meet with someone who can review all the pertinent information, such as expenses (both personal and business), income, taxes, assets, and liabilities and then provide you with a clear picture of your current situation (this should be in the form of a comprehensive and concise written report).

Once you fully understand your own situation, you can begin to look at what potential benefits you would derive from incorporating. At this point you should know where you are and what you need. The next thing is to determine what you want, that is, your goals and objectives, both personal and corporate. In order to maximize your opportunities you must know what avenues are available to you. You might think that a lawyer or accountant would be the person to call upon to assist you with all this, and this might well be the case, however a certified financial planner (CFP) might be a better starting point (many accountants are also CFPs). These professionals can help you explore different models and investigate the various options that are open to you. As a CFP, it is my job to help clients maximize their opportunities and this, of course, includes ensuring they pay only as much tax as is legally required.

Often I come across individuals who say, "If I had just known about that before I...". People make all sorts of decisions without adequate information. Investments are purchased for the wrong reason and turn sour, people go on vacation to new places without knowing enough about them and end up having a bad time, and people make purchases without doing adequate due diligence. An extension of this is, "If I had known that before I bought it, I could have had the company pay for it." These are cases where consultation with your financial planner or accountant could go a long way to helping you more effectively use your professional corporation.

Your financial strategy should now address your current situation; what you need and what you want based on the report prepared for you. You can then look at the advantages and disadvantages of incorporating, given your specific situation. If you have no way to analyze what the difference is going to be, you should probably stop and find someone who can show you. At TPC Financial Group, we always provide our clients with at least two models that illustrate the difference between using a professional corporation and maintaining a sole proprietorship. In this way we can compare future results with what we predicted.

At the end of the day, with or without a financial analysis of your situation, if you want to incorporate, contact a lawyer. I would not recommend that you go through this process yourself; you are busy enough with both your practice and your life. Ask the lawyer you've chosen if they have incorporated a physician or dentist before; their prior experience will ensure they know the appropriate steps to follow. Also, contact the governing body in your jurisdiction to get a copy of their bylaws. A list is provided at the back of this book with all the appropriate contact numbers (see Appendix page 347).

You will find a number of situations described in this book, such as how you can benefit from income splitting, or how income is going to save you money, that should be assessed by both a lawyer and an accountant before you embark on incorporation. If you have already incorporated you may want to examine the potential benefits of reorganizing your professional corporation. Don't assume that because you've already incorporated that your situation can't be improved – often it can be.

Once the decision is made to incorporate, you should assemble your team consisting of at least an accountant, a lawyer and a banker. In an ideal world your team would also include a professional coordinator[4], an investment advisor, an insurance broker and a bookkeeper.

---

4   Professional coordinator is a term created by TPC Financial Group for someone who will look at your entire situation and assess whether or not it makes sense for you to incorporate (among other things).

In chapter 14 we'll look at exactly how this process works but for now, think of the professional coordinator as the proverbial quarterback.

This is the person who will help you work through the decision-making process and then make sure that your accountant, lawyer, and banker are all doing their jobs.

I always try to work with my client's existing advisors, but there are circumstances where I recommend changes. As I tell my clients, "You don't hire me to get my opinion. What you hire me for is to give you a complete set of facts from which you can make an informed decision." It's hard to make an informed decision if your advisors are giving you their 'opinion' and not presenting you with unbiased facts.

To me, it all comes down to accountability. I'm accountable to my clients and their advisors, and in turn they're accountable to me. If everyone is doing his or her job, then you, the client, get the best possible result. If someone is out of step, we work toward a resolution.

I've learned over the last thirty years what your accountant, lawyer, banker, investment advisor and insurance broker can and should be doing. If they're not performing, I call them on it. Likewise, if they think we're out of line, they can call us on that as well.

My philosophy is: it's not about being right, it's about doing what's right - what's right for the client.

Now let's take a look at the accountant's role.

Accountant's Role

I hope by this stage of the process that you've had a number of appointments with your accountant. The accountant you choose should have a strong background in taxation and ideally have a number of other clients who are incorporated professionals.

There is a lot of confusion about accountants and bookkeepers and others who fill out tax forms. You need someone who can help you set up the accounting for your professional corporation, give you guidance on an ongoing basis, and prepare your annual financial statements and corporate tax return.

This is probably best left to a CA (chartered accountant) or CGA (certified general accountant).

So, where does this leave the bookkeeper? A bookkeeper has a role in keeping your books, reconciling your bank account and preparing draft financial statements for your accountant to complete. I have a problem, though, with using a bookkeeper or the corner tax preparation company for corporate tax preparation. In your professional life you refer patients to specialists for specialized treatments; in your corporate life you should also employ specialists to carry out specialist work.

Like lawyers, accountants need a whole bunch of information from you; the questions listed below will help you prepare for your meeting. These questions will need to be considered once you have made the decision to incorporate. Previous discussions should have brought you to this point.

Questions Accountants Ask

1. Are you married or single?
2. Do you have any children?
3. If yes, what are your children's ages?
4. Who is your current accountant?
5. Who is your lawyer?
6. How much money do you need to live on?
7. Do you currently have any debt?
8. If yes, what is it and how much do you owe?
9. What are your assets and liabilities?
10. What is your current income?
11. Where does your income come from (are you an employee)?
12. What type of classes of shares are we going to deal with?
13. Are you going to use an investment company?
14. What are your long-term goals?
15. Do you want to provide income to your spouse and children?
16. What year-end do you want to designate for your corporation?

17. Are there any assets that will be moved into your professional corporation?

18. If yes, what are they and what is their tax cost?

19. Are you going to buy shares or assets?

20. Are you going to be borrowing money?

21. Are you, your spouse, or children American citizens?

You may think that using a chartered accountant will ensure that you're getting the best possible advice. Again, I caution you that not all chartered accountants know what they're doing when it comes to dealing with professional corporations. That's why I recommend using a professional coordinator. A professional coordinator will be able to tell you whether the person you're working with knows what they're doing.

By example, while researching this book I came upon an article that was published by a CA firm in Ontario that claimed when you incorporate as a professional you become an employee of the company and are subject to regular payroll deductions. The article left the reader with the impression that you must take a salary from your company and remit income tax, Canada Pension Plan contributions and employment insurance premiums. Is this true? If you incorporate and take a salary, are you required to make all these remittances?

The answer, of course, is no. If you're taking a salary, you are not required to pay employment insurance premiums. As a matter of fact, that also extends to other family members like your spouse or children. If you hired this particular accounting firm they would have had you paying Employment Insurance premiums that you didn't have to pay.

Now that you have your accountant on board, let's visit the lawyer's office.

The Lawyer's Role

When you go to see a lawyer about incorporating you should go prepared to answer some questions; this will save valuable, and expensive, time. Depending on the experience and style of the lawyer you choose, you may be asked questions such as those I've outlined below. Each question helps to establish how your professional corporation should initially be set-up. It is important to note that this is not a one-size fits all situation. In case you are not asked all the questions, take this book with you and ask your lawyer whether anything listed in this section is of importance or relevant in your particular circumstance.

Setting up your professional corporation with the greatest degree of flexibility from the outset can potentially save you tens of thousands of dollars as your practice grows.

Questions Lawyers Ask, For Which You Should Prepare Answers

1. What is your business plan (what business are you in)?
2. What name do you want (have three choices ready)?
3. Who will be the shareholders?
4. Who will be the director(s)?
5. Who is your banker?
6. Who is your accountant?
7. What share structure do you want?
8. How many shares, and what type, do you want issued?
9. Do you want (or need) a trust? If yes:
   a) Who is the settlor?
   b) Who is the trustee?
   c) Who are the income beneficiaries?
   d) Who are the capital beneficiaries?
   e) What is the trust property?
10. Do you own shares in any other private company?
11. Do you want a holding company?
12. What will be the registered address of your company?
13. Where will you keep your minute book?
14. Who will do your annual filing?
15. When do you want your professional corporation in place?
16. Do you have assets to be put in your professional corporation?
17. Do you have a will?

18. Have you made out a power of attorney form so that someone can act legally on your behalf if necessary?

19. Do you have partners?

20. Are you going to set up a partnership agreement or a cost-sharing agreement?

21. Are you, your spouse, or children American citizens?

You may find these questions confusing at first; in fact you may not understand them at all. Don't worry, that's par for the course if you've never been through incorporation before. The first time I heard the term MOBL restoration on #3.6 I had no idea what it meant either. Check the glossary at the end of the book if you are unfamiliar with any of the terms I use.

When I set up TPC Financial Group Ltd. my purpose was to help professionals incorporate and help them get the most from their corporations. We work through these questions with our clients, making the inevitable visit to the lawyer a whole lot less fraught. Get your accountant or professional coordinator to help you answer these questions and fill in the blanks.

Before I go further let me tell you a couple of stories about my experience with lawyers.

Lawyer Story Number One

A few years ago, a physician from Ontario, who had read my book, contacted me about incorporating her practice. After we spoke, she said she would find a lawyer in the area to help her set up her professional corporation. A colleague who had recently been through the same process, recommended a lawyer who she duly contacted. When she spoke to the lawyer, he assured her that he knew what he was doing, and that he had in fact incorporated a number of physicians and dentists.

Feeling confident, she asked him to proceed with her incorporation. He promptly presented her with a recommended share structure and started the incorporation process. After he had completed the process, he sent a copy of the final documents to her and a copy to me. It took just a few minutes to see that the company had been set up incorrectly and did not comply with the current rules and regulations of the province. If enacted, the doctor in question would have faced a number of tax and legal issues. When confronted, the lawyer's excuse was that an assistant had not used the correct rules. Here was a case where my client hired a lawyer, but someone not fully qualified or up-to-date did the work. We, of course, immediately changed lawyers and got a proper structure put in place.

Lawyer Story Number Two

When seeking professional help to incorporate, watch for sharks. While attending the Ontario Dental Conference a few years ago, I was approached by a lawyer who wanted to know if I would consider referring clients to him. He had read my book and thought it would be useful for me to have a legal contact, should an Ontario dentist want to incorporate. At that point I didn't have any professional contacts in Ontario, so building such a relationship might have been advantageous to my clients.

My first question to him concerned the rate he charged for incorporating professionals. The conversation went downhill from that point as he answered, "Oh, about $5,000 - $6,000."

"Wow," I said, "how can you justify charging so much? In B.C. it only costs about $1,500 - $2,000." His answer was along the lines that dentists have no idea what things cost and you can charge them whatever you want - they just pay it!

His answer floored me. Of course, I never referred anyone to him, but the frightening thing is I do know he has incorporated a number of professionals in Ontario. The moral of the story is: be aware of what you're paying other professionals to do for you, and do your best to get a quote before entering into a contract.

It drives lawyers crazy when you ask them for a quote, and then ask them to guarantee it. Many won't do it; they will tell you it's only an estimate. My response is: if you have incorporated other professionals you know exactly what is involved, both in terms of time and costs, so tell me exactly how much you're going to charge me, or I'll find a lawyer who will.

As a guide, it doesn't matter where you live in Canada, you should still be able to incorporate a professional corporation for less than $3,500. Shop around – lawyers are not all equal and in any case it will likely be an assistant doing 90 per cent of the work.

Before I leave this section, let me tell you about one very important job that needs to be done and that is filing section 85 elections. Section 85 of the *Income Tax Act* deals with the tax-free rollover of capital assets. If you are transferring assets into your professional corporation, whether they are assets such as computers or goodwill, there should be a section 85 election filed which defers any tax owing on the asset. Either the lawyer or, more normally, the accountant may complete this form.

The Minute Book

Your lawyer will prepare your minute book, which you will need when you're getting ready to meet with a bank to set up your corporate account; it contains all the legal information about your professional corporation, for instance:

- a copy of the certificate of incorporation
- a list of authorized capital
- the articles of incorporation
- consent to act as director
- subscription for shares
- banking and authorized signing authority
- share certificates
- a share registry
- resolutions appointing officers
- records office for the company
- a roll-over agreement (if necessary)
- tax election forms
- promissory notes
- trust deed (if using a trust).

Your lawyer can keep the minute book, or you can maintain it yourself. It should be kept up to date with special resolutions for things such as dividends and annual reports. My professional recommendation is that you let your lawyer maintain it on your behalf. Remember, though, that it is your responsibility to notify your lawyer when circumstances change, so appropriate action can be taken if necessary (e.g. you get married or separated, one of your children reaches the age of majority, you become financially responsible for a parent, or you are changing jurisdictions).

Every time you pay a dividend there should be an accompanying dividend resolution. The resolution (sample found on page 171) should be made and dated prior to the actual payment of the dividend.

The resolution should be prepared and signed by the director of the professional corporation and filed in the minute book. You or your lawyer can prepare the resolution but ultimately it should be signed and filed.

If the CRA ever audits you, they can check the dividend resolutions in your minute book and then reconcile them to your corporate bank statement. They should be able to see the cheque being written after the date of the resolution.

If you're going to pay yourself dividends for the year, instead of a salary, you can do up one dividend resolution at the beginning of the year for the entire amount (say $120,000) and then draw down on that over the year.

Always try to keep your minute book up to date; not doing so can cost you a lot more time, money and effort in the future if you have to make changes, or for instance if you sell your practice and your lawyer has to go back and reconstruct years of paperwork.

According to a number of accountants I deal with, the CRA is starting to look at minute books as part of their audit process. Try to keep yours current.

How Do I Incorporate?

After you decide to incorporate, the easiest thing to do is contact a lawyer. Before retaining one, ask if they have any experience in setting up professional corporations. Try to use a lawyer who has direct experience in setting up corporations for professionals. I really dislike seeing someone unknowingly pay for someone else's education.

I remember a dentist in a small northern community who had just purchased a practice from one who was retiring. The retiring dentist wasn't incorporated. The new dentist had heard about the benefits of incorporating and asked the lawyer who handled the sale of the practice if he could handle his incorporation. "No problem" was the response. The incorporation took almost four months and cost the dentist about three times the normal amount. Why? Because the lawyer had no experience in setting up professional corporations. He had incorporated businesses but had no experience or knowledge regarding the regulations that are specific to professional corporations. For instance, not only do you need permission from your association (college), but also there are rules in each jurisdiction that set out limitations on the share ownership.

You should also ask the lawyer in advance to provide you with a quotation that includes the estimated cost of setting up your professional corporation. The actual cost will range from about $1,500 to $7,500 depending on whether or not you already own assets. The average cost of a new professional corporation with no assets is about $2,000.

The next thing you need to do is to pick a name for your corporation. The rules governing corporate names vary from jurisdiction to jurisdiction. In all cases, the name of your professional corporation has to include at least your first and middle initials along with your complete last name. You can't use names like PC Acme Medical Limited. As an example, the more common forms look like this: Dr. James Robbins Professional Corporation or James Robbins, MD, Professional Corporation. However, you should check with your association or college as to their specific regulations.

You will also have to decide on the date of incorporation and your corporation's year-end (year-ends are normally up to the accountant). There really isn't a bad day to incorporate, however, it probably doesn't make sense to start using your new professional corporation in December. There isn't any significant tax benefit to having one year-end over another. I like to use December 31 as this makes things very clean and easy to understand. It ties in nicely with other corporate matters like WCB, payroll and dividend reporting. If you are a sole proprietor, you already have a December 31 year-end.

When you incorporate you can use any date in the year as a year-end, but if you haven't incorporated by December you've already earned 11 months of personal income. So, you might as well incorporate and wait until January 1 to start using the professional corporation. The other consideration is that in the first year of incorporation you are pro-rated on the small business deduction[5]. Based on the 2010 small business limit of $500,000 if you

---

5   Small Business Deduction: The SBD is an income tax deduction available to businesses that were Canadian controlled private corporations (CCPCs) throughout a particular tax year. It reduces the Part 1 tax that a corporation would otherwise have to pay. Effective January 1, 2010, the SBD rate is 10 per cent. It applies to the first $500,000 of a corporation's income.

incorporate on July 1 you can only utilize 50 per cent of the small business deduction limit because you are halfway through the year. If you incorporate in December, the maximum amount you could use would be one-twelfth (assuming in both cases that you use a December 31 year-end).

If your year-end is December 31, then you are required to have your corporate financial statements and tax return filed by June 30 of the following year. Something that is extremely important to remember is that even though you don't have to file until June 30, if you owe corporate taxes for the preceding year they are due by March 31. After the first year you are required to pay tax in monthly instalments.

Once your college has approved your incorporation, your lawyer may ask you what kind of share structure you would like. Don't just guess at this, or even blindly take your lawyer's suggestion; retain the services of a good accountant, or financial planner, to assist you in making this decision. Prior to deciding on what share structure is best, I prefer to draw up a complete financial plan and then review it with the accountant. The reason I do this, is that I want first to determine my client's goals so that their corporation can be set up in a manner that will facilitate those goals. There are, however, some limitations to consider which are imposed by certain jurisdictions. It is very important that you understand the regulations applicable to the province or territory you're working in. In Alberta and Ontario for example, you are not allowed to sell shares to holding companies but you are allowed to in B.C. and Saskatchewan.

Moving from one jurisdiction to another can cause problems. Remember Dr. Durrant from the beginning of this book? His practice was incorporated in Alberta and when he moved to British Columbia he decided to keep his old accountant, who had become a close friend. The accountant continued to handle Dr. Durrant's financial affairs as if he was still practicing in Alberta, and that is where things started to go terribly wrong.

It was ten years later that I came on the scene and started working on the doctor's financial plan. I quickly realized that things were not as they should be. I was shocked to see that he was the only shareholder in his corporation and that he had been using after-tax, personal money to fund a variety of things, such as schooling for his children. Had the children been shareholders, the money could have gone to them in the form of a dividend and they could have paid the bills themselves. As students it is unlikely they would earn enough to pay tax. When I spoke to the accountant in Alberta he was unaware of the different rules governing professional corporations in British Columbia. By my estimate, Dr. Durrant had been paying about $50,000 per year more in taxes than was required had he used a different share structure allowable in British Columbia.

The moral of the story is that when you move to another jurisdiction (or preferably before) you should take it upon yourself to contact your new governing body and find out the local rules pertaining to professional corporations - never, never, assume that your current advisors know all the answers.

So, what are these corporate structures that are so important? To get a basic understanding of them the first thing you need to know are the differences between various kinds of shares. All shares fall into two general categories: preferred shares (or preference) and common shares. Each of these types of shares may be further divided by changing the rights and restrictions. Most shares of private and public companies are common shares.

Basic Definition – Common Shares (courtesy of Investorwords.com)

Securities representing equity ownership in a corporation can provide voting rights, and entitle the holder to a share of the company's success through dividends and/or capital appreciation. In the event of liquidation, common shareholders have rights to a company's assets only after bondholders, other debt holders, and preferred shareholders have been satisfied. Typically, common shareholders who have voting privileges get one vote per share and are allowed to elect the company's board of directors. In a professional corporation, only the professional can own voting shares and be a director so non-voting shares have to be available for other family members.

Basic Definition – Preferred Shares

Like common shares, preferred shares represent an ownership stake in a company – in other words, a claim on its assets and earnings. However, as the term suggests, "preferred" shares carry certain advantages. While preferred shares usually don't carry the same voting rights as common shares, it does have priority when it comes to dividends and bankruptcy.

The primary difference between preferred and common shares relates to the order in which shareholders are paid in the event of bankruptcy, corporate restructuring, windup or sale. If the issuing company seeks bankruptcy protection, then the owners of preferred shares take priority over common shareholders when it comes time to pay dividends and liquidate the company assets.

The other main difference between preferred and common shares relates to dividends. Although dividends paid on common shares are not guaranteed and can fluctuate from time to time, preferred shareholders are usually guaranteed a fixed dividend paid on a regular basis. As a result, preferred shares often act similar to bonds.

—◆—

The articles of incorporation set out the number and various types of shares that the corporation can issue. Most corporations have a number of different types of shares authorized for issue, each with its own characteristics. Most lawyers I work with will set up a corporation with two types of preferred shares and three types of common shares but will only initially use one or two types.

The basic share types that most corporations can issue are:

- first preferred voting fixed value shares
- second preferred non-voting fixed value shares
- Class A common voting participating
- Class B common non-voting participating
- Class C common non-voting non-participating.

The corporation may have the ability to issue a number of shares. This is the company's authorized capital. For example:

- Class A preferred 5,000,000 shares
- Class B preferred 5,000,000 shares
- Class A common unlimited shares
- Class B common unlimited shares
- Class C common unlimited shares.

Each type of share must have some "substantial" difference for it to be separate and distinct. This is very important from a tax planning point of view. If the only difference between your A, B, and C common shares are the letters A, B, and C, then the CRA will probably deem that all the shares are the same and tax you accordingly. For example, if you own Class A common shares and your spouse has Class B common shares and there is no difference in the rights and restrictions of those shares, the CRA can deem that both A's and B's are in fact the same; thereby eliminating the income splitting opportunities that would be open to you had the shares been different.

The most common rights and restrictions on shares are: voting or non-voting, growth or non-growth, participating in dividends or non-participating in dividends, par value or non-par value, common or preferred. Your lawyer should provide you with the rights and restrictions of each share class and ensure that each share class is "substantially" different.

When setting up a corporation from scratch (when there are no assets) only common shares are usually issued. The investor, who becomes a shareholder in the corporation and would normally hold voting privileges, purchases these common shares. Common shareholders elect the board of directors and vote on other matters that require the approval of the owners of the company. If a corporation is liquidated, the common shareholders have the right to a share of the assets of the corporation, after any prior claims on the corporation have been settled. A corporation may authorize an unlimited number of common shares to be issued. Preferred shares are a class of corporate capital stock, which normally hold priority over common shares in dividend payments, and in distribution of the corporate assets in the event of liquidation.

As the professional, you are required to have control of the company. This is easily accomplished by having all voting shares issued to you. Other family members or entities, such as trusts and holding companies, can be issued non-voting shares.

A corporation's directors are important. These people have the legal right to act on behalf of the company. When the shareholders decide to do something, such as borrow money, the directors sign the loan contracts with the bank. Professional corporations, on the other hand, have only one director – you. The one exception to this is when you have two or more professionals in the same professional corporation - in this case it is possible for all of them to be directors.

You are also required to have at least one officer of the company – a president. Some jurisdictions require that you have more than one officer; however, with professional corporations it is not uncommon to have just a president. Other officers can include a vice-president, secretary and treasurer. Your lawyer should be able to tell you what's required in your province or territory.

Once you give your lawyer your chosen name, share structure and the name(s) of the officer(s) and director(s), they will go about setting up all the necessary paperwork; the details can be found in your minute book (for further information on minute books, please refer to page 37). Your minute book will contain your incorporation certificate, all the administrative requirements of your corporation, and your shares held in treasury, including all the rights and restrictions on each share class.

The minute book will also name the directors of the company and the officers, detail the shares issued, provide your corporate bank details and contain the registered address of the company. The registered address is usually your lawyer's office but it doesn't have to be. You can use your practice address, accountant's address or your home address if you prefer. The benefit of having your lawyer's office listed, however, is that the annual report papers will be sent there and they can complete them with you. This helps to ensure that they get done every year.

The professional corporation comes into existence once it is registered with the provincial corporate registry. Usually, the first order of business is issuing shares to the appropriate individuals. The shares purchased usually have a nominal value (say $10). The individual writes a personal cheque to the professional corporation for the prescribed amount and the shares are then issued.

Sometimes lawyers use what are called "shelf companies." These are corporations that are set up by lawyers in advance and used when there is a need to incorporate a company quickly. The lawyer usually owns the shares in these companies until a client requires control. Once a client decides that they need a corporation, the existing shares owned by the lawyer are cancelled and new shares are issued. It really doesn't matter if your lawyer uses a shelf company or not. If one day when you're flipping through your minute book you see a cancelled share certificate issued to your lawyer don't be concerned, it just means that they used a shelf company; not that they were ever a shareholder of your professional corporation.

Before you write a personal cheque to your professional corporation for your shares, you need to set up a corporate bank account.

> *I've seen it more then once where the cheque for the shares wasn't actually written. This can be a critical mistake. If you are buying shares for $10.00, then write out a personal cheque to the company for $10.00. If you are buying shares for your family trust, or holding company, write the cheque from the family trust or holding company. And just to be clear, if your spouse, parent or adult children are buying shares in your professional corporation make sure they write your company a personal cheque for their shares. Do NOT under any circumstances write a cheque for them.*

I believe it's important for you to take the time to shop the market before choosing a bank. Banks, trust companies and credit unions have different packages; check which bank offers the package that best suits your needs. Why is all this so important? While reviewing the banking arrangements of one of my clients I noticed that there were two lines of credit from the same bank with different interest rates (one corporate and one personal). There was also a personal loan and mortgage, and corporately they had merchant account services, to allow them to accept Visa. They expected that, because all their banking was with the same bank, they were getting the best deal possible. In fact, this was not the case. After presenting their information to another bank, I was able to reduce their costs on every account and loan. When confronted with this, the current bank tried to match the new bank's offer and keep their client; in this case they were unsuccessful.

All professional fees earned by you prior to incorporation are considered personal income. The professional corporation should, however, bill all subsequent work including everything that took place on the day of incorporation. However, there will very likely be some overlap between pre- and post-incorporation earnings. Ask your accountant to help you decide how to deal with money received during this transition period.

During the year that you incorporate, keep your personal and corporate records separate because any income received prior to incorporation along with the corresponding deductions will have to be put on your personal return (as a sole proprietor). Once the transition year is over things will be far easier.

Let's take a look at holding companies and trusts. Sometimes it's suggested that you set up a holding company (also known as an investment company) at the same time as you incorporate, as it's usually less expensive to do both things at once.

The purpose of a holding company is normally to separate your "active" business assets from your "passive" assets.

Active business assets include such things as your practice, practice equipment and property owned to carry on your business.

Passive assets are things like rental properties, stocks, bonds, cash, life insurance cash values and mutual funds.

In most cases the holding company will hold (own) shares in the operating company and in essence hold the investment assets of the professional corporation.

A holding company will also normally hold shares in your professional corporation to allow for the movement of money between the two companies. Using a holding company can come in handy when selling your practice because it allows you to sell only your business assets and not your investment assets. This is important because it allows you to make use of the capital gains deduction. Certain practices have no saleable value. For instance, the professional corporation of an emergency physician has nothing to sell from a medical standpoint, since an emergency physician doesn't have a saleable patient base, a lot of equipment, or leasehold improvements. So, if you can't sell your practice, a holding company is probably redundant. However, if your practice is saleable you should consider setting up a holding company at some point in time. Seek advice from your accountant and financial planner as to what is best in your situation.

In jurisdictions like Ontario and Alberta, you can only have a family trust hold shares for minor children. When the child reaches age 18 (the age of majority) the shares have to be given to the child outright. Once the child reaches the age of majority, the shares cannot be left in the Trust. So, if there was no apparent tax benefit to the professional (because any income paid to a minor is taxed at the top personal tax rate) why would you bother to set up a Family Trust to hold shares for a minor child?

The answer is twofold. The first reason would be the cost of having to reorganize the corporation when the child or children reach the age of majority, and you want to start to income split with them. Remember our previous example on page 40?

If you set up a professional corporation when you have young children (or no children) and then want to issue shares to them when they're adults, you have to reorganize the company so they can afford to buy shares. If, for example, you start a professional corporation with $100 and are issued 100 common shares and then leave money in the corporation to accumulate, it could be worth $500,000 when your children reach adulthood. That would make the value of each share $5,000.00. You wouldn't want to sell shares of your company to your children for $5,000.00 because they would have the same type of shares as you, which would greatly reduce your income-splitting ability.

In order to maximize your income-splitting ability you want your children, spouse and parents to have a different class of shares so they can receive dividends on their class of shares to the exclusion of the others.

Just to be clear: you, as the professional have to own 100 per cent of the voting shares so you can't issue voting shares to anyone other than another professional (this is allowed when, for example, you have a husband and a wife who are both physicians or both dentists). If you own all the Class A voting common shares, then you would want your spouse, child/children and/or parents to own other classes of non-voting common shares. If you issue 100 Class B non-voting common shares to your spouse and 100 Class B non-voting common shares to your adult child, they would have to receive exactly the same amount of dividends. If you declare a dividend of $50.00 per Class B common share each person would have to get $50.00 x 100 = $5,000.00.

When one or more people owns the same class of shares, they each receive dividends based on the number of shares that they hold. Dividends are always paid per share.

To allow maximum income-splitting opportunities, it's important to try and get a different class of shares into each person's hands. That way you can pay dividends, for example, to your spouse who owns Class B non-voting common shares, and not pay any dividends to you who own the Class A voting common shares, or your adult child who owns the Class C non-voting common shares.

This is easily accomplished in jurisdictions where you can have adults in a family trust, because all you have to do is name your spouse, children & parents as beneficiaries of the trust and then have the trust buy one type of shares (say) Class B non-voting common shares.

What the trust rules allow you to do in this case is pay a dividend on the Class B non-voting common shares to the trust and then you as the trustee decide which of the beneficiaries is going to receive the dividend. Trust rules allow you to pay out income to one or any of the beneficiaries however you decide, as long as the trust is structured that way.

Now back to Ontario and Alberta. Say you're not incorporated and you have a child who's 14 years old; you decide that you're going to incorporate and your lawyer asks if you would like to issue shares to your spouse. You say yes because you want to have the opportunity to income split. The next question is, "do you want a family trust?"

If you want to have the opportunity to income split with your child when he or she reaches age 18, so that you can pay for their education or anything else you may want, it would probably be a good idea to say yes.

You could say no and wait for 4 years but the cost in 4 years could be significantly more expensive than doing it now.

To set up a family trust now might cost $2,500.00. To maintain the trust over 4 years might cost about $250.00 per year or $1,000.00. That's an estimated cost of $3,500.00.

If you wait until they are age 18 and then have to re-organize[6] the company so they can buy shares in your company, the cost can easily exceed $10,000.00.

---

6   A re-organization is when you change the share structure of a company. If you own 100 Class A voting common shares that have a value of $500,000 you have to convert them to Preferred shares to reduce the value of the common shares. If the conversion amount is $500,000, the common shares are then worth zero. Once the value is removed from the common shares you can then sell new common shares at a nominal value, normally about $0.10 per share. Once your common shares have been converted to Preferred shares you can then buy new Class A voting common shares and your adult children can buy Class C non-voting common shares for say $0.10 per share. At the same time, your spouse might buy Class B non-voting common shares for the same $0.10 per share. The reason this is possible is that when you convert your common shares to preferred shares all the value is attached to the preferred shares, making the common shares worthless. When you sell the company in the future the first $500,000 of proceeds (in this example) would be paid out on the preferred shares first and then any additional value would be attached to the common shares.

If you have an analytical mind you might have figured out the second reason why you might want to set up a family trust for a minor.

If you set up a family trust when you first incorporate and say your child is 3 years old, what would the value of those shares be when they reach age 18? As an example, let's say the common shares are worth $500,000 when your child reaches age 18. If you own 100 Class A voting common shares and your spouse owns 100 Class B non-voting common shares, and the trust owns 100 Class C non-voting common shares, arguably the Class C non-voting common shares would be worth 1/3 of $500,000 or $166,666.66.

Not only would you be able to pay dividends on the Class C non-voting common shares, but also you could arrange to buy those shares, or upon sale (or on your death) the $166,666.66 value would follow those shares owned by your child (as well as any other increase in value after age 18).

So, what if you decide you don't want your child to own one-third of the value of your professional corporation, or have any equity in your PC? How do you get around that? Simply – you put a restriction on the shares that your child is going to own that make them non-growth. In other words they will not increase in value regardless of how valuable your professional corporation becomes.

———— ◆•◆•◆ ————

As an example, one of my clients was putting three of her children through university and helping support her mother at the same time. To facilitate this, she was taking about $300,000 per year out of her professional corporation, paying personal tax and then distributing after-tax money. It is in situations like this that an understanding about how professional corporations can be used to your best advantage, is vitally important.

By rearranging the company, we were able to reduce her annual tax liability by about $38,000. To do this, we set up a family trust and listed all family members as beneficiaries. Each year we were able to declare a dividend to the trust and then to pass it along as a dividend to each of the three children and the mother. Because all four had little or no income, we could give each of them about $35,000 per year. The decision to pay dividends to each family member was made after calculating the effect on each individual. In the mother's case we had to make sure it wasn't going to create a claw back of Old Age Security (OAS) or affect other government programs such as the Guaranteed Income Supplement (GIS) or health-care premium subsidies. If the only income is $35,000 of taxable dividends from a Canadian-controlled corporation, then the individual's taxes payable are probably nil because of what is called the dividend tax credit – a credit that is deducted from your taxes.

In some jurisdictions, such as British Columbia, other family members may hold shares directly in your professional corporation. This can be beneficial as it allows you to split income and growth. Say you own 100 per cent of the shares in your company, for which you paid $100, and over the years you grow the company. At retirement, let's say your company is worth $2,000,000 and you sell your shares. If you were the only shareholder (and the shares did not qualify for the capital gains exemption of $750,000) you would be taxed on half of the gain or in this case $999,950. If, however, you sell three-quarters of your shares to your spouse and two children for $25 each, prior to the increase in value, and then sell the company for $2,000,000, you have effectively split the "growth" of that company amongst your family. Each of you would report a taxable capital gain of $249,987.50.

Case Story

A physician was planning on splitting the growth of his company with his family members so that there would be no tax payable if he eventually sold the practice, retired, or died (as long as the practice was not worth in excess of $3m). He issued shares in his professional corporation to his two children and his wife. The idea was to build a clinic and eventually sell the whole business. He knew that if he could build up the value of the professional corporation to over $3,000,000, he could claim the $750,000 capital gains deduction for himself and each family member could then also claim their $750,000 capital gains deduction. In this way his family could walk away with $3,000,000 net of tax on the sale of the professional corporation's shares. But he hadn't counted on his two children getting married and then divorced. Because the children owned shares directly in the professional corporation, they were family property. At the time of the divorces, the shares were valued and divided with the divorcing partners, and the doctor eventually had to buy them back at a significant cost. The entire situation could have been avoided by having a different share structure. In this particular situation, the shares could have been owned by a family trust instead of directly by the children. Simply being a beneficiary of a family trust does not constitute family property.

Different Shareholder Options Across Canada

Jurisdiction	Can Professionals incorporate?	Can non-professionals be shareholders?	Can a trust be a shareholder?	Can shares be owned by a holding company?
British Columbia	Yes	Yes	Yes	Yes
Alberta	Yes	Yes	Yes*	No
Saskatchewan	Yes	Yes	Yes	Yes
Manitoba	Yes	Yes	Yes	Yes
Ontario	Yes	Yes	Yes*	No
Quebec	Yes	Yes	Yes	Yes
New Brunswick	Yes	Yes	Yes	Yes
Nova Scotia	Yes	Yes	Yes	Yes
Prince Edward Island	Yes	Yes	Yes	Yes
Newfoundland	Yes	Yes	No	No
Yukon	Yes	Yes	Yes	Yes
Northwest Territories	Yes	Yes	No	No
Nunavut	Yes	No	No	No

* Shares can only be held "in trust" for minor beneficiaries.

Students And New Graduates

If you are a new grad, before looking at how to incorporate you should determine if incorporation is right for you. This is where the help of a good professional coordinator can save you thousands of dollars.

When most students graduate today they usually do so with student loans, and depending on the courses they have taken, they have both federal and provincial education tax credits. Care should be taken to insure that all of these non-refundable tax credits are used **before** incorporation is considered. Or, if you do incorporate, make sure you take a salary until all your credits are used up.

Before I go any further let me explain what a tax credit is. A tax credit is a good thing. It is a direct reduction in your tax liability (and, it is not dependent on your particular tax bracket).

Federally there are tuition fee credits, textbook tax credits and an education amount.

- The federal **tuition fee credit** is 15 per cent of the amount paid in respect to attendance at a post-secondary institution.
- The federal **textbook tax credit** is 15 per cent of $65/month of full-time ($20/month of part-time) attendance at a post-secondary institution.
- The federal **education amount** is 15 per cent of $400/month of full-time ($120/month of part-time) attendance at a post secondary institution.

In Canada we use both tax deductions and tax credits to determine your tax payable. If you purchase an RRSP (see page 208) for $1,000 and you're in a 30 per cent tax bracket you save $300 in income tax. If you were in a 40 per cent tax bracket that same $1,000 RRSP would save you $400 in income tax.

But, if you are eligible for a $500 tax credit, it is deducted directly from your tax payable and therefore is of no greater or lesser value regardless of your personal tax bracket. The more tax credits you have, the less tax you pay – so, as I said earlier, tax credits are a good thing.

When I mentioned above, that the federal textbook credit is 15 per cent of $65.00 that means that the tax credit would be $9.75 (i.e. 65 x .15). So where did they come up with the 15 per cent? Well, it just happens to be the lowest federal tax rate.

Each province and territory then calculates its own taxes based on taxable income, although they too convert your tuition fee credits, textbook tax credit and an education amount into provincial credits.

To give you a good idea of what you may see when you graduate, let's look at a real example of a 2010 personal tax assessment shown below.

> According to this assessment, you have $105,663 of federal unused tuition, education and textbook amounts available to carry forward to a future year. For more information, see the explanation at line 323 in your income tax guide.

According to this assessment, you have $107,560 of unused Saskatchewan tuition and education amounts available to carry forward to a future year. For more information, see the explanation at line 5856 in your income tax forms book.

Even if you have little or no income you should file a tax return each year to gain access to "refundable" tax credits. The federal government and some provinces have refundable tax credits, which are payable to you even if you have no earnings and have paid no tax. This means they will send you a cheque for the tax credit (a common one is a GST or HST refund).

Student Loans and Lines of Credit

Not too many years ago, there were student loans and "parent" loans. Today these things still exist but the new kid on the block is the student line-of-credit.

Go to any university campus during the first couple weeks of September and you'll see a virtual midway of financial institutions trying to sign up new customers. Student bank accounts, credit cards and lines-of-credit are all available (complete with a handy tote bag). If you have a student line-of-credit then you've probably already figured out that, unlike a registered student loan, the interest is not tax deductible. This includes lines-of-credit or loans that were used to replace existing student loans.

Interest rates on these financial products vary greatly and should be reviewed regularly. Most have floating rates so be careful when you are shopping around. Make sure you understand the terms of the contract.

Tax planning and cash flow management have to be considered, especially post graduation. If you're going make a change, take the time to review the current and future effects of the change. If you don't know how, contact my office and we'll give you some help.

Depending on who, if anyone, is helping to fund your education, he or she may be able to use some of your education credits while you're in school. To the extent that you're unable to use them all yourself, you can transfer credits to a spouse, parent or grandparent (or the parent or grandparent of your spouse or common-law partner).

The maximum tuition, education, and textbook amounts that is transferable is, $5,000 minus the amount that the person funding your education has used, even if there is still an unclaimed part. Tuition, education, and textbook amounts that the student carried forward from a previous year cannot be transferred.

Depending on the program you graduated from and the amount of income you generate in the first couple of years, you may not have to pay personal income tax.

For most, the primary objective should be to get out of debt. Even if the interest is tax deductable, the principal payments are not.

When you borrow $100,000, you're borrowing after-tax money. If you didn't have to pay tax, you would have to earn $100,000 to pay back $100,000. Unfortunately, once you start to pay tax, the amount you have to earn to pay the debt back is significantly greater.

If you're earning more than $127,000 per year and are in a 45 per cent tax bracket the amount you have to earn to pay back $100,000, is $181,818.

I'm often asked if you can transfer your student debts into a professional corporation; the short answer to that is no. You can only move debts into a professional corporation to the extent that you transfer an equal or greater amount of assets into the company.

One thing that both students and new grads have to be careful about is the amount of debt they take on.

As a professional, the banks are very willing to lend you money, but unless you want to spend the majority of your career being a slave to the bank, don't be fooled by their apparent generosity.

If you graduate with $200,000 in student loans and then go out and buy a new car for say $50,000, and then buy a house for say $750,000, and then want to buy a practice for $500,000, your debt would balloon to $1,500,000 and that's assuming you don't buy any furniture.

Excluding interest, the amount you would have to earn to pay this back would be about $2,727,272.

Assuming interest of 4 per cent, your loan interest might look like this:

Loan	Net Interest [7]	Gross Interest [8]
Student Loan	$8,000	$8,000
Car Loan	$2,000	$3,636
House Mortgage	$30,000	$54,545
Practice Loan	$20,000	$20,000
Total	$60,000	$86,181

As a general rule when someone says something stupid like, "its okay it's tax deductible" that's usually a good time to slowly back away.

If you're currently working with a personal budget, congratulations. If not, it's time to start. The sooner you start using one, the easier your life will be.

Right now you have an opportunity to have it all: the cars, the house, the club membership, the yacht, the plane. It really can all be yours, if you do it the right way.

So what's the right way? The right way is to be patient and systematic about what you're doing. If you learn how to control your cash flow and manage your income and expenses, then all those material things you want can be yours.

Most people take years to figure this out. I'm giving you an opportunity to learn it now. You've spent years taking tests and I know you've passed them because you're here, so take a minute and write one more test. It's just one question. Ready?

Q. **If you buy a pair of shoes for $100 (including all taxes) how much did the shoes cost you?**

A. *If you disregard the amount of money you have to earn to net $100 the number might look like something like $1,842.02.*

Do you have any idea where that number came from? I can reference at least two famous people, Albert Einstein and Warren Buffet.

Albert Einstein was quoted as saying "The most powerful force in the universe is compound interest." And, Warren Buffet is famous for not

---

7   Net interest is the amount you have to pay.
8   Gross interest is the amount you have to earn to pay the interest.

spending money, not because of what its present value is, but because of what it's future value could be.

Let me clarify the point here, if you are 25 years old and don't spend the $100 today but invest it, the future value of your $100 by the time you are 75 (given 6 per cent growth) will be $1,842.02.

Whether you're spending money or paying taxes, you're not only giving up the present value but you're also giving up the future value.

If you're not keeping it and investing it, someone else is. Check the effect of this in more detail in my new book The Financial Navigator – A Professional Guide to Keeping More of What You Earn.

Choosing The Right Corporate Structure

The diagrams below demonstrate four of the more common corporate structures from the simplest of all, where you own all the shares issued in the professional corporation, to one that utilizes an investment company.

Before selecting the appropriate structure, you have to know what the incorporation rules allow in your particular jurisdiction (you can set up the basic structure in all jurisdictions). Once you've established what the rules are, then you have to think about your current, and future, circumstances.

Basic Structure (1)

Professional owns 100% of all shares issued in the professionalcorporation

Available in all jurisdictions.

Basic Structure (2) Utilizing Inter-Vivos Family Trust

Professional owns 100% of all issued voting shares in the professional corporation. Family trust owns some or all of a single class of non- voting common shares in professional corporation. Family members including professional are beneficiaries of trust.

Basic Structure (3) Utilizing Investment Company

Professional owns 100% of all issued voting shares. Investment company owns some or all of a single class of non-voting common shares. Professional owns all issued voting shares in investment company. Spouse owns some or all of a single class of non-voting common shares in investment company.

Basic Structure (4) Utilizing Inter-Vivos Family Trust and Investment Company

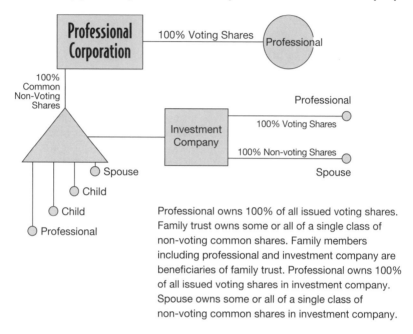

Professional owns 100% of all issued voting shares. Family trust owns some or all of a single class of non-voting common shares. Family members including professional and investment company are beneficiaries of family trust. Professional owns 100% of all issued voting shares in investment company. Spouse owns some or all of a single class of non-voting common shares in investment company.

Diagram 1 shows a basic structure. In this case, the professional owns all the shares. This structure would probably suit those who are not married and have no immediate opportunity to income split.

Diagram 2 makes use of a family trust. The professional still owns 100 per cent of the voting shares with the trust owning a class of non-voting shares. If you live in British Columbia the beneficiaries of the trust can include all immediate family members including yourself. If you live in Alberta or Ontario, however, only minor children can be beneficiaries of the trust.

This structure is normally best suited to professionals working in jurisdictions that allow all family members into the trust.

The third structure (diagram 3) makes use of an investment company. Again you can see that the professional owns 100 per cent of the voting shares, and in this case, the investment company owns a class of non-voting shares.

This structure allows you to separate your active business assets from your investment assets. The benefit of doing this is explained later in the book.

The fourth structure (diagram 4) provides the greatest flexibility and the most beneficial opportunities. It makes use of both a family trust and an investment company.

This structure works particularly well for those professionals who might have the opportunity to sell their professional practice at some stage. Unfortunately, this structure is not available in all jurisdictions.

Changing An Existing Corporate Structure – How To Add Family Members, Trusts And Holding Companies

As rules change in various jurisdictions, the questions I get asked surrounding corporate reorganizations become more frequent. So, here is an overview of the current situation at the time of writing (November, 2010).

Let's use the latest changes in Alberta (i.e. where the opportunities to income split have recently become easier) as a good example. A single shareholder corporation in Alberta can now have multiple shareholders. However, in order to get shares into the hands of family members, the setting up of a family trust or an investment company requires an existing professional corporation to be reorganized.

Before I actually explain the process of a re-organization, I should mention that jurisdictional rules don't have to change to necessitate a corporate reorganization. Changes of circumstances such as marriage or a child reaching the age of majority are examples of situational changes that lead to the same requirement.

When you see the term 'reorganization' you may wonder what exactly is being reorganized; the answer is the share structure. If you have one shareholder and you want to add another you can either sell them new shares, or sell them some of yours. In both cases the price of those shares would be equal to the value of the company divided by the total number of shares that are issued.

If you owned 100 shares (for which you paid $10 when you started the company) and the company is now worth $1,000,000, each share would be worth $10,000[9]. If you sold half of your shares, the selling price would be $500,000 and you would have a capital gain equal to the difference between

---

9   This is called 'fair market value'.

the selling price and the price you paid for them (i.e. if you paid $10 for 100 shares, then the 50 you're selling would have cost you $5.00).

If you get married and want to get shares into the hands of your spouse, you probably won't want to make them pay $500,000 for half of your shares. Besides not being a very loving thing to do, it also creates a couple of problems. The first problem is that you, as the professional, must own all the voting shares, so if you only own one class of shares they would have to be voting shares – and your spouse, unless also a professional, in the same profession, can't own them. Second, if you and your spouse do own the same class of shares it restricts your income splitting ability because dividends have to be paid equally to each shareholder based on their class and number of shares. If both you and your spouse own 50 Class B common non-voting shares, each time you declare a dividend on Class B shares you would have to each get the same amount of dividend. If you owned 75 and your spouse owned 25 Class B shares, every time you declared a dividend on those shares you would have to receive 75% of the total dividends declared and your spouse would receive 25%. This distribution ratio cannot be changed. Dividends are always paid as a dollar amount per share.

Using the same $1,000,000 example, if you live in Alberta and you want to issue a different class of shares to your spouse, the result would be the same, they would still have to pay fair market value. For instance, if you own 100 Class A common voting shares and you issue new Class B common non-voting shares to your spouse, they would still have to pay $500,000 for those shares. But, by issuing 100 new Class B common shares, there would be 200 common shares issued (the 100 Class A common shares you own and the 100 Class B common shares you issued to your spouse). The company would still be worth $1,000,000 but now each common share would be worth $5,000.

I could go on to explain what would happen if your spouse didn't pay you the $500,000 for their shares but I don't think that's particularly relevant and would require several pages of explanation. It's the conclusion here that's the most important thing. You don't want your spouse, children or parents to have to buy shares at fair market value unless that value is extremely low.

Now just to stop some of you from jumping to your own potential tax solutions, you need to know that you can't just pick some arbitrary low value when selling shares to family members. Because you have to prove the reasonableness of the valuation, many people have the company valued by a business valuator, or practice valuator. This service can cause costs to escalate.

If you're an incorporated physician who works in a hospital (say, an E.R. doctor) and just have a corporate bank account with $200,000 in it, the value of your PC would be $200,000 – it's that simple! But what if you're an incorporated dentist who owns half a strip mall (where your clinic occupies only 10% of the total space), your practice has a gross income of $1,200,000, you have all new equipment, and along with all these things inside your professional corporation, you own shares of a private company that produces mouth guards? How would you put a value on that PC?

You could pick a number and hope that the CRA never questions you about it, or you could hire a business valuator who will probably charge you $10,000 - $20,000 to come up with a number. The more complicated the valuation, the more it costs to come up with a number.

At this point you may think it's not worth the expense, but I assure you, if you find yourself being audited and you can't prove that the numbers you used were reasonable, all your planning may not only prove to be useless but even worse – the CRA can reverse everything you did up to that point. Always remember, in tax court the only thing that matters is what you can prove.

If you get an independent valuation done when you're reorganizing your company, or selling shares to a family member, and the CRA subsequently challenges it and wins, chances are they'll just adjust the figures and determine what the difference is. Such an adjustment would normally result in a tax amount owing and an interest charge. This may be bad, but it shouldn't be terrible. On the other hand, having no backup to some arbitrary value you chose could result in a tax nightmare.

When dealing with clients, I like to be blatantly clear. My warning to them goes like this: "Before you go ahead and start issuing shares to family members, fully understand what costs you will incur and realize that everything has to be done exactly in accordance with the prevailing rules and regulations both in your jurisdiction and federally."

Remember earlier in the book I recommended that when you incorporate you should have your lawyer set up multiple share classes? The reason for this, I hope, now becomes clearer. If after you incorporate you want to issue shares to other family members (a holding company, or family trust) you have to have them available. One of the first things we do in my office when we start working with a new client is to review their minute book (if they're already incorporated). If we see that there are multiple types of shares available, we know we have planning opportunities open to us. If the minute book reveals only one class of shares, we know that the company is going to have to be changed (reorganized). This creates additional legal work and expenses, and therefore has to be factored into the cost benefit of reorganizing a corporation.

By now you may be asking yourself, "What is the purpose of a reorganization? All I see are costs and complications."

Okay, let's look at why it's so important. The primary purpose is to get shares of your professional corporation into the name of someone else so you can income split. The secondary purpose is to defer taxes that would otherwise be owed, assuming your shares have increased in value since you bought them or set up your PC. Reorganization will also allow you to structure the PC in such a way that your family members, holding company or trust can afford to purchase the shares.

Let's look at how the reorganization of a professional corporation might look. We'll call it, Dr. Brooklyn Williamson Medical Corporation.

When examining the minute book of Dr. Brooklyn Williamson Medical Corporation we see the following:

Share Capital

Class A common shares	Unlimited[10]
Class B common shares	Unlimited
Class C common shares	Unlimited
Class D first preferred shares	Unlimited
Class E second preferred shares	Unlimited
Class F third preferred shares	Unlimited

There are currently 100 Class A common shares issued with a paid-up capital (PUC)[11] amount of $10.00. On the date of the reorganization let's assume the fair market value of the company is $500,000.

---

10 Unlimited means the company can issue an unlimited amount of shares.
11 Paid-up capital is the amount you paid for the shares.

In order to remove the value from the common shares, you have to exchange them for preferred shares. At the time of the reorganization you can normally set the value of the preferred shares. Again, look at the minute book. If your company was set up to issue preferred shares and they don't have a predetermined value, then you can set the value when they're issued.

There is a section of the *Income Tax Act* that allows for a transfer from one share class to another without triggering tax. If you exchange 100 Class A common shares worth $500,000 with a PUC of $10.00 for 1,000 Class A first preferred shares worth $500,000, and a PUC of $10.00 you're in a neutral tax position. You still own $500,000 worth of shares with a PUC of $10.00.

When this exchange takes place, the value of the common shares is reduced to zero because all the value has been transferred to the preferred shares. It's at that moment that all interested parties should buy common shares. The price for the new common shares being issued will be decided at that time. If you issue 100 shares that have a purchase price of $0.10 per share, you would pay $10.00 for the 100 shares. This initial price that you pay for the new common shares has no bearing on taxes, if all the value has been moved to the preferred shares.

As an example, if you, as the professional buy new Class A common shares for $10.00, your spouse can buy Class B common shares for $10.00 and your holding company or trust can buy Class C common shares for $10.00 (this is just an example – the actual classes of shares that are issued and the price paid will depend on where you live and what you're allowed to do).

To follow through with this example; if the Class A, B and C shares were all eligible for dividends, then you can decide how much in dividends will be paid on each share and class. This is how you income-split. As long as the rights of the shares allow for dividends to be paid on one class of shares, to the exclusion of the others, you could declare a dividend on the Class B shares only. The dividend in this case would be paid to your spouse.

When you sell the shares of your PC, or upon death, the first $500,000 will be attributed to your preferred shares and any increase in value since the reorganization will be split between the common shareholders, unless one or more of the classes of common shares were non-growth[12] shares.

---

12 Non-growth shares are shares that do not increase in value.

There can be significant benefits to reorganizing your professional corporation but you have to know what the cost of such reorganization is going to be. One last word of warning: always be prepared for a cash outlay before a cash benefit.

Picking A Year-End

One of the questions you will be asked (or have already been asked) by your lawyer and accountant is: 'what year-end do you want to use?'. If this confused you, or you didn't really understand your hired professional's suggestions, then read on and all will become clear.

Personal taxes are paid based on a calendar year January 1 to December 31. Incorporated companies however, have what is referred to as a "fiscal" year. A fiscal year can be any 12-month period. Most corporations are allowed to pick any year-end they want. If you choose June 30 as your year-end, your fiscal year would be July 1 to June 30.

So, the question is, does it matter when your year-end is? From a tax point of view it may be marginal, depending on your business. For instance, if you have a lot of income above the small business limit, you may want to declare that money as a bonus before the company year-end in order to get the deduction for the company. If your year-end is July 31 or later in the year, you can declare the bonus in the current company fiscal year and not have to take the money into personal income until the next calendar year. This is because the payment of bonuses declared by a company prior to year-end can be deferred by up to 179 days. This means the company gets a deduction this year and you take the bonus into income next year.

I have an incorporated dentist as a client who chose a corporate year-end of September 30. Last year she made $625,000 of income after expenses and before taxes. In order to reduce her corporate income to the small business limit of $500,000 we declared a bonus to her of $125,000 on September 29. The company deducted the $125,000 last year and she was able to take it out this year. This allowed her to defer paying the personal tax on that money for six months. If she left the entire $625,000 to be taxed in the professional corporation, she would be paying tax in the current year on $125,000 at the high corporate rate. Remember that only the first $500,000[13] is eligible to be taxed at the small business tax rate.

---

13 $400,000 in Manitoba, Nova Scotia and the Yukon.

More companies are using December 31 as their year-end just to make things simple; however, if your accountant has any input into picking the year-end they will probably suggest an "off" calendar year-end. Why will they do this? In most cases they do this to provide you with better service. If everyone had a December 31 year-end, things could get very backlogged at the accountant's office. Corporate taxes are due 90-days after the company year-end and personal taxes are due by April 30. Imagine all the work that has to be compressed into the first four months of the year. The thinking is that if you choose an August 31 year-end, your accountant will have more time available for you.

So, should you buy into this apparently logical approach to choosing a year-end? No, regardless of what your accountant may want, I strongly recommend that you pick a December 31st year-end, no matter when in the year you incorporate. The reason has everything to do with tax reporting.

Every tax certificate is issued between January 1 and March 31. This includes T-3, T-5 and a whole collection of various tax slips. If you have a July 31 year-end, how do you calculate how much income from your investment trust is interest, or dividends, or a return of capital? I speak from experience when I tell you that it will drive you crazy trying to figure out what to tell your accountant when they ask you what your investment income was in the last fiscal period. I'll be spending more time on this in my new book, The Financial Navigator.

Once you've got your professional corporation organized, you have to set up your corporate bank account. Just remember that you can't set up a corporate bank account until after you're incorporation has been completed!

Let's take a look at what should, and hopefully will, happen at the bank.

```
Re: Is my accountant right?
From:
To: tim@tpcfinancial.com

Hi Tim

I met with my accountant yesterday and she recommended
I bonus out all the money I made from the date of
incorporation to December 31st. I thought the idea was
to leave some money in the PC. I only incorporated
September 1st so I don't understand what she's doing.
Does this make sense?
Sven
```

Re: Re: Heathrow Chance Meeting
From: tim@tpcfinancial.com
To: Sven Hansen

Hi Sven

How are you managing up there in the frozen north? A
big change from South Africa I suspect. Are the boys
enjoying the snow?

In your case, it does make sense. From the time you
incorporated last September until January you took
nothing out of your PC. You had enough money in the
bank to live on during that time so all the income that
was paid to your PC is taxable to it. We decided on a
December 31st year-end, so without a bonus all the net
income would be taxable to the PC and due March 31st.

Being that yesterday was January 18th, we're into a
new calendar year. As we decided, you are going to
start taking a salary this month so you're going to be
taking money from your PC anyway.

If you declare a bonus for last year in the first 60
days of this year, you can deduct that bonus from the
previous year's income and take it into personal income
in the current year.

Specifically, in your situation, between September
1st and December 31st your PC had taxable income of
$80,000. If you left everything in your PC you would
have to pay $12,000 in corporate income tax.

The salary you decided on for the current year was
$120,000. By declaring a bonus of $80,000 now, your
PC can deduct the $80,000 against last year's income
resulting in zero tax payable by your PC. You will take
the $80,000 into your personal income this year along
with an additional $40,000 for a total of $120,000.

Call me if you want that explained further. I'll be
going into a lot more detail in the book – I'll send
you a copy as soon as it's available.

Keep warm.

Tim

P.S. I now have a Facebook page and plan to use it to discuss the questions and challenges that seem to most often crop up with my clients. Check me out at http://bit.ly/tpc-facebook

The Banker's Role

Let me begin by saying that all banks may be created equal, and work within the same regulatory framework, but whether you have a good experience or a bad experience will totally depend on the individual you talk to. I don't think it's appropriate to comment on the pros and cons of specific banks in this book, but what I can do is give you a few examples of what I've experienced in the last 30 years.

Case Study: Interest rate blindness

Some time ago, I was reviewing a physician's financial information; she had been in practice for 20 years and had two personal lines of credit with the same bank. She was using both, but they showed different interest rates. Given her financial record and current situation the rates were high – prime plus 2 per cent on one and prime plus 3 per cent on the other. When I questioned her about the different rates she said she had never really paid much attention to them. After our meeting she called the bank and was told that it was simply an oversight at their end and that they would change them to the same rate. When she questioned them on the exact rate they were going to use and asked that it be set at prime, they again stated that it was an oversight at their end and that prime would be no problem.

So, for about twenty years she had been overpaying interest! Interestingly, when the bank was challenged on this point they agreed to back pay interest if she could calculate how much they had overcharged her. The problem was that they said that they could not provide records, and because she did not keep her records, no back interest was paid. The result was that she moved banks.

How did this situation occur? The original line of credit was given to her upon graduation. She was a new graduate and just grateful that the bank gave her a credit facility at all. They charged her a risk premium of plus 3 per cent on this initial line of credit. A few years later they gave her a second line of credit for her practice. This second line of credit was set up with a risk premium of 2 per cent and no offer was made by the bank to reduce the charge on the original line of credit. Over the years these credit facilities were not reviewed and not once did the bank offer to reduce the risk premium.

I'm constantly amazed at how often I see situations in which banks could have reduced rates for customers, but instead appear to try and get away with whatever the customer is willing to pay.

The previous example shows how things can just drift if we don't keep an eye on them. The following story illustrates the fact that we shouldn't take for granted that a so-called 'expert' knows what they're talking about!

Case Study – The account manager who couldn't get a good deal even for herself!

Another situation involved two dentists, a husband and wife who both had successful practices. They were moving to a new house and required bridge financing. The amount involved was $100,000. I suggested they go talk to their bank and get their existing line of credit increased from $50,000 to $100,000 and at the same time ask for a new interest rate of prime instead of their current prime plus 1 per cent. I subsequently received a call from their banker while they were in her office. She asked if I was the one who told them they could get a line of credit at prime. I said I was and she proceeded to explain to me that no one gets prime and that I had no business telling my clients that. "As a matter of fact," she said, "I work at the bank and I don't get prime." My initial reaction was to tell her to go work at another bank. My clients certainly were eligible to get prime and did when they changed to a bank that was happy to give them a $100,000 line of credit at prime.

In the following example, a bank is unreasonable concerning the amount of collateral, or personal guarantees it was demanding.

Case Study – When is enough collateral, enough already?

I was recently involved in the partial sale of a dental practice. One dentist was selling half his practice to an associate. Both dentists used the same bank. The bank put the financing package together and then asked the selling dentist if he would co-sign the loan to the purchasing dentist. What? No way!

After having the selling dentist as a client for 20 years, the bank knew what the practice was worth; there was no reason to ask him to co-sign the loan. I suggested that the purchasing dentist talk to another bank. He did, and as a result got the loan package we were looking for, without a personal guarantee from the seller. It's not uncommon for a bank to ask for as much collateral and personal guarantees as it can get away with. The bottom line is that you need only provide them with sufficient collateral to ensure that you will be able to continue to make the loan payments or pay off the loan in case of disability or death.

I have dozens of examples of dubious practices and poor customer service from banks, but here is a final doozy.

A client with millions of dollars of investments, both personal and corporate, was purchasing a second home. His best financial strategy was to sell one of his company's investments, remove the money from the company as a shareholder loan, and then have the company borrow money to buy the same investment back. This would allow him to get the money he required now, buy back his corporate investment, and write off the interest on the money the company borrowed to re-purchase the investment in the company. When the first home was sold, he would use the proceeds to pay off the shareholder loan. This seemed like an easy way to get the money for the second house and not lose the opportunity that his company investment provided.

I met with the client and his banker in my office and it was agreed that there were sufficient assets to cover such a loan. We agreed on the terms and conditions of the loan and the banker left. The following week, I received a call from the client and his lawyer. They were reviewing the paperwork sent over from the bank and it showed them using every asset the client owned as collateral for the loan. The ramifications of this were that we would require permission from the bank every time we wanted to change an investment. In our meeting with the banker, it had been agreed that we didn't have to use all the assets. In fact, we had agreed exactly what specific assets were going to be used. When the lawyer called the banker he stated that it was a mistake at the bank's end and that the paperwork was incorrect. They reissued the paperwork to reflect what was agreed at the original meeting. That was all well and good, but what if no one had reviewed the documents before they were signed? The bank would have gained control over all the client's assets.

> **Rule of Thumb Buster:** All banks are created equal. Not true, not even the branches are created equal. Shop around.

Working With Your Bank – Not For Your Bank

Dealing with banks is not always full of trials and tribulations; I do have excellent working relationships with two bank managers. Even though they work for different banks, I know I can call on them at any time to advocate on behalf of my clients. I never ask for anything that is not realistic, but on the other hand, I never assume that their first offer is their best offer. For example, the physician I mentioned earlier with two lines of credit at different rates also had a mortgage. When I approached one of the bank managers I deal with, I told him that we wanted one line of credit, not two. I wanted it increased from $75,000 to $100,000, and I wanted the interest rate reduced from prime plus 2 per cent to simply prime. I was also prepared to offer the mortgage as part of the package on renewal in 2010. The first offer came back with the increased line of credit approved at prime and the mortgage was left as is. When I received word from the doctor that the line of credit was in place, I phoned the bank manager and asked him to consider doing something with the mortgage. It took a few days but he was able to put together a new mortgage at his bank with a lower blended interest rate[14] (even after the penalties were factored in). This 'package' will save my client several thousands of dollars over the next five years.

The point here is that you have to take the initiative. If you don't feel comfortable, or qualified to carry out this type of negotiation, ask your accountant or financial planner to help you (we negotiate loan arrangements on a regular basis for our clients). Banks are changing all the time and new services and programs are offered almost daily; just because something was appropriate for you ten years ago, or even last year, doesn't mean it's the best thing for you today. Finally, don't assume that the bank will call you and tell you they are going to reduce your rates – you need to be proactive.

Bank fees are another issue and can vary from account to account. I've always found it interesting that what I pay $12.00 for as an individual; I pay $36.00 for as a business. Most fees and charges are negotiable. I've heard every bank say that something is not negotiable only to find that, well, maybe it is. This also includes legal and appraisal charges. While negotiating a loan for a client I was told that the legal fees absolutely had to be paid by the client. After pressing the issue I got the client a "refund" equal to the legal costs. Yes, the client paid the fees but the bank gave her the money to do so.

Never forget that you are the client; the bank wants your business. As a professional you have a lot of power because of what you do. If one bank will give you something, all the others will probably do the same, and more. You

---

14 Blended basis: A blended rate is an interest rate determined by averaging out two different interest rates, usually your current rate used to calculate your payment and today's rate, taking into account the remaining term of your current mortgage.

can save tens of thousands of dollars over your working lifetime by working with your bank – not for your bank.

When it comes to loans, the bank structures things to their advantage, but how would you like to turn the tables on them?

Most people know that making weekly mortgage payments saves interest when compared to monthly payments. However, most people don't know that loans (and remember a mortgage is just a loan) are calculated with interest payable from the day the money is advanced and what's worse automatically assume that the first payment is at least thirty days out. This brings us to the secret of the missing first loan payment.

The Secret Of The Missing First Loan Payment

When I got my first mortgage in 1982 the interest rate was 16.5 per cent. My banker (a friend of the family) told me that the money would be available on the closing date, which was May 1, and asked when in the month I wanted the mortgage payment to come out. I said that the 15th would be perfect. "No problem," he said. "Because this is your first house and you have other expenses, why don't we start the payments on June 15?" I said, "Great" as this seemed to make perfect sense. However, when I got my first annual mortgage statement in May 1983, I owed more money than the original amount borrowed. I'd paid nothing down on the principal and owed an additional $1,700. How on earth did that happen? The thing is, the bank charged me interest on the amount I borrowed as of May 1 when they advanced me the money. By the time I made the first payment on June 15, I was already behind. I owed interest on the mortgage for the first 45 days (May 1 to June 15). That mortgage interest was now on top of the principal, but my mortgage payment was based on the original amount borrowed. I had no way to catch up. When you are borrowing money personally or corporately, make sure you are aware of how loans are structured.

Could this problem have been avoided? Absolutely. Have I ever been in that situation again? No. Do our clients run into this problem? Never, not on our watch. When you get any loan (unless it's an interest-only loan for investment or business purposes) always make sure you make an extra payment as soon as you can. I love to make a lump sum payment on mortgages or loans equal to the interest owing for the year. This extra payment goes right to principal and shifts the repayment schedule in my favour. Payments are based on the amount borrowed; if you pay off part of the principal in the first month, the payments you will be making are automatically higher, and you therefore pay off the principal faster. If you're ever going to make an extra payment, try to make it the first one.

I have to say that I have more challenges dealing with banks than with any other group; the reason for this is that banks are there to serve their shareholders and not their clients. It is a good idea to remember this when you are dealing with your friendly account manager. Here are a few more examples of banking lunacy.

Not too long ago, I was talking to a client who was planning to get a loan to pay for renovations (leasehold improvements) to her practice's offices. I asked her to have her bank put a loan proposal together and then send it to me for review.

When the proposal arrived, I noticed that the loan rate was prime +2 per cent, which I thought was excessively high. I asked her to call the bank and tell them that the rate was unacceptable and that she wanted it reduced to no more then prime + 0.5 per cent. She told me she wasn't comfortable doing that and asked if I would talk to them on her behalf. No problem I said, and asked her to contact her bank and tell them that I would be calling to discuss her loan proposal. She did and I subsequently made the call to her "account manager."

Before I could even ask a question I was told that I had no right to discuss the client's loan details with the bank, not because I wasn't given permission, but because according to the "account manager" it was between the bank and the client. Now just to be clear, what they were saying was that the client was the only one who had the right to negotiate with the bank. They would give me her account balances or loan details, or anything else I wanted to know but I was not allowed to negotiate the loan arrangement for the client. According to them I had no right to. My view on this can be summed up in the euphemism - male cow dung. I've negotiated hundreds of loans for clients and had never been told I can't – until then. Do not let banks bully you. Remember, you are the client and the bottom line is that they probably don't want to lose you!

Last month I was visiting a client who had a mortgage coming up for renewal. Like always, I like to get the existing bank to give us a quote before we take it into the market for a rate comparison. Being busy, the client asked if I could take care of dealing with the bank and report back later in the month; again no problem, I was more than happy to oblige.

"Do you have the name at the person at CIBC that you work with?" I asked.

"Sure, I'll call them tomorrow and make arrangements for you to deal with them directly" my client assured me.

"Excellent. I'll take it from there."

Now just to be fair I'll quote you the e-mail I got from CIBC exactly as I received it.

> "Sorry for the delay, but this is an unusual request and I had to check with CIBC Audit & Control to see how to proceed (i.e. what letter would be required). Since the letter would need to be very specific as to what could be disclosed and would be the same detail as outlined in an account printout, I would prefer to forward you a banking summary. I would not be able to discuss financial planning matters as it would relate to the information and, of course, not take any instructions from the advisor themselves.
>
> Given all of these restrictions, I would only feel comfortable providing you with your account details. After you review it with the advisor, perhaps you could email me with specific questions. From a banking printout, normally an advisor would have enough information to formulate a financial plan."

Now, does this sound like a bank you'd like to work with?

Here's the interesting thing. Two months ago I did the exact same thing with a client in Saskatchewan with CIBC. I worked with the account manager and we did everything together. The fellow was terrific. So what's with the 180-degree switch in attitude? I have no idea but what I will say is that you have every right to expect your advisors to work together. If they won't, then I recommend you change advisors.

Leasing Companies – Are They Banks' Evil Cousins?

Before we finally leave the section on banks and bankers, let me warn you about their sometimes-evil cousin - the leasing company. I've seen some great leases and some really horrible ones. The great ones are normally with car companies, and the horrible ones are usually with equipment lease companies. Lease companies will sometimes offer loans for things like leasehold improvements. These can be extremely punitive and difficult to get out of, to the point that if you pay back early you have to pay all the interest due for the entire term of the original loan.

If anyone who reads this book can avoid a horrible equipment lease (this can also extend to lease hold improvements), then I feel it was worth my time and effort.

So, how do you protect yourself from a bad lease?

First – never sign a lease that you haven't read. This may sound simple but the fact is most people don't read the stupid things because they're long and boring.

Second – never sign a lease that's not completely filled in. Again this may sound like absurd advice, but believe it, it happens. What can happen is the leasing agent tells you it takes too long to fill in all the paperwork, so they'll do it later and send you a copy.

Third – always know what the terms of the deal are. Clients are always asking me if they should buy this or lease that. My first question to them is always "what's the deal?" Know what the terms are, know what the interest rates are, and finally find out what you can and can't do concerning prepayments.

Forth – if possible, before you sign any lease, make sure you know what other choices you may have. You may be better off to arrange financing of equipment purchases and leasehold improvements through your bank.

Leasehold Case Study

A new dentist was buying part of a practice. He wanted to replace the equipment and so was given the name of a dental leasing company. Before the lease was signed the dentist sent me a copy of the lease agreement. My first thought was wow – what a complete rip off!

The lease was set up over seven years with a floating rate of prime + 3 per cent. There was no prepayment option and once you signed you were committed for the seven years. By comparison, at that time, Scotiabank was willing to give the dentist an equipment loan at prime with no prepayment restrictions. So the question is, why would anyone consider signing such a lease? In this case it was because my client's partners didn't want to approach their own banks for the loan.

I just had to know the answer, so I called the leasing company representative that had made the offer. I asked him why anyone would sign such a lease? He told me it was because the lease was fully deductible. So, that was their justification for the prime + 3 per cent rate. Let's take a moment and look at this situation. On a $300,000 lease that's $35,000 in interest charges and no opportunity to get out of the lease if interest rates were to rise. And that was with a floating (or variable) rate. Recently I reviewed a lease that had a fixed rate of 18.5 per cent. You read that right, 18.5 per cent.

Please, be very careful when you're dealing with leases. In some jurisdictions it's perfectly legal for the leasing companies NOT to disclose the lease rate in the paperwork.

I've picked on lawyers a bit in this chapter so now let me take a passing shot at accountants. I've been in practice for over three decades and have had the pleasure of working with some excellent accountants, but there are certainly a number out there who frighten the life out of me. One particular horror from Ontario deserves particular recognition.

My client was a physician who moved from Ontario to British Columbia, and who asked his accountant to continue handling his finances. The accountant, of course, said there would be no problem in this cross-province arrangement and indeed eight-years passed with no obvious problems. Until, that is, the physician sat in on one of my seminars on family trusts, and afterward asked me if I would review his situation and let him know if he would be a candidate for a family trust. When the information arrived I noticed that he had two children in post-secondary education, which he was paying for. In a subsequent conversation he told me that he had already put two other children through school, and that at least one of the remaining children would be going on to do post graduate studies.

The fact that he was a candidate for a family trust was not in question; the big issue was that he should have set one up eight years ago. So why hadn't he?

It was time to find out. I called the accountant in Ontario and asked him why he wasn't using a family trust to pay for his client's children's education. His response was, "they're illegal." I thought I must have misunderstood him and asked him to repeat the statement – again he came back with the comment that, "they're illegal." I could sense he was somewhat perturbed by my line of questioning and he went on to tell me that trusts are illegal in Ontario and that as a chartered accountant who had been practicing for over 25 years he should know what he's talking about. The fact of the matter was, he had no idea what he was talking about and that although the use of a family trust in Ontario in this case was out of the question, I assured him that trusts were not illegal.

Here is a case where the accountant's lack of knowledge relating to the different incorporation rules pertaining to the various provinces and territories was highly detrimental to his client's financial wellbeing. When the physician moved from Ontario to B.C. his corporate structure should have been changed, plain and simple. By not using a family trust over the eight-year period in question, the doctor paid a minimum of $200,000 in unnecessary taxes.

There are two morals to this story. First, never trust that your accountant always knows what they're doing and second, having an expert advise you doesn't mean that you shouldn't have a good understanding of the financial opportunities open to you. Reading this book, of course, is an excellent start!

Before I leave this section on accountants I want to just touch on fees. I've seen outrageous fees and others that are very reasonable. There doesn't seem to be any standard. Like dealing with lawyers, you should ask your accountant what he or she is going to charge and what they're going to do for the money. For instance, some accountants will send you a bill every time you ask them a question and others won't. What you don't want to see is a big nasty surprise at the end of the year.

Your accountant is a very important member of your team and so you have to feel good about the relationship, and the value for money they represent. Don't be afraid to question what's going on. If you feel like you're being overcharged, ask a few colleagues what they're paying. Most accountants are pretty fair, but like the lawyer I encountered at that dental conference, there are those who will try to take advantage.

Here's an inside tip. Check whether your accountant is charging you the same, or even more, as they always did, but for less work.

It's not unusual to have an increase in fees. One local accounting firm I know was taken over by a larger national firm and their fees went up 30 per cent. If that happens to you, you might want to shop around for a new accountant. But that's not the type of change I'm talking about.

What I'm referring to is a situation where you're not giving your accountant any more work and your accounting should actually be getting easier, yet the accounting bills are the same or higher.

Here's a case in point, I have a client who had a professional corporation and a holding company. The accounting bill for both was $4,800 per year. The client retired and moved all the assets into the holding company and dissolved the PC. Now he only has a holding company.

The first year of retirement, with just the one company, the accounting bill was $4,800. You would think the bill would be less – maybe even half but it was the same.

When I questioned the accountant he told me that the bill was "higher" because of all the changes with the winding up of the PC. Imagine our surprise when the accounting bill the following year came in again at $4,800. What's wrong with this picture?

We ended up changing accountants and the bill dropped to about $2,600, but here's what I learned. It's not unusual for accountants to charge "the same as last year" when they're not sure how much to bill.

Be aware of what your accounting and legal bills are. Call me thick, but in over 30 years I still have no idea how lawyers and accountants bill.

Who Pulls All The Legal And Financial Elements Together?

In my world, we do. For you it may be your accountant, lawyer, financial planner or banker. If at all possible, the one person you don't want it to be is you. Someone has to make sure that everything is done. That someone should have access to all the information and people involved, and possess the right level of experience and knowledge in this specialist area. In chapter 14 "Working with a Professional Coordinator", I take you in detail through how my company handles things. It should give you an idea of what I believe should happen.

For now, here is a brief overview of how all the elements are pulled together.

After meeting a client and deciding that they should incorporate, we contact a lawyer to start the incorporation process. We know what the allowable share structures are in each jurisdiction and therefore recommend the appropriate structure for the client. We also allow for changes by way of extra share classes. We work with the client's existing lawyer or introduce them to a lawyer with whom we can work with.

Our client's accountant is contacted for input, and we work with them to ensure that all proper valuations and tax issues are dealt with.

We negotiate with a number of banks to obtain the best possible deals. In the first instance, we discuss our client's needs with their existing bank, as we recognize that most people would prefer not to move banks if it can be avoided.

We meet with the professional and their spouse to ensure that they both understand what is going to happen, how the incorporation is going to change their lives, and what they can expect from the various individuals they're working with.

In this way, we can assure our clients that the entire process will go as smoothly as possible and that everything will be taken care of. You, as a professional, have enough on your plate without having to work through this process alone. I would advise you to delegate and then hold everyone working on your behalf accountable.

CHAPTER THREE

Buying A Professional Practice

Buying Assets Or Shares

If you are going to purchase a practice, you have to consider what exactly it is you are buying. Because of the enhanced capital gains deduction, most professionals selling their practices prefer to sell shares. As a purchaser, it is usually more beneficial to purchase assets. How then, can you create a win-win situation?

When purchasing assets it's usually just a function of knowing what it's all worth. For example a dental chair or examining table has a value; you pay for the asset and any tax consequences belong to the seller. Some assets may be more difficult to value but there are all kinds of companies and professional business valuators to help you with this task. Assets have the benefit of setting the cost base for you at the price you paid for them. If you pay $4,000 for a dental chair, your cost base will be $4,000. This is the starting value for depreciation. The same holds true for all other capital assets, including goodwill (see page 82, "What is goodwill?").

When you buy shares, it's a different story. In buying shares, you assume whatever cost base was left by the seller for each particular capital asset; you don't have a new cost base, you simply take over theirs. This can mean a significant loss to you if the assets have a low cost base.

Normally, in order to complete the sale, a compromise is reached on the value of the shares. If the selling party is going to walk away with little or no tax consequences and the purchaser is going to lose the opportunity to deduct a large portion of the purchase price, the value of the shares is reduced to deal with this discrepancy. Your practice valuator and accountant should be able to tell you what both situations would look like, so you can reach a mutually advantageous agreement.

Practice Valuations

How business valuators actually value a practice does not fall within the scope of this book. However, there are a number of different valuation methods and services available to determine the value of a practice, but suffice it to say that in all cases the value will be subjective. What a six-year-old dental chair and a nine-year-old examining table are worth is open for discussion. However, like all depreciable equipment, they can be estimated. All assets have a range of values that will be different depending on whether you are the seller or the purchaser. When buying or selling a practice, you might want to get two valuations done to establish a price range.

The following table lists a few of the pros and cons of having more than one valuation done.

Pros	Cons
Accuracy	Cost
Will establish a range	May not be significantly different
Fairness: One valuation can represent the buyer, one the seller	Value may be higher/lower than you want
Peace of mind	

One of the most difficult assets to value is goodwill. Unlike tangible assets, goodwill is totally subjective. The variation in value can be extreme and is usually open to negotiation. Goodwill is discussed further in the next section.

Leasehold improvements present another interesting aspect of evaluating a practice. Suppose you are buying a dental practice from a dentist who is retiring. Leasehold improvements will probably show up on the practice valuation. What are they? They include everything that was put in after the "shell" was built.

When a new building is constructed each floor is usually empty. When a tenant is found, they develop their own floor plan and then have the space constructed, everything that is put into that shell is a leasehold improvement. The more common leasehold improvements are to non-supporting walls, cabinets, bookshelves, built-in desks, carpets and lights.

Dental practices, because the offices are more elaborate, usually have significantly more leasehold improvements than medical practices. When you sell or buy a practice, you usually buy or sell the leasehold improvements. Normally, it doesn't make sense to rip them out and take them with you – but you could! Leasehold improvements belong to you and can be removed if you want to take them somewhere else; however, in reality most people don't want old carpets and walls so they simply leave them, or try to sell them to the new tenant. You can think of leasehold improvements in this way: what the landlord gave you, or what you added, when you moved in is what you have to leave when you move out.

A dentist who was retiring signed a ten-year lease five years previously with the hope that a purchasing dentist would want to take it over at the current fixed lease rate. From a tax point of view, you are allowed to write off your leasehold improvements over the initial term of the lease plus the first renewal option, as long as the combination of the two is at least five years in duration. Theoretically, leasehold improvements are not worth anything at the end of the lease because they have been written down to zero, but in reality that wall you built still has a value.

What Should You Pay?

There is no way to specify what the actual value of any practice is worth. All valuations are subjective. What I can tell you is that generally you shouldn't pay as much for shares of a professional corporation as you would for its assets. When you buy shares you assume the depreciated value of the assets. For example, if a dental chair is old and has a depreciated value of $1,000, then after you purchase the shares of the practice your cost base for tax purposes will be $1,000. You will depreciate the chair at the starting point of $1,000. If, however, the chair is actually worth $3,000 (the value reflected in the valuation) not the depreciated value of $1,000, and you purchase assets, then when you purchase the chair for $3,000, your starting point for depreciation is $3,000. Part of the negotiation, when purchasing a practice should include a comparison for both the buyer and the seller that reflects the difference in tax treatment between buying and selling shares and assets.

What Is Goodwill And Why Should I Pay For It?

When you purchase goodwill, it is treated for tax purposes as an eligible capital expenditure and may be depreciated at a rate of 7 per cent per year. The unfortunate thing about goodwill is that it is extremely subjective when it comes to valuation. In a very well established dental practice, the goodwill value may be high (as much as 80 per cent of the value of the practice): in a brand new practice, it could be zero. Depending on the type of practice you're valuing, the goodwill may or may not be a factor. If you're going to be purchasing (or selling) a practice that has goodwill, you should consider having a least two independent valuations carried out. This should give you a low to high valuation. Based on this range it's easy to conclude that true fair market value would be somewhere between the two valuations.

If you start up a practice from scratch, you don't have any goodwill; although over time, you may create goodwill. When you sell your practice, its value will include the physical assets and some recognition of this intangible asset called goodwill. Most dental practices have goodwill. The amount depends on a number of factors, including, but not limited to, the type and number of patients, the location and the competition.

Recently, I was reviewing a practice purchase that set the value of the practice at $415,000, of which $220,000 was goodwill. This amount was probably not unrealistic when you look at the particular practice. By purchasing the practice, the acquiring dentist would not only be getting the equipment and supplies but also the cash flow created by the existing patients.

Medical practices are not normally sold because they have little or no goodwill. I have seen many situations where physicians have tried, without success, to sell their medical practices. In those cases, the assets were eventually sold and the patients went somewhere else. I believe that one contributing factor in this situation is the shortage of medical doctors. When one leaves or retires, another doctor can easily set up a practice and soon fill it with patients. If attracting patients were a difficult thing to do, then goodwill would have some value.

Goodwill can be the result of legislation. For example, a number of years ago in the Yukon, any qualified physician could practice medicine. Then, the rules changed overnight and the issuing of billing numbers became restricted. This created a situation where billing numbers had a value, as without one you couldn't open a practice, a value defined as goodwill. I personally know of many situations where new physicians paid retiring, or departing, physicians significant sums of money to acquire their billing numbers. Some years later, the rules changed again and today the Yukon does not restrict billing numbers. As a result, there is no more goodwill to be sold. Unfortunately, for those who bought goodwill, they will probably never recover their investment.

Borrowing Money

One of the major advantages of a professional corporation is being able to pay off debt with after-tax corporate dollars, not after-tax personal dollars. The interest on money borrowed to invest in your practice is deductible to you personally if you are not incorporated, and corporately if you are. The principal you have to repay is not deductible.

Let's look at two examples:

Dr. A borrows $350,000 to purchase 50 per cent of a practice. The interest on the loan is 6 per cent. He is not incorporated. The interest on the loan is therefore deductible on his personal tax return. After deductions, his pre-tax income is $200,000. If he lives in British Columbia, he would pay about $67,000 in income tax and make CPP contributions of $4,326 (as a self employed individual you have you pay both as an employee and employer) leaving him with $128,674. If he needs $75,000 to live on, he would have $53,674 available to pay down the principal of the loan. With the top tax rate in British Columbia being 43.7 per cent, Dr. A would have to earn $621,670 to pay off the $350,000 loan. As was mentioned earlier, principal payments are not tax deductible, therefore you have to earn the money, pay the tax and then use the after-tax money to pay off the loan. If you owe $350,000 you have to earn $621,670, then pay tax at 43.7 per cent ($621,670 x 43.7 per cent = $271,670) to net $350,000 ($621,670 - $271,670 = $350,000).

Dr. B also borrows $350,000 (to purchase the other half of the practice). The interest on her loan is also 6 per cent. However, she is incorporated so the interest on the loan is deductible to her corporation. After deductions, her corporate income is $200,000. From this, she takes a gross salary of $110,000, that nets her $75,000 to live on. The company takes a deduction of $110,000 leaving it with $90,000. The company is then required to make a CPP contribution on her behalf of $2,163 (half of the $4,326 as the employer, the other half was taken off her $110,000 salary) and pay tax of $11,857[15]. After CPP and tax, the company would have $75,980 available to pay down the principal of the loan ($90,000 - $2,163 - $11,857 = $75,980). Using the small business rate in British Columbia of 13.5 per cent, Dr. B would have to earn $404,624 to pay off the $350,000. In this case, because you're using after tax corporate dollars, you only have to earn $404,624 inside the company, pay tax at 13.5 per cent ($54,624) to net $350,000.

In both cases Dr. A and Dr. B owed $350,000. In both cases Dr. A and Dr. B deducted the interest. But unlike Dr. A who wasn't incorporated, Dr. B has to earn $217,046 less to pay off the $350,000 because she can leave money in her professional corporation to be taxed at 13.5 per cent instead of paying personal tax like Dr. A at 43.7 per cent.

As a professional, you should never lose sight of the fact that it's all yours. You earn it and you pay tax. If you earn $1.00 and have to pay tax at 43.7 per cent, you'll be left with $0.563. If you earn $1.00 and pay tax at 13.5 per cent, you'll be left with $0.865. When you owe money, it's a lot easier to pay it back when you're working with $0.865 dollars than $0.563 dollars.

As you can see from this example, being incorporated and having your professional corporation pay off your debt can save you hundreds of thousands of dollars. This in turn will allow you to start accumulating investment assets inside your PC sooner.

Before leaving this section let me point out something else about this example that may be less obvious. If you pay off your debt faster by using corporate dollars, you're also paying less interest. Remember the 6 per cent interest? At 6 per cent it would take Dr. A a little over 10 years to pay off a $350,000 debt, if his payments were $3,639.50 per month ($43,674/12). Dr. B on the other hand, would have her loan paid off in about 5 ½ years because she can make payments of $6,331.66 per month ($75,980/12). Over the 10 years Dr. A would pay about $139,000 in interest. Over the 5 years Dr. B would pay about $56,000 in interest. If you add the $83,000 in interest savings ($139,000 - $56,000 = $83,000) to the $217,046 income savings ($621,670 - $404,624 = $217,046), Dr. B would be ahead about $300,000!

---

15 The current small business tax rate in British Columbia is 13.5%. After deducting the $2,163 from the corporate income of $90,000, the net taxable income would be $87,837. You then take the net taxable income of $87,837 and multiply it by 13.5%, which results in corporate tax payable of $11,857.

Re: Opportunity Knocks
From: Lange Zhu
To: tim@tpcfinancial.com

Hi Tim

Things have been going well since we last spoke; I was
saying to a colleague the other day that it seems such
a long time ago since you and I first met in London.
I tell people that a foggy type of karma made you my
financial advisor; it's a good after-dinner story!

Anyhow, as usual I have a question. I have an
opportunity to purchase the building my practice is
in. I'm not sure if I should buy it personally or
corporately. What do you think I should do?

By the way, how's the new book coming along?

Lange

Re: Re: Opportunity Knocks
From: tim@tpcfinancial.com
To: Lange Zhu

Hi Lange

Good to hear from you as always. Yes, I still dine out
on our story; that chance meeting certainly impacted
how I approached the new book. What started out as
a basic update has turned into a major revision and
complete rewrite. I've added a mass of new information
– in part thanks to the questions you and Sven have
been asking, which as we discussed are going to be
featured in the book! Sven says hi by the way! Okay,
let's look at your question.

Purchasing the building where you practice is usually a
great idea. The only caution I have is, ask yourself,
"Is this really a good deal?". If you're paying more
than it's worth, or you have to spend a lot to fix it
up, it may be better to continue renting, or find some
other place to practice. If it is a good deal, then I
recommend that you buy it through your professional
corporation.

Whether you buy it personally or corporately, any interest you pay on a mortgage or loan would be tax deductible, so that makes no difference.

What does make a difference is that money borrowed corporately is paid back with after-tax corporate dollars. Remember, 84-cent dollars are worth a great deal more than 54-cent dollars.

To pay off $1,000 personally would take $1,850 of earnings based on your personal tax bracket. The same $1,000 would only require $1,190 of corporate earnings.

The other added bonus of buying the building corporately is that, because it's your place of business, if it's in your professional corporation and you sell the shares of your company in the future, the building can qualify for the enhanced capital gains deduction.

As a general rule of thumb, when you're buying something with borrowed money, it usually makes sense to buy it corporately if you can.

Once you have all the figures, send them over to me and I'll take a look at them.

I'll be coming over to Vancouver in a few weeks time, so why don't we plan to meet?

Tim

Interest Deductibility

The *Income Tax Act* (ITA) contains specific provisions relating to interest deductibility. There are specific rules that determine the criteria that must be met for interest to be deductible, as well as some specific rules that modify the general provisions.

One criterion is that the borrowed funds must be used for the purpose of earning income from a business or property. The CRA has traditionally held that an interest expense would not be deductible, unless the taxpayer realized a profit (i.e. had net income) from the underlying property, or from carrying on the business activity after taking the interest expense into account.

The ITA contains specific conditions that must be met for interest to be deductible:

- It must be paid or payable for the year
- There must be a legal obligation to pay the amount
- The amount must be reasonable and;
- The borrowed money must be used to earn income from a business or property.

Borrowing Money to Acquire Common Shares

The CRA's position is that where borrowing is used to acquire common shares, the interest charges will be deductible on the basis that there is a reasonable expectation, at the time the shares are acquired, that the common shareholder will receive a dividend. This would include private shares like a professional corporation or publicly traded shares like Royal Bank stock.

Borrowing to Make Employer Contributions to Registered Pension Plan (RPP)

The ITA permits an employer to deduct interest related to loans taken out to make contributions to an RPP. This provision allows interest deducted for loans related to both past service and current service contributions. This would include interest borrowed to fund an Individual Pension Plan (IPP).

There are many other specific situations that allow interest deductibility. Borrowing money to acquire revenue property or repaying shareholder loans are two examples. If you're about to borrow money for any investment or business venture, you should check with your accountant before you proceed. Structuring the loan correctly may save you thousands of dollars.

In case you're interested, interest is not deductible if the money was borrowed to fund a Registered Retirement Savings Account (RRSP), Registered Education Savings Plan (RESP) or Tax Free Savings Account (TFSA).

Incorporating After You Have Bought Or Set Up A Practice

What if you've been operating a practice as a sole proprietor and decide you want to incorporate? Can you move the assets and the debt into a new company? Absolutely. As long as the corporation is assuming debt that is equal to, or less than, the tax cost of the assets, there are no income tax concerns. For instance, let's say you borrow $300,000 to purchase a dental practice worth $350,000. If you wanted to transfer the loan and the practice into a professional corporation, you could because the asset value is greater than the loan value. You should check with your tax advisor to make sure there are no sales tax (GST/PST/HST) issues related to transferring assets from a person to a corporation.

Acquiring shares in a non-arms-length situation can cause problems. Most sales of practices involve unrelated parties; occasionally, however, a practice will be transferred to a related party (say father to daughter or mother to son).

For example, suppose a dentist wants to sell the shares of her practice to her daughter. If she sells her shares to her daughter personally, she will generally treat the sale of her shares as a capital gain. However, if she sells her shares to her daughter's professional corporation, the gain will be reclassified as a dividend and not a capital gain.

Although this may seem unfair, section 84.1 of the ITA applies where an individual (the parent's professional corporation) disposes of shares of a Canadian resident corporation (the daughter's professional corporation) with which the transferor does not deal at arm's length[16]. Under section 84.1, this transaction would result in a deemed dividend and not a capital gain. The rationale given for not allowing a capital gain, and thus not being able to use the capital gains exemption, is that "two related person's may not each claim the capital gains exemption on the same shares".

If the daughter was to purchase the shares personally and then try to move the practice and any business loan into a newly formed professional corporation, you'd end up with the same result. If mom were to sell her shares to an unrelated party, the proceeds would automatically be treated as a capital gain. The purchaser would be able to move the practice and the debt into a newly formed corporation without difficulty, as long as it was less than the tax cost[17] of the practice. In cases such as this, always make sure you get professional tax advice before proceeding.

---

16 Arm's length basically means dealing with someone who has no special relationship with you such as a relative or another company you control.

17 Tax cost is defined as the starting point upon which a gain or loss on a sale or exchange of property is determined; typically, the purchase price of an item; also known as a cost base.

CHAPTER FOUR

Setting Up Your Professional Corporation

Payroll Remittances

When you first set up your professional corporation you are required to get a CRA business number. There are two business numbers for professional corporations. The one to make payroll remittances looks like this: 12345 6789 RP001. The other is the corporate remittance number and looks like this: 12345 6789 RC001. Please note that the numbers are constant; only the letters change.

In the year that you incorporate, you are not required to pay corporate tax instalments, however, you are required to make payroll remittances. Once you decide what salaries are going to be paid from your professional corporation, you or your accountant can calculate what the payroll withholdings are going to be. If you are paying wages to yourself or your spouse, you are required to withhold income tax and Canada Pension Plan (CPP) contributions. The CRA publishes several payroll deduction tables to assist you with calculating these contributions. These are available for CPP, Employment Insurance (EI) and income tax deductions and can be picked up at your local taxation centre or they are available online at http://www.cra-arc.gc.ca/tx/bsnss/tpcs/pyrll/clcltng/menu-eng.html. You can also obtain the TOD (tables on diskette) computer program to calculate your payroll deductions by http://www.cra-arc.gc.ca/tx/bsnss/tod-tsd/menu-eng.html.

If you employ others, you are required to withhold EI and contribute 1.4 times your employees' contribution. You are also required to make matching contributions for the CPP.

In 2010, CPP contributions were based on maximum pensionable earnings of $47,200. The contribution rate was 4.95 per cent. Everyone gets a basic exemption of $3,500 (which means that there is no contribution on the first $3,500 earned); therefore, the maximum contribution to CPP is $2,163.15 ($47,200 – 3,500 x 4.95 per cent). Even if your income is above $47,200, you only pay the maximum of $2,163.15. As an employer, you match the employee contribution, meaning that the maximum you, as the employer, would have to contribute is $2,163.15.

Employment Insurance (EI) works the same way. Maximum insurable earnings in 2010 are $43,200. The contribution rate for employees is 1.73 per cent; therefore, the maximum contribution is $747.36 ($43,200 x 1.73 per cent). In the case of EI, however, no basic exemption is applied. Therefore, the maximum employer contribution per employee is $1,046.30 ($747.36 x 1.4). Each year the CRA issues maximum limits for each of these programs.

In both cases above, figures shown constitute the maximums that you pay as an employer; the actual contribution amount will depend on income levels. Each program has different levels of qualifying income and applicable percentage applications.

Let's look at the example of Justin and Brittany who are married and working in an office with two additional staff, Trevor and Adam. Brittany is a physician and Justin works at the office. Brittany draws a salary of $75,000 per year. Justin's salary is $60,000 per year. Trevor is paid $42,000 and Adam, $28,000.

As employers, Justin and Brittany **withhold** from each employee's salary annually the following for CPP:

CPP	
Brittany	$2,163.15
Justin	$2,163.15
Trevor	$1,905.75
Adam	$1,212.75

And they **withhold** the following for EI employee contributions:

EI[18]	
Brittany	$0
Justin	$0
Trevor	$726.60
Adam	$484.40

In addition, they would also have to withhold the appropriate amount of income tax from each employee's wages, based on their personal circumstances. Each employee is required to complete a federal form TD1 to calculate the amount of tax to be deducted. Currently there are eleven different claim levels based on credits. The more credits you have, the less tax withheld at source. For instance, if you are single with no dependents, you will pay more tax than a single parent. If you have a spouse who works and earns more than $1,200 per year, you will pay more tax than someone whose spouse earns less than $1,200 per year. All the necessary calculations to determine how much tax should be withheld from each employee's pay cheque can be found on the TD1 form.

How much you withhold from each pay cheque will also depend on how often you pay your staff. The tables calculate the withholdings based on 52, 26, 24 and 12 pay periods per year.

All payroll withholdings are due by the 15th of the following month. You must remit to the CRA the amount withheld from the employee along with the contributions required by you, the employer.

As employers, Justin and Brittany would **remit** employer contributions as follows:

CPP	
Brittany	$2,163.15
Justin	$2,163.15
Trevor	$1,905.75
Adam	$1,212.75

---

18 Footnote The Employment Insurance Act states that employment is not insurable if the employer and employee are not dealing with each other at arm's length. In certain circumstances it may be possible to have a family member who is eligible but generally family members aren't covered for EI.

EI	
Brittany	$0
Justin	$0
Trevor	$1,017.24
Adam	$678.16

You can see from this illustration that if a husband and wife were both working for the same professional corporation they would be paying $8,652.60 ($2,163.15 x 4) in CPP contributions, based on the employer contribution and the amount paid personally.

Payroll remittances are deducted from wages. Corporate remittances are taxes paid by the corporation based on estimated corporate profits. In the year you incorporate, you are not required to make corporate remittances because there is no way to know how much taxable income the corporation is going to have. Starting the first or third month (depending on which instalment method is used) after your first fiscal year-end, you are required to start making corporate remittances.

If you incorporated in April of 2010 and chose December 31 as your year-end, you would be required to start making corporate remittances by January 31 or March 31, 2011 (depending on which instalment method is used). The corporate taxes you owed for 2010 are due by March 31, 2011. Your accountant can help you determine the amount of corporate remittance you should make. If you are between accountants, it would be safe to send the CRA 20 per cent of your gross income, as your corporate tax should not be higher than this.

Corporate remittances are due on the last day of each month. Some of our clients like to keep things simple and send in post-dated cheques. This might not be a good idea; one of our clients sent in post-dated cheques for the whole year only to have the CRA deposit all of them at the same time. The bank processed them all and charged the client NSF charges. It took months to fix the problem. If you want to get it out of the way, talk to your accountant about making the remittances on your behalf. Many accountants will take post-dated cheques and send them in for you when they are due. Most banks will also allow you to set up online scheduled payments including corporate remittances.

Workers' Compensation Board

As an incorporated professional you may be required to pay Workers' Compensation Board (WCB) premiums in your jurisdiction. The workers' compensation system provides accident insurance for employers and workers. Employers who pay for the system are not directly liable for the workplace injuries or diseases sustained by their workers. In turn, workers injured in the course of employment are automatically entitled to compensation, regardless of fault. However, they give up their right to legal action against a potentially negligent employer in return for the certainty of no-fault benefits. Benefits can range from financial protection, in cases of death or injury, to medical treatment and rehabilitation services.

In Canada, unlike other countries, workers' compensation is a system of social insurance. Coverage is generally compulsory. In situations where compulsory coverage does not apply, there are opportunities for optional or special coverage. Refer to the web sites below for more information if you are considering such coverage. Assessments are levied on employers and gathered into a common fund out of which benefits are paid to workers who are injured as a result of their employment. Administration and adjudication are carried out by the WCB.

The following table outlines the different registration requirements for each jurisdiction.

Province/Territory	Compulsory Registration	Contact
British Columbia	Yes	www.worksafebc.com
Alberta	No	www.wcb.ab.ca
Saskatchewan	Yes[19]	www.wcbsask.com
Manitoba	No	www.wcb.mb.ca
Ontario	Maybe[20]	www.wsib.on.ca
New Brunswick	Yes[21]	www.worksafenb.ca
Nova Scotia	No	www.wcb.pe.ca
Prince Edward Island	Yes[22]	www.wcb.pe.ca
Newfoundland	Yes	www.whscc.nf.ca
Yukon	Yes	www.wcb.yk.ca
Northwest Territories	No	www.wcb.nt.ca
Nunavut	No	www.wcb.nt.ca

The annual maximum contribution varies according to income and jurisdiction. If you are taking only dividends as income, the amount of coverage is based on estimated value of the work. For example, a dentist in the Yukon who must register and is taking dividends instead of a salary would have to estimate the value of his work up to a maximum coverage amount of $77,610 of insurable earnings (2010 figure).

The following table gives the filing deadline for WCB in each province and territory along with the maximum assessable earnings for 2010.

---

19 Yes if you have any employees (including yourself).
20 There are various criteria for eligibility and certain industries are not required to have mandatory coverage. As an example, a doctor or dentist in a general practice can apply for coverage but there are no guarantees that it will be approved. In this case they are not required by law to register with WCB. The best course of action is to describe your business to a WCB account manager and see whether you are eligible.
21 Yes if you have three or more employees. No if you have one or two employees.
22 Yes if you have one employee. No if you are the only one working.

Province	Filing Deadline	Maximum Assessable Earnings
British Columbia	February 28 (quarterly) March 1 – 15 (yearly)	$71,200
Alberta	February 28	$77,000
Saskatchewan	February 28	$55,000
Manitoba	February 28	$89,000
Ontario	March 31	$67,700
Quebec	March 15	$62,000
New Brunswick	February 28	$55,400
Nova Scotia	February 28	$50,800
Prince Edward Island	February 28	$47,500
Newfoundland	February 28	$45,500
Yukon	February 28	$77,610
Northwest Territories	February 28	$75,200
Nunavut	February 28	$75,200

Re: Worker's Compensation
From: Sven Hansen
To: tim@tpcfinancial.com

Hi Tim

I overheard a couple of my associates today talking about registering for Workers' Compensation. One said you had to join and the other said you don't. I just incorporated and don't know what to do. I don't want to if I don't have to. Do you know if I have to register?

Sven

Re: Re: Workers' Compensation
From: tim@tpcfinancial.com
To: Sven Hansen

Hi Sven:

Yes where you live you have to register. The rules vary from province to province but in BC, registration is mandatory.

If one of your associates isn't registered it may just be a matter of time before he's caught; eventually he will have to pay all the back premiums and interest right back to the date of his incorporation.

One of the confusing things about Workers' Compensation in BC is that it doesn't matter how much you pay yourself, or whether you're taking dividends or salary, the amount you pay in premiums is based on the "value" of your work, not how much you're actually paid.

Some people (in this case, maybe your associate) believe that if they don't take a salary, and only take dividends, that they don't have to pay. This is not the case. It is however true that if you're giving dividends to Yolanda, or the boys, that they're not required to register with the Workers Compensation Board, but you do.

If you happen to move to Saskatchewan we'll be having a different discussion because there you don't have to join if you have no employees and no one on payroll.

Tim

Goods And Services Tax (GST) And Harmonized Sales Tax (HST)

On July 1, 2010 the HST came into effect in Ontario and British Columbia, replacing the GST and PST.

Medical and dental services can be categorized into three types for the purposes of GST/HST: exempt, zero-rated or taxable:

1. Services that are exempt for GST will also be exempt for HST. This includes uninsured services that are consultative, diagnostic or health-related. Input Tax Credits (ITC's) cannot be claimed for exempt services, which means that medical practitioners and dentists must absorb the cost of the HST on these services. For those expenses that are not currently subject to PST, this will represent a 7 – 10 per cent increase in overhead costs depending on your province.

2. Zero-rated products/services are subject to GST/HST at a rate of 0 per cent and include medical aids, eyeglasses, hearing aids, canes, crutches, heart monitoring devices, artificial teeth and orthodontic appliances.

ITC's can be claimed for all expenditures related to the supply of these products/services.

3. Taxable services include uninsured cosmetic surgery, consulting services and expert witness fees. GST or HST (where applicable) will be charged for these services and ITC's can be claimed for all expenditures related to the supply of these services. Medical and dental practitioners might want to evaluate the benefits of claiming ITC's if they haven't in the past as the ITC's will be as much as 13 per cent instead of 5 per cent (in Ontario as an example). There were a number of PST exempt products and services that are now subject to HST. If, for example, a service was PST exempt but not GST exempt and you lived in Ontario, you would have paid 5 per cent. When the HST came into effect, that service would probably be subject to HST resulting in 13 per cent tax.

Medical practitioners and dentists with zero-rated and taxable supplies in excess of $30,000 per annum are required to register for GST/HST.

The introduction of HST in Ontario, British Columbia, New Brunswick, Newfoundland and Nova Scotia will have a negative effect on most medical and dental practices in these jurisdictions. This is due to the fact that more goods and services purchased by the physician and dentist will attract the higher HST, with, in most cases, no opportunity to recover these additional expenses.

*Please note – the whole issue of GST/PST and HST is very complex and in this section I offer only a brief introduction. If you have specific concerns or questions relating to this section please consult a GST/PST/HST specialist.

Human Resources

Employment standards (or labour standards) legislation is frequently amended and varies somewhat from province to province. It is not possible therefore to provide a definitive guide in this book, but I'd like to discuss the type and scope of issues that are usually covered by such legislation.

The following examples have been taken from different provinces to illustrate each topic and then show the differences between each jurisdiction. I strongly encourage you to not only familiarize yourself with the statutes in your province but to incorporate it into your practice policy and procedures. Details specific to each jurisdiction are available on the relevant ministry website. In addition, information is provided on how to deal with a dispute involving employment standards. For example, the BC ministry site provides guides for both employees and employers regarding hearings, mediation, enforcement measures and penalties.

This section also touches on the issues of excluded employment and contractors, as these questions frequently pop up during staffing decisions, particularly if you plan to employ family members. Human rights issues are also included, along with a brief overview of human resource management to assist you with hiring employees and reviewing their performance.

Employee Or Independent Contractor?

Since there is some confusion as to whether or not certain employees, such as hygienists, are considered employees or contractors, a brief explanation of how the CRA and the Employment Standards Act treat this issue is provided below.

Both the BC Employment Standards Act and the CRA publish guidelines that help define the employee-employer relationship. The Employment Standards Branch, the Employment Standards Tribunal and the courts have developed a series of tests to determine who is an employee within the meaning of the Act. Similarly, the CRA has developed a similar list of questions, which helps to define the employment relationship.

- *Control.* Is the person under the direction and control of another regarding the time, place, and way in which the work is done?

- *Ownership of tools.* If the person uses tools, space, or supplies and equipment owned by someone else, then an employment relationship exists. It is common, however, for some employers to require that their employees provide their own tools or vehicles. In addition, the employer covers the following costs related to their use: repairs, insurance, transport, rental, and operation (e.g., fuel).

- *Chance of profit.* Does the person have a chance of profit? If their income is always the difference between the cost of providing the service, and the price charged for the service, the worker may be someone other than an employee.

- *Risk of loss.* Is the person at risk of losing money if the cost of doing a job is more than the price charged for it? If not, this would indicate an employment relationship.

- *Integration.* If the worker integrates his activities with the commercial activities of the payer, an employer-employee relationship probably exists. The worker is acting on behalf of the employer (i.e., he is connected with the employer's business and is dependent on it). If the worker integrates the payer's activities with his own commercial activities, a business relationship probably exists. In this case the worker is acting on his own behalf; he is not dependent on the payer's business and he is in business for himself.

Excluded Employment

Generally speaking, an employee pays EI premiums and may be entitled to receive EI benefits. However, if the employment is deemed an excluded employment under the Employment Insurance Act, the employee does not have to pay premiums and is not eligible for EI benefits. Employment may be excluded when a non-arms-length employment relationship exists. This relationship is defined as one between individuals connected by blood, marriage, adoption, or otherwise. A non-arms-length relationship may also exist between individuals and partnerships or corporations.

If the federal Minister of National Revenue, or his representative, is satisfied that the terms and conditions of employment are reasonable, excluded employment can be deemed to be "included" under the Employment Insurance Act. The minister, or his representative, will examine the terms and conditions of employment based on a number of factors, including:

- remuneration paid
- terms of employment (e.g., hours of work, duties)
- duration of work performed
- nature and importance of work performed.

Once the analysis is complete, if the minister, or his representative, is satisfied that it is reasonable to conclude that the employer would have offered a substantially similar contract of employment to an unrelated person, the employment is no longer considered to be excluded.

Employment Insurance (EI)

Beginning in January 2011, self-employed Canadians will be able to access Employment Insurance (EI) special benefits. There are four types of EI special benefits:

1. Maternity Benefits to individuals who are pregnant, have recently given birth, are adopting a child or are caring for a newborn (maximum 15 weeks, a claim can start up to 8 weeks before the expected birth date).

2. Parental Benefits to individuals who are pregnant, have recently given birth, are adopting a child or are caring for a newborn (maximum 35 weeks).

3. Sickness Benefits to individuals who are unable to work because of sickness, injury or quarantine (maximum 15 weeks).

4. Compassionate Care Benefits to persons who have to be away from work temporarily to provide care or support to a family member who is gravely ill with a significant risk of death (maximum 6 weeks).

You can enter into an agreement, or register, with Canada Employment Insurance Commission through Service Canada if you operate your own business or if you work for a corporation but cannot access EI benefits because you control more than 40% of the corporation's voting shares, and are either a Canadian citizen or a permanent resident of Canada.

Application information

There are a few steps to take before being able to receive EI special benefits for self-employed people. You have to register with Canada Employment Insurance Commission, complete a one-time 12-month waiting period (unless you registered on or before April 1, 2010), and finally, apply for EI special benefits and meet the eligibility criteria. More details are available on the Application information page[23].

Dates and deadlines

You can register to participate in the EI program through My Service Canada Account at any time. Remember, you will have to wait 12 months from the date of confirmed registration before you will be able to apply for EI special benefits.

---

23 http://www.servicecanada.gc.ca/eng/sc/ei/sew/application_information.shtml

Calculation of premiums

In 2010, for every $100 you earn, you will need to contribute $1.73 in EI premiums up to a defined maximum—the same amount that employees pay. This means the most you will pay in EI premiums for 2010 is $747.36.

Since Quebec has its own parental insurance program that offers maternity and parental benefits, EI premiums have been adjusted accordingly for that province. In 2010, self-employed people in Quebec who register for the EI program will pay $1.36 for every $100 of earnings, up to a total of $587.52 for the year.

EI premiums are calculated by Canada Revenue Agency (CRA) based on your net self-employment earnings, as calculated under the *Income Tax Act.*

If you are a shareholder of a corporation and you control more than 40% of that corporation's voting shares, the CRA will calculate your EI premiums based on the amount of what would have been your insurable earnings from that employment, if the earnings had been insurable.

Unlike the regular EI program, and because you are self-employed, you will not have to pay the employer's portion of the EI premium.

Payment of premiums

For the first year of participation in the EI program, you will have to pay your premiums by April 30 of the following year. After that, if you pay your income tax by instalments to the CRA, EI premiums may be included in your instalment payments.

When you register, EI premiums will be payable on your self-employment income for the entire year, regardless of the date you register. For example, whether you register in April 2010 or December 2010, you will pay EI premiums on your self-employment income for all of 2010.

Amount of weekly benefits

In 2010, the weekly benefit amount is 55% of the average weekly earnings from the calendar year before you submit an application for EI special benefits. Based on this maximum, you could receive up to $457 per week. The amount of your benefits may decrease if you continue to work or if your business generates earnings while you are collecting EI special benefits.

Before weekly benefits can be determined, your eligible earnings will need to be identified.

If you have earnings from both self-employment and insurable earnings as an employee, you may choose to apply for EI special benefits as a self-employed person or as an employee.

If you are applying as a self-employed person, the CRA will take into account your earnings from both self-employment and employment as an employee when it calculates your weekly benefit amount, as long as your earnings from both sources are eligible. You must provide your Record of Employment to show details of eligible employment earnings.

Cancelling your participation

Once you have registered to participate, you have 60 days in which you may cancel your participation without having to pay any premiums.

After this 60-day period, you may still terminate your participation if you have never received EI special benefits as a self-employed person. In other words, after you receive EI special benefits, your participation will continue and you will have to continue to pay EI premiums for the entire duration of your self-employed career, regardless of any change in the nature of your self-employment.

Note: you will not receive a refund of any EI premiums.

Summary

- You are required to opt into the program at least one year prior to claiming benefits.

- You need to have earned a minimum of $6,000 in self-employed earnings (net income from self-employment) over the preceding calendar year.

- You can opt out of the EI program at the end of any tax year, as long as you have never claimed benefits.

- You must contribute on self-employed earnings for as long as you are self-employed, once you have claimed benefits.

- You will pay the same EI premium rate as salaried employees.

- You will not pay the employer portion of EI premiums, in recognition of the fact that you cannot collect regular EI benefits.

All this may sound reasonable but personally I never enter into any contract where I don't know what the ultimate cost will be. I suggest you think long and hard before signing up for this program and consider the following points. First, as soon as you make a claim, any claim, you have to stay on the program for as long as you work – yes, there is no getting out of this program once you have made a claim, no matter how small. Second, if the government discovers that too many people are making claims, and that they're losing money, they can put the cost of your contributions up – basically you'll have to pay whatever they say! I don't know about you but there's no way I'd agree to those terms.

The Role Of Employment Standards Legislation

Each province or territory legislates its own employment standards, which govern the following issues:

- minimum wage
- annual vacation and vacation pay
- overtime payment
- statutory holidays
- maternity, parental, and bereavement leave
- meal breaks
- paydays
- requirement for keeping employment records
- overtime
- uniforms and special clothing
- deductions
- termination, just cause and severance pay
- handling complaints.

It is important to remember that the Employment Standards Act sets the minimum standard that employers must meet; you can, of course, exceed these standards if you wish and if your company can afford to. You must also keep in mind that if your company sets standards that exceed the Act in your province, the Act can enforce your policy. The Act also applies to those employees covered by a collective agreement if the collective agreement does not address certain issues, or does not meet the Act in that jurisdiction. For example, the standard for vacation time in British Columbia is two weeks for employees after twelve months of consecutive employment. However, you could decide to adopt a policy of providing vacation pay during the first year of employment; then the Act will require you to adhere to this policy in the event of a dispute. Contact information for each province's Employment Standards Branch's web site is provided in Appendix G.

Compensation

As mentioned above, each province legislates its own minimum wage laws that are generally designed to provide a fair wage for unskilled workers. In your professional practice, you will be hiring trained staff with specialized skills, such as medical office assistants, receptionists, certified dental assistants, registered dental hygienists, nurses, etc. You can obtain current salary scales for these employment classes from your provincial association, or the associations for these specialists. For example, the ADSBC (Association of Dental Surgeons of British Columbia) publishes an annual guide that provides compensation information, gathered through surveys, by geographic area and length of experience.

Salary or hourly pay?

The decision to pay by the hour or monthly is up to the employer and will be influenced somewhat by standard industry practice. Depending on what you decide, you will have to pay special attention to the rules governing overtime, averaging agreements and banking overtime.

Minimum wage

Each province or jurisdiction legislates a minimum wage policy designed to provide a minimum standard of living for workers. At the time of writing, the minimum wage in Alberta is $8.80 per hour, while in BC it is $8.00. Each jurisdiction may supplement its legislation with policies that deal with specific issues such as deductions for board and lodging, or specific groups of workers such as students, or temporary employment.

Minimum daily pay

In most provinces, if employees are called in to work or report for work and are sent home for any reason, they must be paid for a minimum number of hours. This is known as the "three hour rule" in Ontario, where an employee who reports for work must be paid whichever is the greater between three hours at the minimum wage rate, or their regular wage rate for the actual time worked.

In BC, an employee who reports for work must be paid for at least two hours, even if the employee works less than two hours. If an employee who is scheduled for more than eight hours reports for work, he or she must be paid for at least four hours. Sometimes, in the event of a power cut or other reason beyond your control, you may have to close your office temporarily – for the day, perhaps. In this case, you would be required to pay your employee for at least two hours, or the actual time worked, whichever is greater.

Hours free from work
Legislation in BC states than an employee must have at least 32 consecutive hours free from work each week. If an employee works during this period, he or she must be paid time-and-a-half for all hours worked.

An employee is also entitled to have eight hours off between shifts unless required to work because of an emergency.

No excessive hours
An employer must not require, or allow, an employee to work excessive hours or hours harmful to the employee's health or safety.

Overtime
In BC, daily overtime pay is time-and-a-half after eight hours worked in a day, and double-time after 12 hours worked in a day. Weekly overtime is time-and-a half after 40 hours worked in a week. Only the first eight hours worked in a day count toward weekly overtime.

For example, if an employee worked six 11-hour days, they would be paid 18 hours of daily overtime and eight hours of weekly overtime.

Banking overtime
Some employees may request that their overtime hours be banked for their use at a later date. Any agreement to this effect should be in writing. Employment standards may dictate when the banked wages or time must be taken. For example, in British Columbia, banked overtime must be used within six months, while in Ontario it must be used within three months. You should also be aware of the method of accumulating banked time. In BC, straight time is used to calculate time banked and the payment, but in

Ontario, banked time is taken and paid out at the overtime rate (or time-and-a-half). Check your province's policy for specific information.

Paydays and payroll records

The BC Employment Standards Act sets out regulations regarding how often employees are to be paid. These details should be included in payroll records, such as pay stubs. Although other provincial acts are very similar, it would be wise to become familiar with the Act pertaining to your province or territory. Here is a short summary from the Act for BC:

- All employees must be paid at least twice a month
- A pay period cannot be longer than 16 days
- All wages earned in a pay period must be paid within eight days of the end of the pay period
- Employees must receive a written or electronic pay statement (pay stub) each pay day, which gives all details about hours worked, rate(s) of pay, earnings and deductions. Employers must keep payroll records for each employee for two years after employment ends
- An employee must be paid in full within 48 hours after the employer ends the employment, or within six days, if the employee quits. This time is by the clock and the calendar - not business hours or business days.

Averaging agreements

Each Province and Territory has its own legislation dealing with work hours. In British Columbia you can enter into an averaging agreement with an employee. In Manitoba you can apply for an averaging permit. The premise is the same. Basically it works like this:

The standard hours of work range from eight (8) hours in a day and forty (40) hours in a week in British Columbia, Manitoba, Northwest Territories, Nunavut, Saskatchewan and the Yukon to forty eight (48) a week in Nova Scotia and Prince Edward Island. Hours worked above these are overtime. In most jurisdictions, employers and employees may agree to increase the daily hours in a 40-hour work week, or to average the hours across a longer period such as 80 hours in a two-week period, or 120 hours in a three-week period, and so on.

Every jurisdiction has regulations governing standard hours, maximum hours, averaging agreements, overtime, right to refuse overtime, time off in lieu of overtime wages, minimum rest periods as well as meal and other breaks.

For example, in every jurisdiction overtime is payable for each hour or part of an hour that an employee works in excess of the standard hours of work. Standard hours of work are defined by the province or territory. If you're going to ask your employees to work hours that do not fall into the standard applied in your jurisdiction, you should get them to sign an averaging agreement, or obtain the necessary permission from the appropriate Labour Standards Officer.

Payroll/employment records

Most provinces require employers to keep records for each employee including identity, rate of pay and hours of work, etc. For example, in Saskatchewan, all employers must keep the following records:

- name and address
- brief job description
- start and end dates of employment
- time at which work begins and ends each day
- break times
- total number of hours worked each day and each week
- regular rate of wages
- total wages paid
- dates on which each holiday is taken
- total wage and annual holiday pay for any period of employment
- all deductions from wages and the reason for each deduction.

If you live in Ontario you also have to record and maintain:

- the employees date of birth if the employee is a student under age 18
- written agreements to work excess hours or average overtime pay
- information contained in an employee's wage statement
- all documents relating to an employee's pregnancy, parental, family medical, organ donor, personal emergency, declared emergency or reservist leave.

Regardless of where you live, it's a good idea to keep a written record of this information, and you may choose to include it as part of the employment agreement, covered later in this chapter. Accounting software, such as Simply Accounting, is designed to record some or all of these details.

Statutory holidays

Although the statutory holidays in each province are very similar, there are some differences. For example, Boxing Day is not a statutory holiday in BC, but it is in Ontario. Each jurisdiction's legislation also describes how to determine if an employee is eligible to be paid for a statutory holiday. The Employment Standards Act defines how employees are to be compensated if they are required to work on a statutory holiday.

If an employer and a majority of employees have agreed to substitute another day for a statutory holiday, the employer must keep records of this agreement for two years.

Deductions

As an employer, you are required to make certain deductions from your employee's wages by law for income tax, EI and CPP contributions. Tables to help you calculate the amounts are available on the CRA agency web site. The employee consents to tax withholding on both the federal and applicable provincial TD1 forms. Many accounting software packages, such as Simply Accounting, calculate the amounts automatically, and you can subscribe to receive the updates automatically online.

An employer's business costs, such as cash shortages, breakages, damage to company property, etc., cannot be deducted from an employee's pay.

Special clothing

Special clothing is clothing that is easily identified with the employer (e.g., clothing with a company logo or unique company colours). If an employer requires an employee to wear a uniform or special clothing, the employer must provide, clean, and maintain it at no cost to the employee. Employers and employees can agree that the employer will reimburse employees for cleaning and maintaining special clothing. The employer must keep records of such an agreement and the amounts paid for two years.

Although there is an allowance in the *Income Tax Act* (ITA) for "special clothing" this does not mean that you can go out and replace your wardrobe and claim it as an eligible business expense. I do see this periodically, but like most tax avoidance matters it's not worth the risk of getting caught.

Meal breaks

In British Columbia, an employee must not work more than five hours in a row without a 30-minute unpaid meal break. An employee who is required to work or be available for work during a meal break must be paid for the meal break.

Termination with notice

All provinces require employers to give employees adequate notice in the event of termination of employment for reasons other than just cause. However, the amount of notice required varies in each jurisdiction. For example, in BC and Saskatchewan, two weeks' notice is required when the employee has completed one to three years of employment. The Employment Standards Act in BC dictates that after three years, one week's notice is required for each completed year of employment, to a maximum of eight weeks. In Saskatchewan, four weeks is required for three to five years of service, six weeks for five to 10 years of service, and eight weeks for 10 years of service or more. In contrast, employers in Manitoba are only required to provide notice of termination equal to one pay period. Most jurisdictions allow notice to be either severance pay, written notice of termination or a combination of the two. In addition, employers are not required to provide any notice of termination for an employment period of 30 days or less.

Voluntary termination of employment

If an employee chooses to leave your organization to pursue other career interests or another job, you should try to meet with them before they leave. At the meeting, determine if the employee was dissatisfied with their work or the environment. Decide if their comments have merit, discuss with other employees, and make improvements where required. Valuable employees are costly to replace.

Involuntary layoff

If you need to downsize your staff to trim costs, you are required to either give adequate written notice to those employees affected or provide severance pay according to the guidelines in the Employments Standards Act in your jurisdiction. As noted above, compensation can be a combination of written notice and severance pay.

According to the BC Employment Standards Act, when you provide written notice of termination of employment, an employee cannot be on vacation, leave, temporary layoff, strike or lockout, or be unavailable for work due to medical reasons during the notice period.

Just cause

Termination of employment with cause, or termination with just cause means that an action or omission by the employee has irreparably damaged the employment relationship between the employer and the employee. Usually, termination with cause occurs when an employee is dismissed for a serious reason related to the employee's conduct.

Not all employment/labour standards define "termination with cause". Those that do refer to:

- serious, wilful misconduct
- assault or harassment of co-workers
- breach of duty
- conflict of interest (especially if it involves provable loss to the employer)
- theft
- serious breach of company rules or practices
- fraud and dishonesty
- chronic absenteeism, or tardiness
- serious undermining of the corporate culture
- unsatisfactory performance.

Where termination of employment is considered for unsatisfactory performance, employers must be prepared to prove that steps have been taken to improve the situation. In BC, these criteria are spelled out as follows:

For your protection, you as the employer should be able to prove that:

- you made the employee aware of an expected standard of performance
- in the event that the employee failed to meet that standard, you made a reasonable effort to assist the employee – by training or otherwise – to meet the expected performance standards

- the employee, despite your reasonable efforts to assist, failed to meet acceptable standards of performance
- you specifically told the employee that dismissal will result if unsatisfactory performance continues.

As a cautionary note, if you're going to fire an employee and you're not sure what the rules are, it may be worth your while to consult a labour lawyer in advance. What you pay for advice at the front end may save you thousands down the line.

Sick Time

All jurisdictions have labour rules covering sick time. As part of the employee's Employment Contract, you should cover your practices sick time policy. Like all things related to labour laws, make sure you know what the rules are in your province or territory.

Vacation time

Most provinces require employers to provide two weeks' paid vacation after one year of employment, with the vacation pay being equal to 4 per cent of gross wages paid in the previous twelve months. As an example, in Ontario, gross wages include: statutory (public) holiday pay; wages including shift premium and overtime pay; commissions; bonuses and gifts that are non-discretionary or are related to hours of work, production or efficiency; allowances for room and board; and termination pay. If employment lasts less than a year but more than five days, the employee is entitled to vacation pay equal to 4 per cent of gross wages but is not entitled to vacation time. In addition, vacation time entitlement may increase with length of service (e.g., three weeks and 6 per cent of gross wages after five years of service). The vacation entitlement year begins on the date of hire, although your organization may adopt an alternative entitlement year. The period between the date of hire and the beginning of the first alternative vacation entitlement year, or the period between the end of the last standard vacation entitlement year and the start of the first alternative vacation entitlement year, is called the "stub" period. Employees earn a pro-rated amount of vacation time during a stub period.

In addition, most employment legislation dictates when the vacation pay must be paid – either a specified period of time before the vacation begins, or included in every pay cheque. Employment legislation will also cover such details as allowing employees a minimum unbroken vacation period, what to pay when a statutory holiday falls during the vacation period, payroll record requirements, giving notice of vacation time to employees, and the requirement to pay accrued vacation time on termination of the employee.

Leave from work

A leave of absence is defined as a temporary absence after which the employee intends to return to work. In general, unpaid leave for maternity, parental, bereavement and jury duty are allowed in most provinces. The labour and employment standards codes for Nova Scotia and British Columbia are used below for examples. Check the website for legislation in your jurisdiction.

Maternity leave

All provinces require employers to allow employees to take unpaid maternity leave of up to 17 weeks. This period of time is usually covered by EI benefits. The Employment Standards Act in Nova Scotia stipulates that only employees with at least one year of service qualify for this leave. You should check the code in your province for qualification requirements (e.g., in BC, an employee does not have to work for a specified period to qualify for this or any other leave). Depending on your provincial code, employees must provide their employers with either written or verbal notice of their planned leave of absence, including the dates when the leave is expected to begin and end. The amount of notice required also varies from province to province. In Nova Scotia, an employee must be accepted back into the same position or a comparable one with no loss of seniority nor benefits when she returns to work. She is also allowed to keep up, at her own expense, any benefit plan to which she may belong.

Parental leave

Parental leave is designed to provide either or both parents with time to spend with their newborns. For the mother, parental leave provisions commonly stipulate that the leave be taken immediately after maternity leave, thereby extending the total leave period. For the father, parental leave provisions allow time off to help with the care of the newborn; in some cases collective agreement language that is gender specific to the father is referred to as paternity leave.

In a nutshell, this is what is provided in the labour standards legislation.

- In all Canadian jurisdictions, employees who meet eligibility requirements are entitled to unpaid parental leave ranging from 12 to 52 weeks.

- Employees must give notice in writing to the employer a few weeks prior to the start of such leave. When they come back to work, employees must normally return to their former position or be assigned equivalent duties with the same salary and benefits.

- In ten jurisdictions, the full parental leave is available to both parents if they are eligible. However, in Alberta, New Brunswick and the Yukon, parental leave may be shared between both parents as long as the total period of leave does not exceed the legislated maximum.

- Some jurisdictions allow employees to continue their participation in benefit plans during the leave, provided they make all contributions they would normally have made, within a reasonable period of time. In some jurisdictions the employee may be required to pay the employer's share of these benefits.

Jury duty or court leave

Employers are required to allow their employees unpaid leave to attend court to serve as a juror for as long as required. Using Nova Scotia as an example again, employees are required to give their employer as much notice as possible.

Bereavement leave

The Nova Scotia Employment Standards Act dictates that employees may take up to three working days consecutively in the event of the death of a spouse, parent, guardian, child, or a child under their care. The code also allows employees to take one calendar day of unpaid leave in the event of the death of a grandparent, sister, brother, or relative by marriage (in-law). This differs from the code in BC, where a bereavement leave of three days is allowed on the death of any member of the employee's immediate family.

Occupational health and safety

In most jurisdictions, health and safety legislation requires employers to take all reasonable precautions to ensure the health and safety of their employees.

Employers must provide safety information, instructions, training and supervision, and must ensure that all equipment is safe. In some jurisdictions, a health and safety policy may be required.

An employee has the right to refuse to perform work that they believe may endanger them or another worker without fear of reprisal.

Human Rights Legislation

Discrimination in hiring and employment practices

According to the Canadian Human Rights Commission (CHRC) "all individuals should have an equal opportunity to make for themselves the lives that they are able and wish to have." It also states that individuals should have their needs accommodated, consistent with their duties and obligations as members of society, without being hindered by discrimination based on the factors or "prohibited grounds" listed below:

- race
- national or ethnic origin
- colour
- religion
- age
- sex
- sexual orientation
- marital status
- family status
- disability
- criminal conviction for which a pardon has been granted.

Protection against discrimination is particularly important in cases where an employee has been away and is planning a return to work. Many of the complaints filed with CHRC arise from these situations. In return-to-work cases, disability is the ground most likely to be at issue. Discrimination following absences due to pregnancy and maternity may also be grounds for complaint.

What is workplace discrimination?

Workplace discrimination means putting an employee at a disadvantage based on prohibited grounds. Discrimination results in barriers to workplace equity because it blocks access to equal opportunities. Discrimination may happen intentionally or inadvertently – workplaces often have policies that apply to everyone, but some employees may not be able to meet certain expectations for reasons concerning a disability or other prohibited ground.

As the CHRC explains, employers need to examine how their workplace rules might affect employee rights, and then take action to prevent discrimination.

Harassment in the workplace

Each province has legislated against harassment in the workplace under certain prohibited areas (as listed below). Harassment is defined as unwelcome conduct related to a prohibited type of discrimination that detrimentally affects the work environment or leads to adverse job-related consequences for those experiencing harassment. In BC, the human rights code makes unlawful any discrimination and harassment on the basis of the following characteristics:

- race
- colour
- ancestry
- place of origin
- religion
- marital status
- family status
- age (covers only those 19 years and older and less than 65 years old)
- sex (which includes pregnancy, breastfeeding, and sexual harassment)
- physical or mental disability (which includes HIV/AIDS and drug or alcohol addiction)
- sexual orientation (being gay, lesbian, straight or bisexual)
- criminal conviction (employment only)
- political belief (employment only).

Dealing with harassment

Harassment in the workplace constitutes grounds for dismissal for just cause under the Employment Standards Act in BC. Check your province's legislation for guidance on this issue. Most organizations have policies and procedures surrounding incidents of harassment; these would include documentation, such as written warnings to offenders, and details of disciplinary measures (such as dismissal), which will be taken if the behaviour continues. As an employer, you are responsible for not only being aware of the legislation but also upholding the rules.

Human Resource Management – The Essentials

Hiring employees

Once you have decided that you need to hire staff, there are several simple steps that will help ensure that you hire the best employee:

1. Develop a job description and a list of essential qualifications before placing the ad.

2. Some of the best employees come from people you know. Ask friends and acquaintances if they know of anyone looking for a job.

3. Consult associations and trade magazines for résumés and advertisements for skilled people who may be looking for work. Advertise in the local newspaper, post a job opening on web sites, at community colleges and universities.

4. Screen résumés for those applicants who most closely match your requirements. Interview several candidates, but only interview a maximum of three or four in one day. Many recruiters use group interview techniques that involve existing staff members in the process, and this can sometimes result in a better hiring decision. Remember to ask the same questions of each applicant, keep the interview focused, and ask open-ended questions that encourage more than yes or no answers.

5. Remember the importance of attitude in employees. Employees with excellent skills and qualifications but a poor attitude toward patients can be more trouble than they are worth.

6. Check references carefully before offering the job to the most suitable applicant.

Employment agreements

Once an employee is hired, develop an employment agreement, or job description, for that employee. At a minimum, this document should contain the following information:

- employee name
- effective date of the agreement
- job title
- reporting relationships
- rate of pay, pay periods (hourly or monthly salary), and details about bonuses or incentive plans
- vacation entitlement
- sick leave entitlement
- breaks
- job status: probationary, permanent or temporary (if temporary, to fill in for an employee on leave for example, the start and end times of the employment should be stated)
- description of benefits, if any, and if they are company-paid, employee-paid, or a combination (keep in mind that a qualification period may apply, set by you or the insurance provider)
- job description: provide a detailed description of the duties of the job, and any projects that the employee is expected to complete, and over what time frame (state whether on-the-job or formal training is required)
- the duration of the agreement, and the length of the probationary period (if applicable)
- reimbursement or compensation for costs and expenses paid by employees, such as automobile expenses
- non-compete clause
- confidentiality clause
- provisions for termination.

The importance of this document cannot be stressed enough. It clarifies expectations and provides a structure against which performance can be measured.

Performance review

During the probationary period, give frequent verbal feedback for positive performance. If required, provide guidance concerning areas that may need improvement privately to the employee – not in front of other employees or patients. Document your comments in the employee's personnel file in readiness for their performance review.

Formal performance reviews should be conducted at least annually, usually on the anniversary of the employee's hiring date. Invite the employee to prepare for the performance review meeting by summarizing their achievements, assessing their own performance, and developing future objectives. Some employers use a rating system to assess performance; others prefer an anecdotal method. Whichever method you choose should apply to all employees within the organization. Conduct the meeting with the employee in private, reviewing areas that may require improvement first so that you can adjourn the meeting on a positive note with recognition of the employee's contribution, achievements, and areas of strength. Where possible, develop goals and objectives with the employee that matches both your organizational goals and the employee's personal goals. A tried and true method of developing objectives is to use the SMART rule: specific, measurable, achievable, relevant and timely (or time-bound).

For best results, prepare a form to help you document what has been discussed during the meeting. Carefully document the areas of performance that may need improvement, what measures have been taken to assist the employee to meet performance improvement objectives, and agree on a date when the next review will take place. Also, take care to document the SMART objectives that have been agreed upon along with dates of completion. It is also a good idea to incorporate these objectives into a new employment agreement that both the employee and you sign. One copy can be stored in the employee's personnel file, and one copy given to the employee for their reference.

For more information refer to the section, "Termination with notice" on page 109.

CHAPTER FIVE

Risk Management

As an incorporated professional you have to provide your own insurance. Unlike people working for a major corporation or government, that provides various types of insurance coverage, you have to seek out and purchase your own.

There are a number of different types of insurance that cover a wide variety of disasters. For the purposes of this book I'll break them down as follows:

- Personal insurance
    - life insurance
    - dependent life insurance
    - term insurance
    - whole life insurance
    - universal life insurance
    - joint life insurance
    - accidental death insurance
    - disability insurance
    - critical illness insurance
    - long-term care insurance.
- Practice insurance
    - office contents, practice interruption and general liability
    - office overhead expense insurance
    - buy/sell insurance.
- Liability and legal insurance
    - malpractice insurance
    - personal umbrella liability insurance
    - legal expenses insurance.
- Staff insurance
    - group benefits.

Personal Insurance

Life Insurance

Life insurance is known by many names including: death insurance, mortgage insurance, creditor insurance, partnership insurance. The basic principle is simple: pay a premium and die, and your beneficiaries receive an insurance payout. For our purposes, the only thing we need to be clear on is that when you die (not if you die) you may need or want to ensure that cash is available for your company or heirs.

There have been volumes written on how to decide on what coverage you need to have, and I'm not going to add to the list. I would suggest that you discuss the matter with a chartered life underwriter (CLU). A CLU is a life insurance representative who is educated about insurance matters. You should have a similar discussion with your accountant.

After you've decided that you need life insurance, and the amount required, you need to figure out the type, who's going to own it, and who is going to be the beneficiary of the proceeds.

Life insurance can be purchased on an individual basis, or through associations and groups. In all cases there is a premium and a benefit. How much you pay will depend on many factors, including mortality charges, expenses, and investment returns. Mortality charges are age and gender specific, meaning that the older one is, the more the premium costs and that females pay lower premiums than their male counterparts. Additional factors considered when establishing an individual's insurability are health, smoking habits of the insured, net worth, income and lifestyle (including things like driving record, dangerous occupations and hobbies, such as parachuting). Underwriting is not a science; it's a best guess by an individual or group of individuals attempting to determine when you are likely to die.

Unlike most things we purchase, life insurance is not automatically approved. Before an insurance company will assume the risk, it will ask you to submit to underwriting. This can range from a few questions to a complete medical and financial workup. The requirements can vary from company to company. Whether you buy individual or association/group coverage may determine whether you get coverage at all.

Rule of thumb buster: When you're turned down for insurance with one company, you're turned down with every insurance company.

Not true. You should always try another company or agent.

Just to be clear, the terms association and group coverage refer to the same thing, just as creditor insurance, credit card insurance and mortgage insurance are all intrinsically the same. The characteristic common to all of these types of insurance is the price, which is based on a group of people, not on one person. When you buy individual insurance it's based on just the one person, the insured (or insured's in the case of joint life coverage).

When I refer to group coverage I'm referring to all types of group coverage, including any coverage provided by your association. When you look at group coverage, the rates vary depending on the program. In an association group, the rates are usually broken down by age category, male or female, smoking or non-smoking and sometimes preferred or regular. When assessing risk, most insurance companies will charge lower premiums when an individual has an excellent medical history and no current medical issues. These lower rates are often referred to as "preferred" rates. Regular (often called "standard") rates, are rates charged by insurance companies based on an average person's health.

With group coverage, from an underwriting point of view, you are usually accepted or rejected. There is normally no option for the underwriter to modify the rates or benefits for one person. You either fit into the group or you don't.

There can be benefits to being in a group plan because the initial price for coverage is usually less expensive. The problem with group plans is that you have little or no control after the insurance is in place, as both the insurance companies and the policyholders are constantly reviewing, and possibly amending, the plans.

The Canadian Dentists' Insurance Program is an example of coverage that is offered through a number of different carriers. In 2010, Manulife Financial underwrote the life insurance and may or may not continue to provide this coverage in the future. Manulife's claims experience, along with the price they want to charge, will influence whether the Canadian Dental Association will continue with them as their life insurance provider. If Manulife were to increase premiums (which can be adjusted annually), then the Canadian Dental Association might decide to get quotes from other insurance providers.

Underwriting is somewhat arbitrary, so you could get a number of different quotes for the same coverage, depending on the company. Past experience, profit margins, and business practices can influence rates quoted by insurance companies.

Group insurance programs regularly change insurers, as employers or associations seek out the best deal for their employees or members. This means that group coverage can change over time depending on how the group policy is managed. The "master" contract can be under constant review and open to negotiation. If you were to go back over the last number of years and look at the coverage and rates of various associations you would find, in a number of cases, that there have been changes – some beneficial, others less so.

Personal life insurance is between you and the insurance company. Once you've decided which firm you want to go with, you ask them if they will provide you with the coverage at their quoted price. A number of different scenarios can result: the first and most desirable is that you get the coverage exactly as applied for; the second is that you get rejected altogether (remember, underwriting is subjective – so, I would encourage you to approach another insurance company); the third possibility is that the policy could be offered to you with modifications.

Modifications can be in the form of increased premiums, exclusion of coverage in the case of death by certain means, or rejection of certain riders. In the case of increased premiums, the insurance company you have applied to may see you as at a higher risk to die sooner than is normal for the population. You may have a medical condition or family history that could affect your mortality. This extra risk is reflected in a higher premium charged by the insurance company.

Exclusions are normally specific in nature and address either conditions or situations. The insurance company might look at your hobby, for example mountain climbing, and decline to award benefits if you should die as a result of a mountaineering accident. If you accept a policy with a mountaineering exclusion and fall while climbing, the insurance benefit will not be paid out.

A rejection of certain riders might result from a situation where your mortality may not be affected but your morbidity is. Mortality is the likelihood of dying; morbidity is the likelihood of becoming disabled. You may have asked the insurance company to waive the premiums on your life insurance if you became disabled; this is known as a waiver of premium rider. The insurance company may have noticed that you have a history of back pain. The back pain may not kill you prematurely but it may disable you; therefore, they are not willing to risk giving you waiver of premium as a rider.

You may have noticed a theme here. Group insurance coverage is often yes or no; you're either accepted or rejected. Individual coverage is more of a negotiation, in which the insurance company may make you an offer based on your specific circumstances.

If you get an offer on an individual life insurance policy and it's not exactly what you applied for, try another insurance company; they may see things differently.

Shopping for insurance can be easy or painful. You can deal with one person or a number of people. If you are buying insurance through your association plan, you will normally deal with one person and will not have access to other insurers. If you are dealing with a captive agent, one who works for a particular insurance company, you are probably only going to have access to one insurance company. The other alternative is to use an insurance broker who represents a number of insurance companies and gives you a variety of choices. This can be helpful if you end up having to apply to more than one company.

As a financial planner, I explore all insurance opportunities. I never discard one option automatically, nor accept another without examining it. Group coverage and personal coverage are considered on their merits, depending on my client's specific circumstances. Frequently, I find that a combination of group and individual coverage is appropriate.

Once your insurance is issued, you can change the beneficiary and the owner. As a professional corporation, you can have the coverage owned personally or by your company. If the owner of the insurance is the professional corporation, then the beneficiary should also be the professional corporation.

It is useful to know that, from the insurance industry's perspective, it's usually a lot easier to underwrite a personal policy than a corporate-owned policy. Experienced life underwriters will often apply for insurance on a personal basis and then change the owner and beneficiary to the professional corporation after issue.

So the question is, why change the owner and beneficiary to the corporation? Let me explain. Gross cost is the biggest reason. Life insurance premiums are normally paid with after-tax dollars. If you're in the top income tax bracket and have a marginal tax rate of 46 per cent, a $1000 premium would cost you $1,851.85 on a gross basis. You would personally have to earn $1,851.85 and pay tax at 46 per cent ($851.85) to have $1,000 after tax to pay your $1,000 premium.

If your professional corporation owned that same insurance policy, that $1,000 premium would cost you about $1,250.00. Your professional corporation would have to earn $1,250 and pay tax at its corporate rate of about 20 per cent ($250) to have $1,000 after tax to pay the $1,000 premium. That represents a reduction in insurance costs of 32 per cent.

This is extremely important to remember, because in both cases, you are the one earning the money. By saving yourself 32 per cent in premiums, you have extra money to invest.

Often, when I talk to professionals about having insurance owned by their professional corporations, they think that they're giving something up; as with most things there are pros and cons.

There can be little difference from a tax point of view. Insurance premiums paid with after-tax money allow tax-free benefits to be paid to the beneficiary. In the case of personally owned policies, the benefits are paid directly to the beneficiary or estate. In the case of corporate-owned insurance, the benefits are paid to the corporation. But, I hear you ask, how does the insurance money get out of the professional corporation? The answer is, through dividends. You may be thinking, but dividends are taxable! Well, they normally are, except when it comes to capital dividends. Let me explain.

A private corporation (your professional corporation) is entitled to maintain a notional tax account, called a capital dividend account (CDA), that keeps track of various tax-free surpluses accumulated by the company. These surpluses may be distributed as capital dividends free of tax to the corporation's Canadian-resident shareholders.

The amount of death benefit that exceeds the adjusted cost basis[24] (ACB) qualifies as tax-free surplus for the capital dividend account. Life insurance policies may have an adjusted cost basis or may not. It depends on a number of factors. Your insurance provider should be able to give you a projection that will illustrate the ACB of your insurance policy. It's important for you to see this before deciding whether or not to have the professional corporation own the policy. If the policy has a large ACB, then the amount that will be credited to the CDA will be smaller, and therefore less money can be removed after your death, tax-free.

The primary disadvantage of corporate-owned life insurance is that the benefits under the policy may not be protected from creditors, of either the corporation or the insured. The other disadvantage is that the insurance proceeds may end up being subject to probate fees. If you live in Alberta or the Yukon, this may not be much of an issue because their probate rates are so low. However, if you live in British Columbia or Ontario it could create a sizable extra cost.

If you do decide to have life insurance owned by your professional corporation, are you allowed to deduct the premiums from your taxes? The answer is maybe; nothing is ever straightforward is it? If the policy is required to secure a loan for business purposes, the premiums may be totally or partially deductible up to specific amounts. In order for premiums to be deductible the policy must be a condition of the loan, the policy must be assigned to the lending institute, and the institute must be the beneficiary to the extent of the loan.

I sense the need for an example. Suppose you went to the bank to get a practice purchase loan for $300,000. The bank requires that you have life insurance to pay off the loan in case of your death. You already have a $1,000,000 term life insurance policy, which is owned by your corporation. Your current annual premium is $1,500. You collaterally assign the policy to the bank and designate it as beneficiary. Because the loan requires life insurance and the policy is assigned to the bank, 30 per cent of the premium would be deductible: 300,000/1,000,000 = 30 per cent. As the loan is paid off, the amount of the deduction will decrease. As you can see, in this example I used a term life policy. When you apply for other types of insurance, like

---

24 The adjusted cost basis of a life insurance policy is calculated using a complex formula that takes into account all deposits into, withdrawals or loans from, dividends and the cost of insurance charges of a policy.

whole life or universal life, the amount of the premium that is deductible is not as clear.

So where does that leave you? What am I advising? Well, in most cases I recommend that the professional corporation owns life insurance in order to keep the cost down. Occasionally, I recommend personally owned insurance when it's important to have the insurance proceeds paid directly to a named beneficiary. Remember, the beneficiary of a corporate-owned insurance policy should be the corporation.

When you are using corporate owned life insurance, it is important to remember that the owner, beneficiary and payer should be the corporation.

Occasionally someone may recommend that you have an individual as the owner and beneficiary, and have the company pay the premiums. This is fine as long as the premiums are declared as a taxable benefit. If they're not and you die, the proceeds of the insurance policy will be taxable to the beneficiary.

Dependent Life Insurance

Dependent life insurance provides funds in the event of the death of your spouse, which will allow your spouse to meet their outstanding financial obligations, funeral expenses, the cost of ongoing childcare, and other expenses. Coverage is also available for dependent children. This life insurance is normally added as a rider to an individual life insurance policy or as an additional elected benefit in a group insurance policy. Depending on the coverage and the insurance company, your dependents may or may not have to qualify medically.

Term Life Insurance

This form of life insurance provides protection against financial loss resulting from death during a specific period of time or "term." The policy pays only if the person insured dies within the given period defined in the policy. The period of coverage is usually one year, five years, 10 years, 20 years, or until a specific age such as 65. At the end of the period, the protection ceases unless the policy is renewed. Travel insurance that you see at the airport is another form of term insurance except the "term" is your flight, not a time frame.

Many term policies contain a renewable clause that gives the policyholder the option of renewing the policy for some predetermined period of time without a medical examination, usually at a higher rate of premium. Some policies have a conversion clause that gives the policyholder the option to convert the term insurance to a form of permanent insurance without a medical or other evidence of insurability.

Term life insurance normally has no residual benefits and no cash value other than the death benefit. It is designed to provide a death benefit only and can be considered the simplest form of life insurance.

Whole Life Insurance

Whole life provides protection for the whole of the insured's life, not just for a specific term. Whole life insurance is a form of permanent life insurance with a fixed annual or monthly premium that is payable for the entire lifetime of the insured. The terms "whole life," "straight life" and "ordinary life" are used interchangeably.

Premiums can be paid on a continuous basis over the insured's life or on any limited basis, such as a single payment or annually for 10 years. With whole life policies, the premium rate is established at the time the policy is purchased and is guaranteed not to increase for the life of the contract.

With whole life, the premium payments are the amount required to pay for the actual cost of insurance plus expenses. Effectively, some of the cost is prepaid or over-funded with whole life. This over-funding gives rise to what the actuary refers to as the policy reserve and the *Income Tax Act* refers to as the accumulating fund of the policy, which is the amount of funds set aside for the policy.

If you look at the following graphs you can see how this works.

With **term insurance** the cost gets higher as the individual gets older.

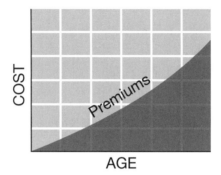

With **whole life insurance** the premiums paid are greater than the amount required for the insurance and accumulate to offset higher costs in later years.

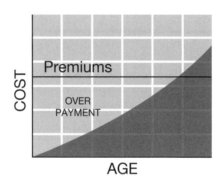

Whole life insurance policies often contain cash values, a portion of which may be guaranteed, as well as contractual reduced paid-up insurance benefits. A paid-up insurance benefit enables the policyholder to cease making premium payments and the accumulated cash value purchases a reduced amount of life insurance on the individual's life with no further premiums.

There are two types of whole life policies:

- **Participating whole life** policies participate in the profits of the insurance company. A participating whole life policy usually receives the payment of dividends on an annual basis. The dividend is essentially a refund of premiums for the previous policy year, the total premiums, or a percentage of the premiums.

- **Non-participating polices** do not participate in the profits of the insurance company.

Term to age 100 can also be seen as a whole life policy. This type of insurance is designed to provide a level insurance benefit with a level premium payable for life. Usually there is no cash value or paid-up value; however, there are versions of this coverage that allow for a limited number of premiums, and do have a cash surrender value. For example, premiums are payable for twenty years only; then no further premiums are due and the policy remains in force until age 100.

Term 100 policies usually feature fixed level premiums that are contractually guaranteed. Upon reaching age 100, one of three things can happen: the policy will continue to remain in force without further premiums, the policy endows, that is the policy's cash value equals its face value, or it expires, depending on the insurance company.

Universal Life Insurance

The primary attraction of a universal life (UL) policy lies in its flexibility. Traditional life insurance policies were bundled, meaning that with the exception of dividends on participating plans, all of the cash and coverage elements of the plan were inextricably tied to each other. The premium and cash surrender value were a function of the initial face amount, and both were established at policy issue and could be predetermined for the life of the policy. Universal life, on the other hand, unbundles these elements and is now at the leading edge of life insurance flexibility.

Universal life is essentially a combination of a life insurance policy and an investment contract, whereby the insured chooses a particular insurance type and a separate and distinct investment vehicle. The insurance component of the policy is commonly based upon either yearly renewable term costs, or a level term cost to age 100. However, mortality charges based on term insurance to age 65 and/or 10-year or 20-year renewable terms may also be available from some companies.

The investment component of a universal life insurance policy allows for a wide range of investments such as a bond or mortgage fund, as well as a number of equity investments that are linked to Canadian, US and international stock market indices. The growth of the investment account fund is tax-deferred until withdrawn, or the policy is surrendered.

Universal life plans offer the policyholder complete freedom with regard to the amount, frequency, timing, and duration of deposits, subject only to the restrictions of the *Income Tax Act* and the need to maintain sufficient value within the contract to pay for all insurance costs and other expenses.

All universal life contracts are subject to annualized expense charges of various types, which are generally deducted monthly. Typical charges include the following:

- provincial premium tax
- mortality deductions
- rider charges
- annual administration fees.

The cash deposits in a universal life plan can be divided into two categories: premiums and deposits. The premium under a universal life policy is the single or periodic payment required to pay the mortality cost, operation margins, administration fees, premium tax, and any increases in the accumulating fund, other than from investment income. A deposit under a universal life policy is an amount paid by the policyholder, whether to pay the premium or to contribute to the investment account.

Universal life policies are either exempt or non-exempt. Let me explain: if the policy is exempt, there is no annual accrual tax; if on the other hand, the policy is non-exempt, there can be a taxable gain that has to be reported. Policies are "tested" each year to determine whether they are exempt or not. These calculations are made using a number of different variables determined by the CRA. If the calculations find that the policy has too much cash on the investment side and not enough insurance on the insurance side, you basically have three choices: take some money out of the investment to bring the policy back into line; increase the amount of insurance to bring the policy back into line; or leave it as it is and pay tax on the gain in the policy. How you actually deal with this problem will be a matter of personal circumstances; however, some insurance companies have defaults built into their polices that automatically trigger an event, for example, paying out the surplus.

Universal life polices have many applications, some of which are discussed in other chapters of this book. For more information on universal life policies talk to your insurance advisor.

Re: Life Insurance as an Investment?
From: Lange Zhu
To: tim@tpcfinancial.com

Hi Tim – I was told that I should buy a life insurance policy and have my professional corporation pay for it as an investment. Does this make sense to you?

By the way, I spoke to Sven and Yo the other day, they seem to be enjoying Dawson Creek, I hear that Henrik is playing hockey, we'll make Canadians of them yet!

Lange

Re: Re: Life Insurance as an Investment?
From: tim@tpcfinancial.com
To: Lange Zhu

Hi Lange

Yes, the boys are really adapting well to living in Canada and they all seem to be settling in very well up there.

With regard to life insurance, when we did your last review we concluded that you didn't need any additional life insurance. Have your circumstances changed at all? If not, then I don't think it makes sense to buy life insurance just as an investment.

When you buy such a policy, the insurance company charges huge upfront costs. These costs have to be recovered, so there is usually little or no gain in the policy for several years. When you're paying for insurance you don't want to see the mortality costs eroding the investment returns of the policy.

Often, insurance agents will tell you that the insurance policy will accumulate tax sheltered, and that you can get money out of the policy tax-free. These statements can often be misrepresented.

> It is generally a correct statement that the cash
> (or fund) value of most policies does accumulate tax
> sheltered, but the actual dollars invested are reduced
> by the cost of insurance. Let me give you an example
> here Lange, if you deposit $1,000 in an insurance
> policy, you may only get $500 invested on your behalf
> in the first year. If you used a traditional investment,
> the actual amount invested would, of course, be the
> full $1,000.
>
> As for being able to remove money tax free, this often
> refers to a death benefit, which is of no use to you as
> a retirement planning vehicle. Other "tax free" options
> are often mentioned, but to the best of my knowledge
> none have been approved by the CRA.
>
> Generally I recommend that you consider life insurance
> only when you need life insurance and make your
> investments elsewhere.
>
> Tim

Joint Life Insurance

Life insurance can also be obtained on a joint life basis. It can either be joint first-to-die, or joint last-to-die. This type of coverage insures two lives but pays only one death benefit.

As the name implies, joint first-to-die pays out on the first death. This coverage is commonly used to cover debts such as a mortgage. When two people are covered under one policy it usually results in a lower cost. If a husband and wife both have individual mortgage insurance, they would, in fact, have their mortgage doubly covered. If they both died, the benefit payout would be double, as both policies would pay out. If the same mortgage were insured under a joint first-to-die policy, there would only be one payout.

In the above example you might think that having both policies pay out would not be a bad thing because it would leave extra money. That's true. However, you were most likely paying an extra premium for the extra coverage.

Joint second-to-die (also known as last-to-die) insures two lives but pays out only one death benefit upon the death of the last survivor. Since the proceeds are payable on the death of the last survivor, the underlying premium costs substantially less than if only one individual were to be insured.

A joint second-to-die life insurance policy is the most cost effective way to provide for liquidity to fund deferred capital gains or other deferred tax. It also works well as a vehicle to provide a transfer of family wealth to the next generation.

When a whole life or universal life policy is utilized to take advantage of the inherent tax sheltering opportunities, the underlying mortality costs can be greatly reduced by using a joint life second-to-die policy. The amount of the premium paid, which goes toward the mortality cost, is greatly reduced, thereby leaving a larger amount to accumulate on a tax-sheltered basis.

Joint second-to-die life insurance can also be a very advantageous option when estate planning for families, in situations where one person has health problems. The policy is designed to pay out on the second death; therefore, the health of one individual will usually not result in less coverage. Instead, the policy will probably have a higher premium than if both individuals were healthy, but still be less than individual coverage.

Accidental Death Insurance

Have you ever wondered why someone is worth more if they die in an accident than if they die of an illness? Accidental death insurance is life insurance coverage that pays out in the event of the insured's dying as a result of an accident. If you look at an autopsy report, it will list the causes of death as natural, homicide, suicide, unknown, undetermined or accidental. One would assume from the list that people die in a lot of ways other than accidentally. If you think about the people you know who have died, most of them, I would suggest, did not die as a result of an accident. So why buy insurance in case of accident? Well, I'm not sure why, myself!

Most people buy it because it's cheap. So, why is it so cheap? Because the insurance companies don't pay out very often. I'll bet, without ever having met you, that you've had accident insurance given to you by your bank. It may be a chartered bank, trust company or credit union – it doesn't matter. Over the last few years banks have been giving clients free accident insurance (usually for $1,000). Do you know why? One reason is because it is cheap (rarely do people lay a claim) but more importantly for them – are you ready for this – it's to get you into their system as an insurance client. The regular banking division can't give client information to their insurance side unless you're an insurance client. This information is very beneficial for cross-selling. The next time you get an offer from your bank of free accident insurance, read the fine print and see what you are agreeing to.

Disability Insurance

Disability insurance provides a monthly benefit to help replace your personal income if illness or injury prevents you from working. From a purely financial point of view, it's the most important type of insurance for you to have. Life insurance protects your beneficiaries; disability insurance protects you. As a professional, your greatest asset is your ability to earn income. Protecting that income is paramount.

Disability insurance can begin to pay out after a variety of time periods (30 days, 60 days, 90 days, 120 days, 180 days and one year); these are known as elimination periods. Benefit periods can range from two years to age 65 and beyond.

Disability insurance can be purchased on a group basis or individually. Who you are talking to will probably determine whether you end up with one or the other. An association representative will promote the group plan. An individual insurance sales person will almost certainly promote individual disability. Both have pros and cons.

Like life insurance, disability insurance varies from program to program and company to company. When comparing group plans to individual plans the most obvious difference is the initial cost. I say "initial cost" because most group plans have increasing premiums, so the older you get, the more you pay. With individual insurance, the premium is usually guaranteed never to change after the policy is issued. A few life insurance companies even offer a return of premium rider, which can also reduce the net cost over time (this rider is described in more detail later in this section).

Group coverage is very sensitive to claims experience. If the insurance company has had a lot of claims, they will increase the premiums to offset the expense. The policyholder will either accept the new premiums or take the contract to market to try to negotiate a better deal for its members. Most group plans have seen an increase in their disability premiums over the last number of years. Some groups have stayed with their existing insurance provider and some have moved. The important point is that you really have no control over the group, nor the policy.

Individual policies are those that are directly available from an insurance company and that can be tailored to provide the specific coverage that an individual requires. Total protection is very expensive because of the high probabilities of disability, and the high costs involved in replacing one's earned income. The only way insurance companies can offer insurance at relatively low cost is to place limitations on the benefits, and restrictions on the conditions they insure.

When you get individual coverage, the policy is between you (the policyholder) and the insurance company. The contracts are normally issued on a unilateral basis, which means that once the policy is issued you are the only one who can change the contract. In other words, you control it.

Signing up for disability insurance is very different from getting life insurance. The underwriting is a lot more detailed and a number of additional factors come into play.

When applying for group disability, the end result will normally be either yea or nay – you will either get the coverage or you won't. With individual coverage you can have so many variations on one application that I can't even begin to list them all. The insurance company can exclude almost anything on an individual disability insurance policy: they can exclude claims if the disability is related to a specific part of your body (your back, your left arm, your right arm, your neck, your left knee, your right ankle, etc., etc., etc.); they can exclude activities (sky diving, mountain climbing, car racing); or they can charge extra premiums for additional risk. I've even seen policies that have both exclusions and extra premiums.

Disability policies can pay out benefits as a result of a total disability or, in some cases, a partial or residual disability. **Total disability** means, "due to injuries or sickness the insured is not able to perform the substantial and material duties of his or her occupation, and is under the care and attendance of a physician." Less comprehensive coverage may specify that total disability requires that the insured cannot perform any job.

Partial disability is based upon time, and means that due to injuries or sickness, the insured is unable to perform either of the following:

- the important duties of one's occupation at least one-half of the time usually required
- one or more important duties of your occupation
- and that the insured is under the care of a physician.

Residual disability is based upon loss of earnings and means that due to injuries or sickness, the insured has a loss of monthly income of at least 20 per cent. The insured must also be under the care and attendance of a physician. With residual disability the benefit amount should be designed to restore the income of the incapacitated individual to the after-tax income earned before the disability.

Whether you apply for disability insurance through a group plan or individually, the limitations are about the same. As an example, if your annual income, after business expenses but before taxes, is $250,000 then the amount of tax-free disability insurance you can have is about $7,600 per month. If the benefit applied for is taxable, this monthly amount may be increased.

Be careful, at the time of application there might appear to be little difference in cost between group and individual coverage, but there can be a significant difference at the time you make a claim. To qualify for $7,600 of benefits with a group plan, you have to provide the insurance company financial information with your application. At claim time, the actual amount paid out is calculated based on either:

- average monthly income during the 24-month period prior to disability, or
- by taking the highest average earnings for any 12 consecutive months in the 24 months immediately prior to the month in which disability commenced.

If your income level is less than the income level at the time of application for the group policy, the benefit amount would be reduced to reflect the lesser amount, even though you were paying for the higher amount. With individual insurance however, the benefit amount is approved at the time of application.

If you are totally disabled at claim time, the total benefit amount will be paid out. For example, you apply for an individual disability policy when your income is $250,000 per year and the insurance company has issued a policy with a monthly benefit amount of $7,600. Three years later you decide to cut back your hours and your income drops to $150,000. If you were to become totally disabled at that time the benefit payout would still be $7,600.

In determining disability, individual contracts will have provisions defining the following:

- causes of disability
- degrees of disability
- provision for own occupation
- HIV benefit.

Ideal coverage would provide protection from disability arising from any sickness or injury. The more comprehensive policies define these two critical terms as follows:

- sickness means a sickness or disease that first manifests itself while the policy is in force
- injury means an accidental bodily injury occurring while this policy is in force.

Less comprehensive coverage excludes certain sicknesses or causes of accident. Exclusions might include:

- injuries that cause a disability for more than 90 days after the injury is sustained
- injuries or sickness arising from pregnancy
- psychoneurotic or behavioural disorders.

Unlike life insurance, where the individual insured is in one of two states, either dead or alive, there are many degrees of disability. The individual may be totally disabled, and unable to perform any job, or partially disabled and able to work on a limited basis, or for a limited time per month. Therefore, definitions of total disability and partial disability are very important in assessing an individual's disability insurance coverage.

Aside from the elimination period and the benefit period, disability contracts can be issued with a number of riders. These additional riders can include:

- future insurance guarantee

- cost of living adjustments

- own occupation

- retirement protection

- return of premium

- health care profession rider

- automatic increase rider

- catch-up rider.

The **future insurance guarantee (FIG)**, sometimes known as a future needs rider (FNR) or a medical insurability rider (MIR), allows the insured to periodically increase the benefit amount subject to income qualification, but not medical qualification. As an example, the FIG option allows you to increase your coverage by 25 per cent (or some dollar amount, such as $1,000) without medical underwriting, when you get married, or upon the birth or adoption of a child. It also allows you to increase coverage on your birthday at ages 25, 30, 35, 40, 45 and 50. This benefit must be exercised within 60 days of any of these events.

I would advise that you have this rider added to your initial disability policy, whether it is group or individual. The best chance you have to get disability insurance underwritten without exclusions or limitations for health is probably when you're younger. By adding this rider on your first disability contract, you are guaranteeing that future disability purchases, when exercising this option, will be free from medical underwriting.

This rider is particularly important for professionals. A common problem that manifests itself, after you start practicing medicine or dentistry, is back pain or discomfort. You can take advantage of your strong, healthy back when you graduate, by getting your disability insurance issued with a FIG rider. If you develop back problems later in life, you can then increase your coverage under this option without having your back excluded.

Here is something else to consider. If your first disability policy is issued through a group plan, you could end up being stuck in that group plan if health issues appear later in life. A good strategy would be to purchase both an individual insurance policy with a FIG and a group policy with a FIG at the beginning of your career. Care should be taken to avoid being over-insured by splitting your disability insurance between carriers, not duplicating it. Over time, you may decide to change all your coverage one-way or the other. Just make sure that you don't over-insure in the beginning because you may end up paying for coverage you can never collect.

You should also keep in mind that you shouldn't add this rider to every disability policy you buy. I've seen dozens of cases where people have increased their insurance (which had this rider) and then had the rider added to the increase. What a waste of money! Some professionals have FIG options that require their incomes to increase tenfold. A FIG rider is designed to allow for increases to your disability coverage based on income, not on health. If you are paying premiums for a rider that would require you to earn 10 times more money, you are paying for too much rider. Say you are have an income of $100,000 annually, and you purchase a $4,500 per month disability policy with a FIG rider for $1,000, As your income increases you can increase your coverage by up to $1,000 at a time (based on your gross income). To get an $8,500 a month benefit, your income would have to be over $200,000 annually. If you were to have $3,000 of FIG rider, you would have to increase your income to about $400,000 in order to take full advantage of the rider. If you don't think your income is going increase by that much, don't buy $3,000 of FIG.

Make sure you review all riders with your insurance representative, paying particular attention to any insurance you are unlikely to use, or can never use.

The **Cost of Living Adjustment (COLA)** increases your benefit each year you are on claim to protect your purchasing power. The increase is usually tied to the consumer price index. The benefit may be compounded or established according to simple interest, and may have a maximum figure or payout, for example double the original benefit amount.

One example of a compounded COLA states that the monthly benefit will be adjusted annually based on the percentage change in the consumer price index. The monthly benefit may increase up to an annual 10 per cent compounded indexing maximum, cumulative from the start of disability. In addition, there is a minimum monthly benefit increase of 2 per cent of the previous year's monthly benefit. Other than the 10 per cent compounded maximum, and the actual consumer price index, there is no overall cap on monthly benefit adjustments.

One example of a simple-interest COLA states that during an extended period of disability, your monthly benefit will be adjusted annually based on the percentage change of the consumer price index. This index amount each year is added to the original benefit amount and is not compounded.

Simple and compound interest compared

If disability payments begin at age 50 and last until age 65, this table shows the effect of different cost of living riders on the benefit payout. What starts out as a $5,000 benefit at age 50 is only indexed to $7,250 at age 65 with a 3 per cent simple interest benefit compared to $10,349 benefit at age 65 with a 5 per cent compound benefit.

Age	3 per cent Simple Interest	3 per cent Compound Interest	5 per cent Simple Interest	5 per cent Compound Interest
50	5,000	5,000	5,000	5,000
53	5,450	5,463	5,750	5,787
56	5,900	5,967	6,500	6,697
59	6,350	6,519	7,250	7,751
62	6,800	7,122	8,000	8,941
65	7,250	7,781	8,750	10,349

The monthly benefit may be increased up to an annual 4 per cent simple maximum, cumulative from the start of disability. Ideally, the benefit will keep pace with inflation. This is extremely important when you're young.

I have a client who became permanently disabled at age 31 as a result of MS. His benefit amount was $4,000 payable to age 65. Without COLA, his benefit, assuming 2 per cent inflation, would have been worth $2,745 at age 50 and $2,040 at age 65. This loss of purchasing power can be catastrophic over time. In my opinion, all disability contracts should be issued with COLAs.

An **own-occupation** rider ensures that you continue to collect disability benefits if you are unable to engage in your regular occupation, or perform the main duties of that occupation. As a professional, I believe this is a must.

You've spent years educating yourself, why would you want to be forced into some other occupation if you happen to become disabled? I've witnessed dozens of situations where this one rider could have made all the difference in people's lives.

For instance, I once knew an emergency physician who was told that his disability coverage would protect him if he could not engage in his regular occupation. When he became disabled (he hurt his back) he put in a claim, only to have it rejected on the grounds that he could still practice medicine. According to the insurance company, he was a physician who happened to work in the emergency department of a hospital. He could still practice medicine because his disability prevented him only from lifting patients. The back injury was not severe enough to lay him up, but was significant enough to impede his work. A properly worded own-occupation rider could have prevented this problem. I say, "properly worded" because I reviewed this case with two different insurers and one insurer agreed with the definition in this case, and the other did not.

I currently have a client, a dentist, on disability who is unable to work because of a tremor in his right hand. He was first diagnosed with a disabling illness three years ago and has since sold his practice; he will not practice dentistry again. With his own-occupation definition, he can explore other career opportunities without having to worry about being "cut off." Even if he does get another job, he will continue to receive his benefits in full.

After thirty years, I still hear people argue about whether or not it's worth paying for an own-occupation definition. Many insurance agents don't see the need. I don't agree and here's why.

You've made a huge investment in your career. If you become disabled (regardless of what you may or may not be able to do), if you can't do what you were trained to do, why should you be penalized? If you have disability insurance without an own-occupation rider, I would consider replacing it, or at the very least when you get additional insurance make sure you add it to any new policies.

Retirement protection provides a monthly contribution during a total disability to an account set up for your retirement. It allows you to continue saving for your retirement when, because of your total disability, you do not have earned income that enables you to contribute to an RRSP.

A **return of premium (ROP)** provides for a return of up to 65 per cent of the money you have paid in premiums at preset return dates if you do not become disabled, or if your claims are minimal. Return dates and refund amounts vary by company and are only available on individual policies. Here is an example of how it works. Assuming an annual base premium of $1,000, the example below outlines the significant premium reduction you can realize by adding the ROP to a disability policy.

Annual policy premium without ROP	$1,000
ROP premium (50 per cent of $1,000)	$500
Total policy premium with ROP	$1,500
Total policy premium paid over 8 years	$12,000
Amount of ROP benefit payable after 8 years (62.5 per cent[25] of $12,000)	$7,500

In the example above, the net premium after 8 years is $4,500 (the $12,000 gross premium less the $7,500 premium return). With the return of premium benefit, the average annual premiums are effectively reduced to $562.50, or a little more than half the $1,000 per year you'd be paying without ROP. If the policy premiums were paid with after-tax dollars, the ROP benefit is a tax-free refund.

Health care profession rider. If a health care professional becomes infected with HIV, hepatitis B or hepatitis C, it can have career limiting implications. Although the health care professional may be fully functional, the nature of the infection could mean that restrictions might be imposed upon the practitioner. In such a case, it is uncertain whether disability benefits could be claimed. The health care profession rider removes doubt.

If, as a result of HIV, hepatitis B or hepatitis C infection, a law or medical authority prohibits the performance of the important duties of the regular occupation, total disability benefits are payable as if caused by sickness. The person insured must not be working in any other gainful occupations. The 75 per cent loss of income qualification for total disability and benefits payable under the own-occupation rider are not applicable to the healthcare profession rider.

---

25 The 62.5 per cent is based on a return of premium benefit of "5 back". Five back is an option where you choose to get five of the eight years of premiums refunded. If you chose "4 back" you'd get back four of the eight years of premiums paid and you would pay an increased premium of 40 per cent, not 50 per cent.

If the requirements for disability benefits are met, the waiting period will be waived. Additionally, the regular care and attendance of a doctor will not be required.

An **automatic increase rider** (**AIR**) increases the monthly benefit automatically for the first several years. For example, an AIR might allow for an automatic 4 per cent increase in the monthly benefit for the first five years. The increase usually happens automatically unless you notify the insurance company that you do not want to exercise the option. Your corresponding monthly premium will increase with each increase in benefit. The idea behind this rider is to "inflation proof" your monthly benefit. At the end of the five-year period, you are asked to provide new financial information to ensure that your income can continue to support the increased amounts.

A **catch-up rider** is designed to allow the insured to catch up on benefits that were not received during the exclusion period. If the exclusion period is 90 days, no benefits are paid out during that time. With a catch-up rider, the insured will be paid for those 90 days, if they are totally disabled for at least six months.

Benefits can be level or "stepped." A level benefit pays the same amount each month during the disability period (after the elimination period and excluding any cost of living increases). A stepped benefit starts at a lower amount and then increases after a specified period of time. A disability benefit, for example, after 90 days of $3,000 per month, might increase to $5,000 after 180 days.

A step benefit can be useful in keeping down the cost of your disability insurance while at the same time ensuring that you will have sufficient coverage in case of a long-term disability.

Critical Illness Insurance

Critical illness insurance pays you a lump-sum tax-free benefit equal to the amount of your coverage, if you are diagnosed for the first time in your life with a serious medical condition such as the ones listed below. The lump sum benefit amount is tax-free; however, if the policy is corporately owned, the beneficiary is the corporation. The proceeds are paid to the corporation tax-free but would be taxable to the individual if removed. You can get an offsetting deduction personally, if proceeds are used for an eligible medical expense.

The critical illness condition must persist for at least 30 days after the first diagnosis or any longer time period specified in the definitions in the insurance contract. Depending on the insurance company, the list of insurable conditions includes:

- heart attack
- cancer
- blindness
- stroke
- multiple sclerosis
- Parkinson's disease
- Aortic surgery
- heart valve replacement
- major organ failure (on waiting list)
- motor neuron disease (e.g. ALS)
- benign brain tumour
- major organ transplant
- coronary artery bypass surgery
- loss of independence
- paralysis/loss of limbs
- coma
- deafness
- loss of speech
- Alzheimer's disease
- severe burns
- renal (kidney) failure
- occupational HIV infection.

Options and riders include:

- child critical illness protection for children up to their twenty-first birthday
- premium payback benefit, which provides for a full refund of premiums at a specific age or time period (age 75 or 10 years)

- conversion option, that allows you to convert to a level premium regardless of health
- waiver of premium, that allows coverage to remain in effect in the event of total disability
- return of premium upon death
- charitable contributions, through which a $500 donation is made on every claim to the charity of the policy owner's choice.

Policies can be issued with a number of different insurance options including renewable (five or 10-year) as well as level payment programs. The rate structure works in the same way as with life insurance. Renewable contracts start out being less expensive and then increase in cost over time. Level cost contracts bear a fixed premium throughout the lifetime of the contract.

> **Rule of thumb buster:** If I have disability and overhead insurance, I don't need critical illness insurance.
>
> **Not true.** It may be to your advantage to also have critical illness insurance.

I've had many people say that they don't need critical illness insurance because they have disability insurance and overhead coverage. I do not believe this to be the case. Critical illness insurance can have many uses. It can be used personally for medical expenses, replacement of lost income for a caregiver, to retire debts, for travel or purchases one might want prior to death, or for asset protection. Corporately, it can be used to stabilize the business, pay off debt or buy out a partner.

Dr. Marius Barnard, the creator of critical illness insurance, stated, "survival is expensive." Health care costs are ever increasing. Waiting lists for treatment are getting longer. Having choices for health care can be life saving. If you are diagnosed with a critical illness, such as cancer, having a lump sum of money available gives you options. If you want to use a private clinic, or go outside of the country for treatment, these choices are available. Having cash also allows you to explore alternative treatments and drugs. For example, stem cell treatment can cost $25,000. Other costs, like necessary upgrades to your home, can also cost tens of thousands of dollars.

Long-Term Care Insurance

Long-term care insurance helps to pay for the care or services that other medical plans don't provide, or works to bridge the gap between what is provided and the extra care or services you might prefer. This extra care can be either in your home or in a facility, for a period ranging from a few years to lifetime coverage. Long-term care insurance helps to cover the costs relating to care, which means that you have more choices around the kind and amount of care you receive. Its flexibility allows you to decide whether you want professionals or family members to provide the care. It also allows you to preserve your savings and investments.

There are three types of plans currently available:

- *Income plan.* Once you are eligible to claim, you receive a predetermined weekly benefit. You are free to use the benefits for whatever long-term care services you wish.
- *Reimbursement plan.* Once you are eligible to claim, you must submit proof that you received services that are covered under the plan. Eligible expenses are reimbursed up to a predetermined daily maximum.
- *Indemnity plan.* Once you are eligible to claim, you receive a predetermined daily benefit if you prove you received a covered service.

Plans are normally sold on a daily unit basis, for example $50, $100 per day. Coverage is available from as low as $10 per day to as high as $300 per day.

This may be something you might want to purchase for yourself or your parents. Escalating costs and shortages of facilities, and home care workers, will continue to put a strain on personal finances.

Practice Insurance

Office Contents, Practice Interruption And General Liability

Office contents insurance covers items in your office that are stolen, damaged by fire, vandalism, or other insured incidents. All equipment, leasehold improvements, supplies, furniture, fixtures, interior and exterior signage, office equipment, and personal effects are included.

Besides damage to the contents of your office, such as equipment, you will also have coverage in the event of losses caused by an insured incident in the following special categories:

- valuable papers, such as patient records

- accounts receivable – for reconstruction of records, uncollectible accounts and extra expenses related to collection procedures

- extra expenses – for additional costs incurred while your office is being restored and to cover extra expenses incurred due to computer loss, damage or breakdown resulting from an insured accident

- rental value – covers your practice rent while office restoration keeps you from practicing in your usual premises

- additional lease – covers increased expenses if you have to sign a new lease at a higher monthly rate

- money and securities

- gold and precious metals

- employee dishonesty – for losses caused by staff, and for professional accounting fees to substantiate loss resulting from an employee's dishonesty

- counterfeiting - for counterfeit money orders and paper currency

- depositor forgery

- credit card forgery

- personal property – for damaged or stolen personal property belonging to you or your staff

- fire extinguisher recharge – to recharge a portable fire extinguisher that has been used to combat a covered fire

- arson reward – for information leading to an arson conviction in connection with a covered fire loss

- elevator collision – for specified property that is damaged by accidental collision with an object in an elevator, or with the elevator itself

- clean-up of polluted water and land – for the clean-up of pollutants from water or land on your premises, if the release of pollutants is occasioned by loss or damage to property insured at the premises under the office contents coverage caused by an insured peril, is sudden, unexpected and unintended, and first occurs during the policy period.

Practice interruption coverage covers fixed expenses and reimburses you for loss of income (normally for a maximum period of 12 months) when your office use is interrupted or interfered with for one of the following reasons:

- fire, theft, vandalism or other insured peril (including computer damage or theft)
- repairs in progress when your office is being restored after damage or loss from an insured peril
- lack of access when you are prohibited from entering the premises by order of police, fire department or other government authority.

General liability coverage covers legal costs and damages, if personal injury to others or damage to a third party's property arises out of your practice (excluding malpractice). If you are incorporated, the policy should cover both you and your professional corporation.

Office Overhead Expense Insurance

If you become personally disabled, office overhead expense insurance is designed to cover certain specific business expenses.

The elimination period for this coverage is usually shorter than for individual disability insurance (usually 14 days or 30 days). In addition, the benefit period is shorter than for individual disability insurance, normally 12 months.

Office overhead coverage can be level or stepped, like disability insurance, except that with office overhead, coverage is normally stepped down, that is, the initial benefit amount is larger than the secondary amount. This option is designed to keep the cost of the coverage lower while acknowledging that some expenses may be reduced over time. For example, you might have an initial benefit of $10,000 per month for the first three months, reduced to $6,500 for the next six months and then finally reduced to $4,000 per month for the remaining three months.

Office overhead insurance can be issued with a future insurance rider and own-occupation rider.

- Eligible expenses might include:
- staff salaries and benefits
- utilities
- office maintenance
- laundry
- rent or mortgage interest payments
- interest on loans, depreciation, and/or rental
- accounting and legal fees
- practice insurance premiums
- association membership dues
- business taxes
- telephone, answering service, pager.

Your professional corporation should own the office overhead insurance, if you're incorporated. I've seen too many situations where professionals have incorporated and not changed the owner of their overhead coverage to their professional corporation. Make sure you make the change after you incorporate. You want the benefit to be paid to the one paying the bills – your professional corporation.

Buy/Sell Insurance

Buy/sell insurance acts as a funding mechanism for a buy/sell agreement. The policy provides a lump-sum benefit in the event that one of the principals of the business dies, or becomes permanently, totally disabled. Buy/sell insurance helps make sure that the interests of all partners are protected if anything should happen to one of them. It:

- protects all members of a business partnership from financial hardship in the event that a partner dies or becomes disabled
- provides the surviving partners with money to buy the deceased or disabled partner's share of the business
- ensures that money is available to the surviving partners at a crucial time, so that the business can sustain a secure financial position and continue operations without undue disruptions.

Premiums for this coverage are normally level throughout the term of coverage. The normal waiting period for this coverage is 365 days before the lump sum payout.

Liability And Legal Insurance

Malpractice Insurance

As a licensed professional, you are legally responsible for the services you, or your staff, perform. If you are accused of malpractice, error, or mistake while you are practicing, you have to bear the significant financial consequences that can accompany such charges. Malpractice insurance can protect you in the event a patient makes a claim against you, or your practice, arising from professional services rendered. In addition, malpractice insurance provides claims assistance and legal representation.

As an incorporated professional, you are legally liable both personally and corporately. Your malpractice insurance should cover both you and your corporation.

Personal Umbrella Liability Insurance

Personal umbrella liability insurance can provide coverage in case a large lawsuit award goes beyond the limit of one of your primary personal insurance coverages. For example, if a third party is awarded $5 million in a car accident covered by the plan, and the liability limit on your automobile policy is $3 million, then the primary policy pays the $3 million limit on your policy, and personal umbrella liability insurance will pay the second $2 million.

Umbrella coverage applies to liability claims under all of the insurance policies listed below, when they carry $1-million or more of liability coverage:

- homeowners
- condominium
- tenants
- vacation properties
- boats

- personally owned or leased automobiles
- recreational vehicles
- other motorized vehicles.

Personal umbrella liability insurance may cover some third-party liability claims that are not covered by your primary policies. Types of claims covered include those for defamation of character, libel, slander, invasion of rights or privacy, false arrest, wrongful detention, wrongful eviction, mental injury and malicious prosecution.

Legal Expense Insurance

Legal expense insurance reimburses you for the costs you incur from initiating or defending claims, or legal proceedings, that are covered by the plan and approved by the insurer. It pays fees, expenses and other costs charged by your appointed legal representative, including the costs of expert witnesses.

The plan covers specific legal proceedings that result from delivering your professional services and a wider range of personal legal proceedings for both you and eligible members of your family.

Legal expense insurance can cover:

- someone testifying at a coroner's inquest as a witness
- expenses resulting from a legislated investigation, tribunal or inquiry
- fees arising out of divorce or matrimonial matters
- expenses due to an investigation launched by your board, college or association, concerning your licensing or fitness to practice
- expenses arising from a disciplinary or complaint hearing undertaken by your board, college or association or disciplinary board (provided you are acquitted, or the charges are dismissed or withdrawn)
- expenses arising from a criminal or statutory hearing (providing you are acquitted, or the charges are dismissed or withdrawn)
- expenses arising from an appeal or judicial review arising out of any of the above situations.

Staff Insurance

Group Benefits

Group insurance is available to small groups with as few as three employees. Group insurance premiums can be paid for by the employer, employee or by both on a split basis. All group insurance premiums paid by the employer are tax deductable, however the tax treatment to the employee will vary depending on the specific benefits the employer is paying for. The following is a list of benefits available, and the taxability of those benefits, to the employee.

The basic benefits provided by most group insurers include:

- *Life insurance* – provides a payment to the named beneficiary in case of an employee death. If the premium is paid for by the employee, the death benefits are received by the beneficiary tax-free. Employers are permitted to pay the cost of up to $10,000 of benefit without impairing the tax-free status of the benefit. If the employer pays for insurance above this figure, the excess is taxable to the beneficiary.

- *Dependent life* – provides a payment to the named beneficiary in case of a death of an employees' spouse or dependent children.

- *Accidental death and dismemberment* – provides a payment to the named beneficiary in the case of accidental loss, or loss of use of:
  - one or both hands, arms or feet
  - entire sight of one or both eyes
  - speech
  - thumb and index finger on either hand
  - thumb of the dominant hand
  - index finger of the dominant hand
  - thumb of the non-dominant hand
  - index finger of the non-dominant hand
  - all toes on one foot
  - joint between two phalanges or phalange of thumb or index finger of dominant hand
  - partial loss of sight of one eye (loss of 30 per cent or more of visual acuity)

- *short-term disability* that provides disability benefits after normal one, seven or 14 days of disability with benefits normally payable for 17, 26 or 52 weeks

- *long-term disability* that provides disability benefits after short-term disability benefits expire or after employment insurance disability benefits expire; normally benefits are payable to age 65

- *medical insurance* that provides benefits to supplement provincial or territorial health care; coverage can include:
  - drugs, nursing care, emergency ambulance, hospital and medical services and supplies
  - eye care services
  - out-of-province or out-of-country emergency medical coverage
  - emergency travel protection
  - out-of-province referral
  - two-year survivor benefit
  - supplemental hospital benefit (semi-private or private hospital room coverage)
  - nursing home benefit (for active treatment or convalescent care provided by a nursing home)
  - pay direct drugs
  - paramedical services
  - vision care benefit
  - foot orthotics benefit.

Dental coverage provides employees and their families with preventative and diagnostic treatment, including root canals, and may also include major dental procedures, like bridges and crowns. Orthodontic coverage is also available with some plans.

Group benefits can be an excellent additional reward for your staff. Packages are available through associations and directly with various insurance companies. Premiums can be split between employer and employee or paid entirely by the employer. Some group benefits are better paid by the employee such as life and disability coverage so that in case of claim, benefits are received tax-free. Some group packages have mandatory benefits that must be taken while others provide for more customization.

As an alternative to the traditional group benefit program, you can also take advantage of cost plus arrangements and health spending accounts. These two programs provide a dollar amount directly to an employee and can be used at their discretion to pay for additional medical and dental expenses. The difference between the two is that the cost plus plan allows for payments of medical and dental procedures not covered by the standard benefit plan and may be an additional benefit to only key employees, whereas a health spending account provides each employee with a personal account used to pay for additional medical and dental expenses. Also see page 186 for a discussion of health and welfare trusts.

Summary

This chapter touches only briefly on all the different types of risk management tools available to you as a professional. The various programs and details of each policy vary and you should have your particular choice fully explained to you by an insurance professional.

Many of the programs I have outlined are combinations provided by various insurers. The actual products on the market may not cover all the conditions listed in each example. My goal is to provide you with an overview of the type and variety of product available to you to help you make the right decision for your particular circumstances.

Note that the taxation of insurance is a highly complex issue and should be thoroughly discussed with your tax professional. Each program listed in this section is either deductible or non-deductible and the benefits received from each may be taxable or tax-free. Many factors contribute to the tax status of these programs, including whether you are incorporated or not and who is receiving the benefit. You will need professional help to ensure you are using these programs to your best advantage.

Liability insurance should be owned and paid for by your professional corporation. This includes all office and malpractice insurance. The premiums paid by the company are tax deductible.

Overhead expense insurance should be owned and paid for by your professional corporation. The purpose of this insurance is to pay for office expenses during a period of disability. These policies vary from company to company and are offered both on a personal and association basis. It's worth your while to ask your insurance advisor to explain the differences. Don't assume that all coverage is created equal. For example, some contracts are refundable (if you don't make a claim the insurance company will refund part of your premium). The premiums paid by the company are tax deductible.

Disability insurance is often where you find differing opinions and biases. Disability insurance can be owned personally or corporately. The premiums can be paid personally or corporately. However, normally the premiums are paid for personally. The main difference between corporate and personal payment of premiums is the taxability of the benefit. Let's investigate the differences.

If the professional corporation is the owner and pays the premiums, the benefits are taxable to you if you become disabled. If the owner is you and the professional corporation pays the premium on your behalf, you can declare the premium as a taxable benefit on your personal tax return. This would make the benefit to you tax-free in the event of disability. If you are both the owner and pay the premiums personally the benefits are tax-free in the event of claim.

As with overhead coverage, there are many different types of disability insurance coverage. We don't have space to discuss all the options and carriers, but a well-trained insurance advisor can assist you in creating the best disability plan for your particular circumstances. I will say that no matter which disability policy you choose, you should always get the own-occupation rider and indexed cost-of-living rider. It's your responsibility to ensure that these two benefits are contained in the policy. Ask the agent to highlight these two clauses in your policy contract. And don't let anyone tell you that you don't need them; I could tell you dozens of stories of professionals who wished they had taken this advice.

A case in point involves a dentist I met 12 years ago who was unincorporated and had a variety of personal and association disability coverage. After incorporating her we reorganized all her insurance so that the appropriate policies were put in the professional corporation and others left to be held personally. Some policies had own-occupation, others did not, some had cost-of-living, simple interest, others had cost-of-living, compound interest. A few policies had no cost-of-living at all. After reviewing all the various policies, it was decided that all would be kept and any increases in coverage would include own-occupation and compound cost-of-living benefits. We retained all the existing policies due to the high cost of getting new ones, and the fact that it might result in higher costs due to the client's current situation. Disability policies are normally less expensive the earlier you buy them, so replacing the existing policies would cost more. The other reason was that at the time of issue the dentist had no health issues and the policies were issued "clean" (i.e., no exclusions or ratings). Since issue, the dentist has been seeing a chiropractor; any new policy would have had a back exclusion in it.

As time passed, new policies were added with different companies as a result of changes in definitions, and medical insurance rider options coming due. It was also necessitated by the consolidation of the insurance companies.

Just prior to her fiftieth birthday, she became disabled. After numerous tests, it was determined that she would no longer be able to work as a dentist, so after two years, she sold her practice. During that time she had interaction with three different insurers. One was very cooperative, one was very difficult and the third was inconsistent, depending on whom she talked to.

The insurer who issued the policies with own-occupation riders was only concerned with whether she could, or could not, continue practicing dentistry. Once satisfied that this was the case, they were very cooperative and paid the claim monthly and on time. The only requirement going forward was confirmation that there was no change in status. The dentist could go out and do whatever else she wanted to earn income without jeopardizing her benefits, as long as she wasn't practicing dentistry.

The second insurer had issued their policies without own-occupation riders. The dentist had been told that because they were using a loss-of-income formula, having an own-occupation definition was unnecessary. Unfortunately what happened at claim time was the insurer not only wanted to know if the dentist was disabled but also wanted to know what else she could do. The disability did prevent her from practicing dentistry, but it did not prevent her from doing other work. They have consistently come back to her to see how she can be retrained and have, on occasion, withheld benefits for non-compliance.

The third company has been inconsistent when dealing with the claim. There were a number of policies, some having own-occupation and any-occupation definitions. The policies with own-occupation are paid regularly and the others are not.

I'm not saying that in all cases a policy with own-occupation is handled better than one without; however, with own-occupation, the fact that the only thing the company has to be assured of is that the individual cannot practice their profession makes claims significantly more straightforward.

The other issue centered on the cost-of-living benefit. The dentist had three main disability contracts in force at the time of her disability. One had an initial monthly benefit of $10,000 and a compound interest cost-of-living rider (which keep pace with the consumer price index). After five years the benefit had risen to $12,166. The second policy was for $4,000 and had a simple interest cost-of-living rider. After five years the benefit had risen to $4,800. The third policy was for $2,000 and had no cost-of-living rider.

By the time the dentist reaches age 64 her $10,000 policy with compound interest cost-of-living rider is guaranteed not to be paying less than $18,008. Her $4,000 policy with simple interest cost-of-living rider will be paying her a minimum of $6,400 and the $2,000 policy will still be paying $2,000.

You can see from this example how important cost-of-living benefits are in ensuring that you maintain the purchasing power of your disability benefits.

It is a common practice for life insurance agents and brokers to recommend using various types of life insurance for investment purposes. The pros and cons of this are outside the scope of this book but are covered in my book, "The Financial Navigator – A Professional's Guide to Keeping More of What You Earn".

CHAPTER SIX

Administering Your Professional Corporation

Unlike a sole proprietorship, a professional corporation is a separate legal entity and has to remain separate and distinct from the individuals who own it. Once you've incorporated, you have to perform a number of administrative duties in order to comply with all legal and tax regulations. These administrative duties are described below, starting with the annual filing.

Annual Filing

Every year most jurisdictions require you to file an annual report with the provincial corporate registry. The number can be found in your local telephone directory, or just Google "corporate registry + the name of your province." Your annual report confirms the names and addresses of all directors and officers of your professional corporation. There should be a resolution adopting the financial statements of the company, a resolution of the annual meeting, and perhaps a waiver of appointment of an auditor (if applicable).

These resolutions can be prepared by your lawyer and filed with your annual report. Copies should also be kept in your minute book.

Record Keeping

Any corporation carrying on business must keep books of accounts and records, that provide the ability to calculate taxes payable. These books and records must be supported by "source documents" which substantiate the figures in the books of account. Source documents include (but are not limited to) invoices for purchases and sales, deposit slips, cheques, and contracts.

For income tax purposes, many books of accounts, records, and source documents have to be retained for a minimum of six years after the end of the last tax year to which they relate. In the case of records relating to capital purchases, the last tax year to which they relate will be the tax year in which a disposal of the capital property occurred. The purchase records will be required to calculate the gain or loss on the disposal. Thus records regarding capital property should normally be kept until six years after the end of the tax year in which the capital property was sold. Further information on this topic is available on the CRA web site (http://www.CCRA-adrc.gc.ca/; under forms, look for IC78-10R5).

Bookkeeping

Bookkeeping is the recording of the information required to complete financial statements and corporate tax returns. An accountant, a bookkeeper, yourself, or anyone you feel has the ability can do this. I would normally suggest hiring a bookkeeper to keep the cost down and get the job done correctly. If you prefer to try it yourself, or have a family member do the bookkeeping, you can buy easy-to-use programs like Simply Accounting or QuickBooks. The most important thing is getting it done correctly and in a timely manner.

Credit Cards

I'm often asked if it's important to have a separate corporate credit card. The quick answer is no but I do recommend that you use a separate credit card. If your bank is willing to give you a separate credit card for your professional corporation that's fine as long as it doesn't cost you more then a regular personal credit card.

It always amazes me that what you pay $20 for personally often costs $75 corporately. So be careful about costs.

It's a lot easier to keep track of your business expenses if you're using a separate credit card. If you want to make your accountant's life (and yours, too) easier, do the following:

Get a separate credit card for your business expenses. When you buy something with the card, keep the actual store receipt and the chit. Each month when your credit card statement comes in, reconcile the receipts with the statement then attach the receipts to the statement – done. If you're ever asked to produce an actual receipt, you know where to find them and all you have to remember is the rough date the transaction took place.

Write on the chit, or cash register tape, the nature of the expense, for instance whether it is a gift, business dinner, event or for any expense capable of being seen as personal in nature. The CRA will characterize as "personal" virtually every expense that could be seen as personal unless the business connection is noted. Also, the typical CRA auditor will attempt to disallow every expense where your only proof is a credit card statement.

So remember, unlike criminal court where you're innocent until proven guilty, in tax court you're guilty until you can prove yourself innocent. So always think, "what can I prove?"

Reimbursement Of Expenses

Occasionally you will find yourself paying for business expenses with personal money. This can be in the form of cash, personal credit card or personal cheque. As long as the expense is business related, your professional corporation can reimburse you. The important thing, as always, is to keep your receipts.

The easiest way to do this is to take the receipt, make sure you can determine what it's for, and then submit the receipt to the company. The company should write a cheque to you personally and record the reimbursement under the appropriate accounting category. If the receipt is for dining, write on the back who it was that joined you for the meal, and the purpose of the meeting. If you're not sure if a receipt is deductible, keep it in a separate envelope and discuss it with your accountant.

What Happens If Money Is Paid To The Wrong Entity?

Occasionally you may end up being in receipt of money that should have been paid to your professional corporation. This can happen in a number of ways, for instance, when cheques are written to you personally or someone pays you cash for services rendered. This isn't a problem as long as you put the money into your corporate bank account and record the payment. The other choice is to keep the money personally and record it as income from business on your personal tax return. It is however, easier to simply deposit the money directly into your professional corporation's bank account.

Annual Maintenance

Directors and officers run corporations, with the highest legal responsibility placed on the directors. When corporate decisions are made or contracts signed, it is ultimately the directors who are legally bound. Directors also have responsibility to the shareholders.

Every year the corporation is required to file an annual return. The annual return consists of a resolution, or number of resolutions, verifying that the company has:

- notified all voting shareholders of the annual meeting
- held an annual meeting
- approved the financial statements
- appointed the director or directors
- waived the appointment of an auditor.

Personal Taxes

If you've been working for a while and have not been an employee (or incorporated), you've been operating your business as a sole proprietor. As a sole proprietor, your tax return is due June 15th. However, any income taxes are due April 30th.

Because no one is deducting income tax from you, you are probably making quarterly tax payments. Taxes paid in quarterly instalments are personal taxes paid in the current calendar year and due on March 15, June 15, September 15 and December 15. These instalments are generally calculated based on your previous year's income and applied to the current year's taxes. When you set up a professional corporation, you can decide to be paid a salary or receive dividends, or a combination of the two.

There are in fact three different methods of calculating instalment payments.

The first method is to take last year's actual taxes paid and divide that number by four. For example, if in 2009 you paid $36,000 in income tax, each of your instalments in 2010 will be $9,000. This is a calculation you do yourself; therefore, you will not get instalment notices from the CRA. The second method is to follow CRA notices that are sent out twice a year, in February and August.

The third method is based on an estimate of the current year income. This method requires some calculation, because once you've estimated what your current year's income might be, you have to calculate the estimated tax liability. For example, if in 2010 you estimate that your income is going to be $100,000, the tax liability is about $30,000. Based on the estimated tax liability of $30,000 your instalments in 2010 would be $7,500 per quarter.

One cautionary note with the third method, if your estimates are low and you do not remit enough taxes, you will be charged interest by the CRA on the difference between what you should have paid and what you did pay.

The CRA has this to say about interest and penalties, "deficient payments of income tax and tax instalments are subject to an interest charge, which compounds daily. The rate of interest is set quarterly, based on the prescribed rate plus 4 per cent."

You are entitled to an interest offset on deficient tax instalment payments if you prepay subsequent payments; however, early payment of instalments will not generate refundable interest. Therefore, if you have underpaid, you can prepay to avoid interest charged on the underpayment.

In addition to interest charges, a penalty is imposed for late or deficient tax instalments. The penalty is 50 per cent of the interest payable on instalment shortfalls for the year (net of interest offset) less the greater of $1,000 and 25 per cent of the interest you would have had to pay for instalment shortfalls, assuming no payments were made in the year.

Interest is paid on tax refunds at a rate equal to the prescribed rate plus 2 per cent compounded daily. For corporations, interest is not compounded until the due date of the return, or the actual filing date of the return, whichever is later. If tax returns are filed later than three years after the end of the taxation year, the CRA has no obligation to refund overpaid tax or pay interest.

Once you incorporate, your personal tax return is due April 30th.

If you decide to take a salary from your professional corporation, you are required to deduct income tax and CPP contributions. If you only take dividends, you are not required to source deduct income tax or CPP. You are, however, required to continue making your quarterly instalments. Using the second method of instalment calculations, the amount is calculated and sent to you by the CRA. If you pay it as required, on time, and you owe more tax at the end of the year, you are not charged interest. If, however, you do not pay the required amount or are late making the payments, you are charged interest on any late amounts, assuming you owe more tax when you file.

I was once asked, if instalments are due in March, June, September and December and, if you were required to make instalments of $2,500 per quarter, could you make payments of $1,000 in March, June and September and then make one for $7,000 in December and not be charged interest? The simple answer is probably no.

The good news is that individuals are entitled to an interest offset on deficient tax instalment payments if they prepay subsequent payments or overpay the amount they were required to pay; however, early payment of instalments will not generate refundable interest. Therefore, if you underpay you can either pay subsequent instalments early or overpay them and get interest on those payments, which can be used to offset interest charged by the CRA on the underpaid amount.

Another question I get asked is: are you required to make quarterly instalments and source deduct your salary? Maybe, but the quarterly instalments will probably be less than was originally required. If you incorporate halfway through the year you will have six months of income as a sole proprietor and six months of wages from your professional corporation. You must, however, take the net (after expenses) pre-tax income from the first six months and add it to the six months of wages you are going to receive in the last half of the year. This total income is then used to estimate your total tax liability for the year. If the total taxes you have paid are greater than, or equal to, what's required, then you don't have to make quarterly instalments.

Let's look at an example. Suppose you are making quarterly payments of $16,000 and decide to incorporate on June 30, 2010. On June 30 you calculate that your income to date has been $90,000, after expenses. From July to December you are going to be receiving a wage from your professional corporation of $5,000 per month. Your estimated income for the year will be $120,000: $90,000 + $30,000 ($5,000 x 6). The estimated tax liability for the year based on an income of $120,000 is $38,000. You will have made instalment payments of $16,000 in March and June; therefore, you have already remitted $32,000. The tax deducted from your $5,000 per month wage will be about $1,200 or, $7,200 from June – December ($1,200 x 6). Based on your estimated tax remittances for the year of $39,200 ($32,000 + $7,200) and your estimated tax liability of $38,000, you can skip the September and December quarterly instalments.

Your accountant can help you determine the appropriate amounts if you decide to incorporate. As you can see, there is a planning opportunity here, depending on when, during the year, you incorporate.

I met an unincorporated physician a few years ago who was making about $275,000, after expenses and before tax. He was required to make instalment payments of about $29,000 per quarter. His living requirements were $10,000 per month net after tax. After incorporating him in June we started paying him and his wife wages of $63,000 and $42,000 (based on her job) respectively. The after-tax income was not sufficient to meet their monthly living requirements, so instead of taking more wages or dividends in the current year, we used a shareholder loan (see page 188) to make up the difference until the next year. The following year, we were able to increase their monthly income by using dividends and eliminating the shareholder loan over the next two years. This allowed us to reduce the taxable income in the current year and defer the income to future years.

By converting from a sole proprietorship to a professional corporation and taking a salary, we were able to skip the September 15 and the December 15 instalments. His instalments were calculated using the second method and therefore were based on his income from two previous years. He had just moved from a different jurisdiction and his income had initially dropped. His instalments from March and June were sufficient to pay his new estimated tax bill for the whole year and therefore when he filed his tax return the first year after incorporation he ended up getting a refund.

Re: Why did I get a personal tax demand!
From: Sven Hansen
To: tim@tpcfinancial.com

Hi Tim

I'm confused. When I went onto paying myself through
dividends I thought I only had to pay corporate tax.
Why then did I just get a personal instalment reminder
from the CRA?

By the way, we went out into the country the other day
and saw the Northern Lights, or I suppose I should use
the scientific name, the Aurora Borealis. They were
incredible - there's a lot to be said for living up
here in the wilds!

Sven

Re: Re: Why did I get a personal tax demand!
From: tim@tpcfinancial.com
To: Sven Hansen

Hi Sven

I'm glad you got to see the lights, did you know that
some Inuit people call them "aurora aqsarniit?" It
means football players; they say it's the spirits of
their ancestors kicking around the head of a walrus.

Makes all this tax stuff seem mundane doesn't it?

But, down to your very interesting tax question.
When you were taking a salary from your professional
corporation, your taxes were withheld and remitted
monthly. You weren't required to pay tax instalments
because the withholding tax was enough to cover your
tax liability.

When you pay yourself via dividends there is no payroll
tax being withheld. Your PC is indeed making corporate
remittances, but no tax is being paid on your behalf.
So, based on the amount of dividends you're receiving,
you will still owe some personal tax. These taxes
are due on a quarterly basis and are payable by you
personally, not by your PC.

The first year you go on dividends you won't get a remittance reminder unless you owed tax from the year before. Remember when we decided to change you to dividends, I told you we would give you an extra dividend to cover your taxes? Well the quarterly instalments are part of those taxes.

The CRA has estimated your taxes owing this year based on last year's taxes owing. At the end of each tax season they estimate what you should pay in quarterly instalments for the current year. If you follow their schedule they won't charge you interest even if you owe them in April.

To sum up, when you're on salary the company makes payroll remittances and corporate remittances. When you're only receiving dividends the company makes corporate remittances and you make personal quarterly remittances (instalments).

I hope this brings some 'light' to this issue.

Tim

Corporate Taxes

In the year you incorporate, you are not required to make tax instalments for the simple reason you have no idea how much taxable income your professional corporation is going to have.

A simple rule is to set aside 20 per cent of your gross income. After expenses, this should easily cover what you may end up owing.

If you incorporate on March 4th and decide to make your year end December 31st, your taxes for the first year will be due by March 31 of the following year.

As strange as it may sound, if you owe the CRA money, they want it within three months of the year-end, even though they give you six months after the year-end to file your corporate tax return. So, you may have to start making instalment payments for your second year even before you pay your balance due, or file your first return. If the amount of tax owing from the first year is greater than $3,000 you are required to make instalments.

Instalments may be made monthly or quarterly but in order to qualify to pay quarterly you must have:

- a perfect compliance record
- claimed a small business deduction in the current or previous tax year
- taxable income of $500,000 or less
- less than $10 million taxable capital

There are also three different ways to calculate your instalment amounts; you can base them on:

1. current year estimated earnings (if its lower than the previous year – you better be right or instalment interest will apply)
2. the previous year
3. a combination of the previous year and the year before the previous year.

Once you and your accountant have established if you have to make corporate instalments and the amount, you should make the first payment. If you happen to be late with your instalment payment, you can offset the interest the CRA charges by making another instalment in advance.

For example, say your PC owes $20,000 in instalments for 2011 and you pay nothing for the first 6 months. If you make a lump sum payment of the entire $20,000 right at the 6 month mark, there will be zero instalment interest because you effectively made the July-December payments early offsetting the January – June ones that were late.

Until you know exactly when and how much you should be making in instalment payments, you should estimate your taxable corporate income for the previous year and start remitting from the month after your year-end.

In the example above, that would be January 31st.

Corporate instalments (unless quarterly) are due at the end of every month. Unlike payroll remittances that are due by the 15th of the following month, corporate remittances are due in the current month.

If you're not sure how much to remit in the second year, use the 20 per cent rule; send the CRA 20 per cent of your gross corporate income. After your accountant has figured out exactly what you should be paying, you can adjust your remittances. Doing it this way should keep you away from that nasty late instalment interest.

Another thing to be careful about is, when you make an instalment payment, be careful about what year it's credited to. If you're making a current year instalment, make sure you mark the cheque and the remittance form with the current year. For example, if you're making an instalment in January for the current year, then indicate (for example) 2011. If you're paying an amount owing for say 2010, make sure you mark on the cheque and remittance form, "to be applied to 2010". If you don't, and you make the payment in 2011, they will automatically apply it to the current year and then you'll have to go through the process of having the transaction reversed.

If you decide to use an off calendar year-end like June 30th, the same rules apply. Your taxes owing have to be paid by September 30th and your first monthly instalment in your second year will be July 31st.

Payroll Tax

Most professional corporations are required to remit payroll deductions from their employees' paycheques, along with the employer's portion of Canada Pension Plan (CPP) contributions and Employment Insurance (EI) premiums, to the CRA by the 15th of the following month.

If your average monthly remittance two years ago was less than $15,000, or you are a new remitter, you are considered a regular remitter. You have to remit your deductions so they are received on or before the 15th of the month, following the month you made deductions. If the 15th of the month is a Saturday, Sunday, or statutory holiday, your remittance is due on the next business day.

If your total average monthly withholding amount (AMWA) is between $15,000 and $49,999 or the company has more than one payroll remittance amount and the combined average withholding is between $15,000 and $49,999 (for example a dental practice and a hygiene company), you are a Type 1 accelerated remitter.

A Type 1 accelerated remitter is responsible for remitting payroll deductions taken from an employee between the 1st to the 15th of the month and the employer's portion of CPP and EI by the 25th of the same month.

A Type 1 accelerated remitter is also responsible for remitting payroll deductions taken from an employee between the 16th to the last day of the month and the employer's portion of CPP and EI by the 10th of the following month.

If you're taking a salary from your professional corporation, your accountant should provide you with a payroll remittance schedule. This schedule should be strictly followed. If you have other employees, I recommend that you use a payroll service to pay you and your staff. They will make payroll remittances as part of their service.

Just so you understand how important this is, I'll quote directly from the CRA website on the subject of "Late remitting/Failure to remit":

We can assess a penalty of up to 20 per cent of the amount you failed to remit when:

- you deduct the amounts, but do not remit them; or
- we receive the amounts you deducted after the due date.

If the remittance due date is a Saturday, Sunday, or public holiday, your remittance is due on the next business day.

The penalty is:

- *3 per cent if the amount is one to three days late;*
- *5 per cent if it is four or five days late;*
- *7 per cent if it is six or seven days late; and*
- *10 per cent if it is more than seven days late or if no amount is remitted.*

Dividend Resolutions

Dividend resolutions should be passed prior to the paying of any dividend. The resolution should be signed by the director/s of the company and filed in the minute book. The following is an example of a dividend resolution.

RESOLUTION OF THE DIRECTOR OF

DR. GAIL MARY PROFESSIONAL CORPORATION

CONSENTED TO IN WRITING BY THE

SOLE DIRECTOR EFFECTIVE

JANUARY 17, 2010

BE IT RESOLVED

THAT a dividend of $50.00 per share for a total of $5,000.00 upon the outstanding Class A Voting Common shares of the Company be declared payable on the 1st of February 2010 to shareholders of record at the close of business on such date, such shareholders being:

Gail Mary 100 Class A Voting Common Shares

I, the undersigned, being the sole Director of the Company, do hereby consent to and approve all the foregoing business and resolutions and waive the necessity of calling and holding a meeting of Directors.

_____

Dr. Gail Mary – Director

January 17, 2010

What Is A T2?

A T-2 is a corporate tax return. Within six months of the company year-end you must file a T-2 return. Unlike a personal return (called a T-1), which is due April 30, or a self-employed person's return (also a T-1), which is due June 15, T-2s have a different filing deadline depending on your company year-end. When he is preparing your T-2, your accountant will also prepare your corporate financial statements.

When your T-2 is filed, a general index of financial information (GIFI) usually accompanies it. The GIFI is an index of items found on the balance sheet, income statement, and statement of retained earnings. Financial statements of professional corporations are usually not audited and contain a "notice to reader" to this effect.

Understanding Financial Statements

Financial statements are usually broken down into six sections:

- Section 1 – Notice to Reader or Review Engagement.
- Section 2 – Balance Sheet.
- Section 3 – Statement of Operations and Deficit or Income and Expense.
- Section 4 – Statement of Cash Flow (optional).
- Section 5 – Summary of Significant Accounting Policies.
- Section 6 – Notes to Financial Statements.

Notice to reader

The notice to reader is usually a statement that indicates that the financial statements were completed based on the information provided by the company owner, and that the information was not audited, reviewed or verified unless otherwise stated.

Review engagement

The review engagement is a more comprehensive financial statement preparation procedure. The financial statements are not simply prepared with the information provided by the client. A typical review engagement report will look like this:

To the Shareholders of Dr. Fred Davis Inc.

We have reviewed the balance sheet of Dr. Fred Davis Inc. as at March 31, 2010, and the statements of operations and retained earnings and cash flows for the year then ended. These financial statements have been prepared in accordance with Canadian generally accepted accounting principles using differential reporting options available to non-publicly accountable enterprises, as described in the summary of significant accounting policies. Our review was made in accordance with Canadian generally accepted standards for review engagements and accordingly consisted primarily of enquiry, analytical procedures and discussion related to information supplied to us by the company.

A review does not constitute an audit and consequently we do not express an audit opinion on these financial statements.

Based on our review, nothing has come to our attention that causes us to believe that these financial statements are not, in all material respects, in accordance with Canadian generally accepted accounting principles.

Balance Sheet

The balance sheet lists all assets and liabilities of the company and indicates the shareholder equity of the company.

Statement of operations and deficit

The statement of operations and deficit, sometimes known as the income and expense statement, lists all revenue earned by the company as well as all expenses incurred. This statement may differ from your tax return in that it accounts for all expenses, regardless if they are tax deductible or not, and can also include revenue that is not taxable, like holdbacks or work in progress (see 'What Are T-2 Add-backs', page 185). At a quick glance, this statement will usually tell you whether your company is profitable or not.

Statement of cash flow

You may or may not have a statement of cash flow. This statement indicates the cash position of your company and all related operating, financing and investing activities.

Summary of significant accounting policies

The summary of significant accounting policies tells the reader about the nature of the business and lays out the significant accounting policies used in the preparation of the financial statements.

Notes to financial statements

The notes to financial statements document is very important in that it gives the reader insight into specific items in the financial statements. It can include items such as the breakdown of capital assets and the depreciation numbers, the share capital of the company, and any other relevant information that the accountant wants to convey about specific items. Many accounting firms do not do notes for a "Notice to Reader" financial statement.

What Does It Mean To Bonus Down?

When corporate income exceeds the small business deduction limit, most accountants in the past would have recommended that a bonus be paid out to reduce the taxable income to that amount. In 2010, the small business deduction limit (in most jurisdictions) was $500,000.

Let's look at this a little more closely. Suppose your pre-tax income, after all expenses have been written off, is $650,000 and you live in, say, Saskatchewan. If you leave the entire amount in your professional corporation, you will pay tax on the first $500,000 at the low corporate rate of about 15.5 per cent and a higher rate of 30.0 per cent on the next $150,000.

If you take $150,000 as a bonus, the company gets a deduction in the current fiscal year and this income is not exposed to the higher corporate rates. If the amount is left in the corporation, it will be taxed at the higher rate.

What if you don't have enough cash to pay out a bonus? You can declare a bonus at any time via a corporate resolution up to the fiscal year-end. Often the bonus is recorded as a bonus payable on the financial statements of the company and must be paid out, within 179 days of the year-end. At the time the bonus is paid out the appropriate source deductions must be remitted to the CRA.

In my previous example the income amount was $650,000. Let's say that the professional corporation's year-end is August 31. A bonus is declared in August and the appropriate corporate resolution is made stating that the bonus will be $150,000. The bonus is recorded in the books as a bonus payable. The bonus is paid out in January of the following year. The company has a deduction for $150,000 in the current fiscal year (say 2010) and you have an income inclusion in the following year (2011). But what if you still don't have the cash? The company can borrow the money, pay out the bonus, including the appropriate deductions, and then you can put the after-tax money right back into the company as a shareholder loan.

You do not declare the bonus money as income until 2011. However, in order for the bonus to qualify as a write-off for the company in the previous year, the income tax on the bonus must be paid when the bonus is paid out. This remittance of tax is due with the next regular remittance.

One important thing to note is that this only works if your professional corporation's year-end is after June 30[26].

At a later time, when the company has extra cash, you can remove the money you put back in the company tax-free by paying off the shareholder loan.

With the introduction of eligible dividends (see eligible dividends on page 181) in 2006, the question of bonusing down doesn't seem to be as clear.

The decision to bonus or not will ultimately depend on whether you need funds personally. If the answer is "no" then there is a very compelling argument to not bonus. Of course, not bonusing will come with some downsides (such as increased corporate income tax instalments, and increased cash in the company) but such cons can be easily dealt with by way of good cash management and additional planning.

The Transition Year

The transition year is your first year of incorporation. If your professional corporation year-end is December 31, then your fiscal year and calendar year are the same. This can make things easier in that your personal tax year and your corporate tax year are the same.

Up until the date of incorporation, all income earned is personal income and should be reported on your personal tax return. Income earned after the date of incorporation should be paid to the company.

Depending on when in the year you incorporate, and your personal income requirements, you may choose not to take anything out of your professional corporation until the end of the calendar year.

You should check with your accountant or financial advisor to determine the amount and type of income you should take from your professional corporation in the first year.

---

26 If your year end is before July 1st this strategy won't work because in order for the company to get a deduction in the current fiscal year the bonus has to be paid out within 179 days of the year end. It only works if you can deduct it corporately in the current fiscal year and take it into personal income in the next calendar year.

CHAPTER SEVEN

How Your Professional Corporation Can Save You Money

The Difference Between A Tax Saving And A Tax Deferral

A tax savings is simply tax you don't have to pay. When you look at T-2 add-backs – the amount that is added back to your income when your corporate tax return is filed – they are usually tax savings. If you have a corporate-owned life insurance policy and your premium is $1,000, your corporation will have to earn $1,250 to pay that premium ($1,250 - 20 per cent tax = $1,000). If that same policy were owned personally, you would have to earn about $1,818 to pay the premium ($1,818 - 45 per cent personal tax = $1,000). The tax savings in this case would be $568 ($1,818 - 1,250).

Tax deferrals are taxes that you will pay at a later date, such as taxes on retained earnings. When you earn money in your professional corporation and do not remove it, it is taxed at the corporate rate. The money that remains can be invested and removed at a later date. If you leave $100,000 of corporate earnings in your professional corporation, it will be taxed at about 20 per cent. The $80,000 remaining could be invested. When it is removed at a later date, the balance of the taxes owing (such as personal taxes) will be paid at that time. If you were to remove the $100,000 in the beginning you would pay about 45 per cent personal tax and have only $55,000 left to invest.

Tax deferrals can be a powerful tool. Imagine the wealth accumulation if you could defer sending $50,000 per year to the CRA. If you are 40 years old and invest that amount of money annually at 5 per cent until you are 65, you will accumulate $2,386,354. Even if you cashed it all out at one time and paid 37 per cent tax on the whole amount as a dividend you would still have $1,503,403 net. That is over $1.5 million dollars that you have for your retirement or family as a direct result of deferring taxes. The key to maximizing this strategy is not having to pay annual income tax on your investments.

Tax deferrals can also be in the form of a capital cost allowance (CCA) or depreciation. Capital assets generally go into CCA pools[27], but certain assets must go into separate pools. Computers, as an example, generally go into a pool. Buildings over $50,000 go into their own pool.

For example, suppose you bought a revenue property for $500,000, with the land valued at $300,000 and the building at $200,000. Each year you are allowed to depreciate – write down – the value of the building against the income you receive. Depreciation is an allowable expense that recognizes that capital assets, over time, wear out and have to be replaced.

However, if the asset does not lose its value or even increases in value, the amount you deducted has to be added back onto your tax return in the year of sale. Let's go back to my example. If in the first year you wrote off $4,000 and the following year $6,000, these amounts are deducted from the total value and therefore reduce the amount left. So, if you started with $200,000 after two years you would have $190,000 left. If you were to sell the property after two years for $600,000, you would have to include, in income, a capital gain and you would have to recapture depreciation. The amount included in income would be 50 per cent of the gain, $600,000 - $500,000 = $100,000 /2 = $50,000. In addition, you would have to include the $10,000 you wrote off in the previous two years because the value of the asset did not depreciate; rather it gained in value. The same would hold true if the asset value didn't change and you sold it for $500,000. You wouldn't have a capital gain because the asset didn't increase in value, but you would have recaptured depreciation because the asset didn't decrease in value.

This is different than pooled assets. If we use computers as an example, every time you buy a new computer it goes into the same pool. Suppose you buy a

---

27 Pools are groups of assets that are similar.

computer for $3,000 and when it's added to the other computers in the pool the total depreciated value of the computers equals $20,000. Then, after a few years, the computer is depreciated down to $500 and you sell it for $1,500. In this case there is no recapture because the individual assets of the pool are not recognized. Instead, the pool is reduced by the proceeds of $1,500, which in turn reduces future write-offs.

How Do I Pick A Salary Amount? Salary Or Dividends?

As an incorporated professional you can decide to take a salary or dividends, or both. There are a number of different factors to examine before making this decision. Circumstances can also change, which can affect what you are currently doing. In British Columbia, for example, the BC Medical Association (BCMA), which pays doctors, began a registered retirement saving plan (RRSP) matching program. The program matches on a dollar-to-dollar basis RRSP contributions made by the physician, up to certain limits. It's a great program that makes it beneficial for doctors to buy RRSPs. However, this can only be accomplished if they have a salary. Dividends are not considered "earned income" for RRSP purposes.

Before you decide on taking either a salary, or dividends, you should understand what they are. A salary (or wage) is compensation received for the performance of the regular duties of a position or office. It is fully tax deductible to the corporation and fully taxable to you.

A dividend is a distribution of after-tax corporate profits that is paid to shareholders, usually in the form of cash. It is not tax deductible to the corporation. In your hands, "other than eligible" dividends will be grossed up (see glossary) by one-quarter and eligible for a dividend tax credit, which is two-thirds of the amount of the gross-up.

As an incorporated professional, whether or not you pay yourself a salary is a tax planning decision. The first thing you should do is determine what you need for household income. This can be accomplished by preparing a budget or cash flow statement. In undertaking this exercise, don't worry about how you are going to get money out of your professional corporation, just calculate what you need on an after-tax basis to go into your personal bank account to meet your average monthly expenses.

If you choose to take a salary, you are required to make income tax and CPP contributions on a periodic basis, as described on page 214. When you pay out dividends, you are not corporately responsible for remitting payroll tax and you do not make CPP contributions. If you decide to take dividends instead of a salary, you will not be able to make RRSP contributions and you will not be contributing to the CPP. One has to weigh the benefits of contributing to the CPP before opting out through the use of dividends. See page 215 for a discussion of CPP benefits.

The jurisdiction you live in can also influence your decision. If you are allowed to have non-professional shareholders, you may choose to have dividends paid to them while you take a salary. If, according to law, you can't have non-professional shareholders, you may hire them and pay the corresponding reasonable wage to them while you take a dividend. Review your options with your financial planner and accountant to ensure that you maximize the movement of money between you, your family and your professional corporation.

If you decide to use dividends instead of drawing a salary, you should still pay yourself a one-time annual wage of $3,500. We recommend that our clients do this each December. The $3,500 is the maximum amount you can be paid without having to withhold tax and CPP contributions. This amount is deductible to the corporation and allows you to make a small RRSP contribution of $630.00. You may also choose to take a salary, or bonus, in order to take the corporation's income down to the small business limit.

Types Of Dividends

Since 2006 there have been two types of dividends in Canada, eligible dividends and other than eligible dividends.

Eligible dividends are tax preferred, in that the rate of personal tax applied to eligible dividends is less than the personal tax rate on other than eligible dividends.

If a professional corporation receives a dividend from a publicly traded company (say common shares of the Royal Bank), it is deemed to be eligible as the dividend was paid for by a company that paid tax at the high corporate rate (or what is said to be the "general" corporate rate).

These particular dividends are recorded on your corporate tax return and added to the GRIP (General Rate Income Pool).

A GRIP is a notional account that allows a shareholder to declare an eligible, or other than eligible, dividend to the extent of the GRIP balance.

In other words, if your professional corporation (PC) receives $1,000 in dividends from your Royal Bank shares, $1,000 is credited to the company GRIP. If, during the year, you take a taxable dividend from your PC of $1000, or greater, you can declare that up to $1,000 was an eligible dividend. If you choose not to declare an eligible dividend, the $1,000 stays in the GRIP and any future Royal Bank dividends will be added to the balance.

If you have no GRIP balance, and you pay out a taxable dividend, those dividends are said to be "other than" eligible dividends.

In Ontario in 2010, the top marginal rate of tax on eligible dividends was 26.57 per cent, whereas the top marginal rate on other than eligible dividends was 32.57 per cent.

In my second book "The Financial Navigator – A Professional's Guide to Keeping More of What you Earn", I spend a lot more time explaining how to plan and use eligible dividends.

Income-Splitting Opportunities

The Canadian tax system is not based on family income but on individual income. A couple earning $60,000 each will pay less tax than if one of them earned $120,000 and the other didn't work. This occurs as a result of individual marginal tax brackets, and the different tax rates applied to each bracket. The federal government currently has four personal tax brackets. The tax rate ranges from 15 per cent in the lowest bracket, to 29 per cent in the highest bracket. Each province and territory has its own brackets and rates range from 4.0 per cent to 17.5 per cent. The idea behind tax planning is to try to split income equally between spouses. The best-case scenario is having both spouses taxed in the low bracket. The worst-case scenario would be to have one spouse in the higher bracket and the other spouse with no income. After you decide what income you require, work with your accountant and financial planner to decide what is the best income split between you and your spouse, and whether or not you should take a wage or dividends.

Dividends can be paid to shareholders and are not based on the amount, or type, of work you do for the company. If you have more than one shareholder, you can split income. Most commonly, a husband and wife are both shareholders in a professional corporation. Dave is a dentist and Sue is a stay-at-home mom. Their annual income requirement is $100,000. Dave could take the whole amount himself and pay tax, or they could split the income by paying Dave $75,000 in wages and paying Sue $25,000 in dividends. If Dave takes it all himself, he will pay $28,000 in taxes whereas if he splits the income with Sue, they will pay $19,476. This example assumes they have the proper share structure to allow Sue to receive dividends to the exclusion of Dave.

Trusts and investment companies can also be used to split income. This is, however, dependent on where you live. Check the table found on page 51 to determine if you can use a trust or investment company to hold dividend-paying shares in your professional corporation. See chapter nine (page 221) for ideas on how to use a trust or holding company.

So, exactly how much can you pay your spouse or children, if you aren't able to pay them in dividends? The simple answer is as much as you would pay an unrelated person to do the same job. Say your spouse is working in your office as a receptionist. Her pay should reflect the value of that work. If the going rate for receptionists in your area is $32,000 per year, your spouse should be paid that amount. There is nothing preventing you from paying more if the nature of the work is more extensive; however, it should be well documented in her employment agreement (see page 117). This rule also applies to children. If your 13-year-old child comes to your office periodically to file and clean, you shouldn't be paying them $40.00 per hour. The amount should reflect the market value of that work.

I once heard a story about a physician who was paying his spouse $48,000 a year for doing office management, bookkeeping, banking, and payroll. After he filed the corporate tax return, the CRA had a query and called the contact number on the return. They reached the spouse, who on paper was responsible for dealing with such issues, and her response was honest but deadly – "You'll have to call my husband. He handles all that stuff." If you can't justify the wage, don't pay it. If you are paying wages to family members, make sure they understand what their job is and ensure they are capable of both performing those tasks and actually carrying them out. Ideally, always have an employment agreement.

It's My Money, Why Can't I Have It?

When you earn money as an incorporated professional, the income is paid to the company. Once the money is in the company, you have basically two ways to get it out, salary or dividends. You are allowed to borrow money by following very strict rules, but in the end you are going to be faced with paying yourself a wage, or declaring a dividend. Let's look at these two methods in more detail.

As an employee of your professional corporation you are entitled to a salary or wage (these terms are interchangeable) the same as any other employee. However, as an employee/shareholder, you are not required by law to take a salary from your professional corporation. If you take a salary, it is taxable to you personally and deductible to the company. Let's say your professional corporation makes $550,000; if you decide that you are going to pay yourself $75,000, the company will deduct the $75,000 and pay taxes on the remaining $475,000. You, on the other hand, will pay tax personally on the $75,000.

If you take a salary of $75,000 and then decide to later pay yourself a "bonus" of $15,000, the company will take a deduction in the current fiscal year and you will pay tax on the bonus as additional salary.

Active business income, above the small business tax limit of $500,000, is taxed at the high corporate rate; the rates in 2010 range from 28 per cent to 34 per cent depending where you live in Canada. If you bonus-down, you avoid having active business income being taxed at these higher rates. For example, if a professional corporation has a pre-tax income after expenses of $550,000, it can pay out a bonus of $50,000. The corporation takes a deduction and reduces its taxable income to $500,000, which will be taxed at the low corporate rate.

The company can defer paying the bonus to you for up to 179 days and still take a deduction in the fiscal year. For example, if your company year-end was August 31, you could declare a bonus payable to you, deduct it from the company in the current year, and choose to defer receiving it until after December 31. You only have to pay tax on the bonus personally when it is received. In this example, you would be deferring the personal tax payable to the following calendar year.

Following through with this example the company will now have a taxable income of $460,000 ($550,000 - $75,000 - $15,000). Assuming a combined (federal/provincial/territorial) corporate tax rate of 16 per cent, the company will pay corporate taxes of $73,600. The income left in the company will be $386,400.

The $386,400 belongs to the company. Now, if you are the only shareholder you could argue that it is your money; however, a professional corporation for tax purposes is a separate entity and any money left inside the company belongs to it. So how do you get money (that was taxed at the low corporate rate) from this entity if not by wages? The answer is through "other than eligible" dividends.

"Other than eligible" dividends are after-tax corporate profits distributed to shareholders. They are not tax deductible to the company (i.e., they are not an expense). For tax purposes they are grossed up[28] by 25 per cent and eligible for the dividend tax credit.

Dividends received from a Canadian corporation are taxed in a way that is designed to reflect the fact that the corporation paying the dividend has already paid tax on its profits. The amount included in the individual's income is grossed up to reflect the total amount of pre-tax income that the corporation is presumed to have earned. The individual then receives a tax credit to offset the tax the corporation has paid.

Canadian "other than eligible" dividends received are grossed up by one quarter, that is, you add 25 per cent to the amount received, and show the total as income from dividends on your tax return. The offsetting federal dividend tax credit (see glossary) is then two-thirds of the amount of the gross-up, two-thirds of that 25 per cent, or, to look at it another way, 13.33 per cent of the total you report as dividend income. Similar credits are available at the provincial level.

For example, Grant has retired early and lives on the beach, and he has only dividend income to report. Last year he received $24,000 in dividends from his shares in Canadaco. On his 2010 tax return he declared a taxable dividend amount of $30,000 (24,000 x 1.25). His tax is calculated based on the $30,000. From the tax, he deducts his regular credits and the federal dividend tax credit of $4,000 (two-thirds of the $6,000 gross-up). He then calculates his provincial dividend tax credit. The net result is that there is no personal income tax due.

---

28 To gross up is to add 25% to the amount of dividend received, and show the total income from dividends on your tax return.

Currently, if you have no other income, you can take up to $35,000 (this may be higher in some provinces and territories) in dividends from a professional corporation and probably not pay personal income tax. This is because the company has already paid tax on the income. The purpose of the dividend gross-up and subsequent dividend tax credit is to integrate the personal tax rates and the company tax rates.

If we change our earlier example (see page 184) to wages of $75,000 and dividends (rather than bonuses) of $15,000, the company would deduct the $75,000 and not deduct the $15,000. The individual would have a taxable income of $93,750 ($75,000 + $15,000 + the grossed-up amount of 25 per cent or $3,750). The company has already paid tax on the $15,000; therefore, you would get a dividend tax credit of about $2,500. You would have to take out $18,750 as a bonus from the company to be in the same tax position as taking $15,000 in dividends.

If you took only wages you would take $75,000 + $18,750 = $93,750. The company would deduct $93,750 and you would pay income tax personally on the full amount. If you use wages and dividends you would take $75,000 + $15,000 in dividends and after the dividend gross-up your taxable income is $93,750, resulting in the same amount. In 2010 eligible dividends paid to individuals, resident in Canada, will be grossed up by 45 per cent and the federal tax credit will be 18.97 per cent.

An eligible dividend of $15,000 would show up on your personal tax return as $21,750 ($15,000 x 1.45 = $21,750) and the resulting dividend tax credit would be $4,125.98 ($21,750 x 18.97 per cent = $4,125.98).

Remember tax credits are, to quote Martha Stewart, "a good thing".

What Are T2 Add-Backs?

There can be significant differences between your professional corporation's financial statements and your corporate tax return. When you look at your income/expense statement, you will see things like insurance, meals, entertainment and auto expenses.

A T-2 add-back is an amount that is added back to your corporate income when your corporate tax return is filed. For example, only 50 per cent of meals and entertainment costs are deductible for income tax purposes. If you look at your income/expenses statement, it may read meals and entertainment $1,000, but when your accountant files your corporate tax return they would add $500 back to the professional corporation's income, and you would pay tax on that amount. There is a benefit to having a professional corporation because T-2 add-backs are taxed at corporate rates, not personal rates. If you have T-2 add-backs of $10,000 you would pay about $1,350 in corporate tax. Assuming a top personal rate of 45 per cent, you would pay $4,500 in personal tax, if you weren't incorporated – same expenses, but with a professional corporation you save $3,150 in taxes.

Health And Welfare Trusts

A health and welfare trust is a plan, put in place by employers, to cover the medical and dental expenses incurred by their employees. The trust is basically a bank account that is specifically set up and used solely for healthcare spending.

Health and welfare benefits for employees are sometimes provided through a trust arrangement, under which the trustees receive the contributions from the employer to provide such health and welfare benefits that have been agreed to between the employer and employees. To qualify for treatment as a health and welfare trust, the funds of the trust cannot revert to the employer, and they have to be used to provide health and welfare benefits for which the contributions are made. In addition, the employer's contributions to the fund must not exceed the amounts required to provide these benefits. Once set up, the payments by the employer must be made within the rules and regulations of the trust. They must be enforceable by the trustees should the employer decide not to make the payments required. The trustee or trustees act independently of the employer, as opposed to an arrangement initiated unilaterally by an employer who has control over the use of the funds.

A Cost Plus Arrangement

A "cost plus" arrangement, or a private health services plan, is similar. Companies have used cost plus arrangements for years to allow the employer to cover those costs incurred by an employee in excess of traditional group coverage for dental, medical and vision care. The employer pays the cost of claims plus the contractual costs of administration. In a cost plus plan, as explained by the CRA, "an employer contracts with a trusteed plan or insurance company for the provision of indemnification of employees' claims on defined risks under the plan. The employer promises to reimburse the cost of such claims plus an administration fee to the plan or insurance company."

The great thing about both health and welfare trusts, and cost plus arrangements, is that the medical, dental and vision care expenses paid through the plans are not taxable to the employee, yet all costs to the employer are tax deductible as an employee-benefit expense. Coverage under either program can be extended to include employees' eligible dependents.

What makes these arrangements different from a traditional group plan is that they do not restrict benefits (except where required by law). They are totally flexible and designed even for a one-life group, and they allow the employer complete cost control for each class of employee.

See also group benefits on page 152.

Borrowing Money From A Professional Corporation

One of the most attractive ways of getting funds out of a corporation is to borrow them. The tax cost will be much lower than if you take salary or dividends, although the loan must be repaid.

A loan to a shareholder is acceptable and will not be treated as income, if it is repaid within one year from the end of the year in which it was made, and if it can be established that the loan was not a part of a series of loans and repayments. This provision of the *Income Tax Act*, used occasionally and judiciously, can offer some very useful tax planning flexibility.

Corporate loans are allowed for longer periods in certain circumstances. These include:

- loans from a corporation in the business of making loans
- loans for the purchase, by the employee or shareholder, of a home – the loan must be in conjunction with a purchase and cannot be used to pay down the mortgage on an existing home
- buying stock in the corporation or a related company
- buying a car to be used in the business or employment.

To avoid having the CRA add the value of the loan to an individual's income, which would negate the tax benefits, arrangements for repayment must be made with the corporation.

The caution here is that these provisions provide for loans to employees and shareholders. If you are the only employee and shareholder, or if you do not extend the same loan options to other employees, the CRA can claim that the loan was made as a shareholder and therefore is a shareholder loan and must be paid back within the prescribed time (one year from the end of the year in which it was made).

The loan will be subject to imputed interest for tax purposes at the CRA prescribed rate of interest in effect at the time the loan was made. You do, however, get credit for any interest actually paid. For example, if you borrow $100,000 from your professional corporation at no interest, and the prescribed interest rate happened to be 4 per cent per year, you would report $4,000 as income on your personal return. The actual cost of the loan to you will be the $1,800, tax bill, assuming 45 per cent marginal tax rate ($4,000 @ 45 per cent) – for an effective borrowing rate of 1.8 per cent.

In the first quarter of 2011 the prescribed interest rate on shareholder loans was at an exceptionally low 1 per cent!

Are Shareholder Loans An Asset Or A Liability?

Shareholder loans are one of the most confusing things that show up on financial statements. They can be listed as an asset or liability of the company. If you, as a shareholder, borrow money from the company, then it is an asset of the company because you owe it money. If you lend the company money it's a liability because it owes you money.

If you borrow money from your professional corporation you have to pay interest, or you have a deemed interest benefit. The interest rate must be no less than the prescribed rate (see glossary). If the amount borrowed is not repaid within two fiscal years, the amount is added to your personal tax return. Suppose you borrow $50,000 on January 1, 2010. If the prescribed rate is 1 per cent you will pay the professional corporation $500 for the year. The alternative would be to include in your personal income, $500. If the company year-end were December 31, 2010 it would show a shareholder loan listed as an asset on your balance sheet for $50,000. If you pay back the loan on December 31, 2011, you will pay $500 for interest and $50,000 to repay the loan. However, if you do not pay back the loan by December 31, 2011, you will have to add the loan amount on to your 2010 tax return. There is no deemed interest benefit, but you will be charged interest by the CRA because you owe them taxes from 2010.

If you do have a deemed interest benefit, it may be deductible depending on what you use the money for, for example, if the loan is used for investment purposes.

If you lend money to your professional corporation, you can choose to charge interest or you can lend it on a no-interest basis. If you charge interest, the company can deduct it and you must declare it as income. When the company pays you back, you will not be taxed on those funds because you are simply getting your money back.

Shareholder loans can be created in a number of different ways. It doesn't necessarily mean that you put cash into the professional corporation. Moving assets into your professional corporation, including your practice, can create shareholder loans. Suppose you've been running your dental practice since the beginning as a sole proprietor, you have no debt, and your practice is worth $300,000. When you purchased the practice, you paid $250,000. In this simple example, if you transfer your practice to your professional corporation for $250,000 you would not trigger any tax and the professional corporation would owe you $250,000. You can then earn money in your professional corporation and remove it on an after-tax basis tax-free. If you can't wait long enough for your professional corporation to earn the money to pay you back, the company can borrow the $250,000 inside your professional corporation, from the bank. You take it out from your professional corporation tax-free and then write off the interest corporately. Money borrowed to repay shareholder loans are deductible business expenses.

I recently did some work for a physician who owned her principal residence and a revenue property. When we incorporated her we rolled the revenue property into her professional corporation, which created a shareholder loan equal to her equity. She had paid $175,000 for the property and its current value was $200,000. The outstanding mortgage was $85,000. By moving the property into her professional corporation and using a value of $175,000, there were no taxes owing and her shareholder loan balance was $90,000. She happened to owe $90,000 on her principal residence mortgage, so we borrowed the money from the bank to pay off the shareholder loan and she used the money to pay off her house. She now has clear title on her principal residence and a tax deductible "mortgage" inside the professional corporation.

Re: Financial statements query
From: Sven Hansen
To: tim@tpcfinancial.com

Hi Tim

Just a quick question; I think I know the answer but would like some clarification.

Last year when I picked up my Financial Statements there was an asset listed "Due from Shareholder". This year there is a liability listed "Due to Shareholder". Are these shareholders loans?

Sven

Re: Re: Financial statements query
From: tim@tpcfinancial.com
To: Sven Hansen

Hi Sven

I like quick and easy questions. Yes and yes. Both are shareholder loans.

Okay, I suppose I should explain a little more.

The one listed as an asset last year was money that you borrowed from your professional corporation to buy your car. If you look at your financial statements from the previous year you'll see that neither was listed.

When you borrowed money to buy your car last year, we left it as a loan owing to the company and we added some interest to your personal tax return. This year we wanted to remove the loan from the company and so we declared a dividend to you. When we did that it reduced the loan to zero and you'll pay tax on it next April.

```
The amount you see listed as  "due to shareholder"
under liabilities, are expenses that you paid for
personally in the last year, which the company still
owes you for. In essence, when you pay for something
personally, that's actually for the company, you are
lending it money thereby creating a shareholder loan -
that is, you the shareholder are loaning money to the
company.

Shareholder loans can be either an asset or a liability
of the company depending on who the lender is and who
the borrower is.

I hope that's clear, if not call me.

Tim
```

Loans To Family Members

Sometimes people try to get creative. They decide that in order to avoid paying tax on money removed from their professional corporation, they will simply loan the money to some other family member. Unfortunately, the CRA has long since learned to deal with this manoeuvre. If you loan money to a non-arm's length person, the same rules described on page 188 apply and the deemed interest benefit is taxable to you. Furthermore, the money still has to be repaid within one year from the end of the year in which it was made. If it is not repaid within that time, it is taxable in the hands of the recipient.

Tim Cestnick, in his book *The Tax Free Zone,* brought to light a very interesting side benefit to this situation. "If you own a corporation that makes a loan to a student (who is at least 18 years of age) who does not deal with you at arm's length (say, one of your kids), and that loan is not repaid within one year of the company's year-end, the amount of the loan will be taxed in the hands of the student. The student will likely not pay much tax on that loan if he or she has little other income. Here's the real benefit: When the child graduates and starts earning more income, he or she can pay back the loan and get a deduction for the repayment."

On a personal note, I thoroughly recommend Cestnick's books. He is one of the most creative tax authorities in the country and writes in a style that makes even tax law bearable.

Death Benefits From Your Professional Corporation

The CRA allows employers to pay out a tax-free death benefit to deceased employees up to $10,000. In order to take advantage of this one-time opportunity you should have, in your minute book, a corporate resolution that states something like this:

SPECIAL RESOLUTION

The following special resolution was passed by the under-mentioned company on the date stated:

Name of Company: Dr. James Pollock Professional Corporation

Resolution:

RESOLVED as Special Resolution that:

DR. JAMES POLLOCK PROFESSIONAL CORPORATION has agreed to pay a $10,000 death benefit to James Pollock upon his death in recognition of his service to the company.

Dated this 7th day of December 2010

James Pollock
President

DR. JAMES POLLOCK PROFESSIONAL CORPORATION

If you wish to take advantage of this tax-free death benefit with other employees, you can do it upon their death, there is no need to have the resolution done in advance. This is only required when you pay out.

The Company Car

As an incorporated professional you are, by definition, an employee of your corporation. As a result, your right to use a company car falls into one of following categories:

- If a car is clearly a business asset and is used 100 per cent for business purposes, the expenses will be treated like normal business costs and will be fully deductible (you should still keep separate kilometre and expense records). For example, a vehicle might be used during the day to visit patients or to run errands for the business and then left on the business premises at night.

- If you are a partner and use your own car in carrying on the partnership's business, this requirement must be clearly stated in your partnership agreement. You must maintain detailed records of the expenses incurred and the kilometres driven for business purposes.

- Employees who must use their own cars in performing their duties, must meet the following conditions in order to deduct automobile expenses:

  - you must ordinarily be required to work away from your employer's place of business, or in different places

  - you must be required, under your employment contract, to pay automobile expenses incurred in the course of performing your employment duties

  - you must not receive a tax-free car allowance.

For 2010 the allowable reimbursement is 52 cents for the first 5,000 km of business travel and 46 cents per km for business travel over 5,000 km. For the Yukon, the Northwest Territories and Nunavut, the rate is 56 cents/km for the first 5,000 km of business travel and 50 cents for each additional km.

If your professional corporation buys or leases the vehicle then additional rules apply. Because the vehicle is available to you for personal use, you are considered to have a taxable benefit from employment (referred to as a "standby charge").

Once you've determined that you should be keeping records, you'll want to ensure that you're tracking everything that's deductible. When using your car for business, you normally incur two types of expenses: fixed costs and operating expenses. Operating expenses include gas, maintenance, oil changes and repairs, car washes, insurance, licenses, and registration fees. Fixed costs are amounts that relate to the vehicle itself and do not vary with kilometres driven; they include capital cost allowance (tax depreciation), interest expenses for purchased vehicles, and lease payments for leased vehicles.

If you buy a more expensive car, there are rules that restrict the amount you can deduct when claiming capital cost allowance. What's the definition of a more expensive car? According to the CRA, an expensive car is one that cost more than $30,000 plus GST and applicable provincial sales tax (PST) or HST.

If you borrow money to buy your car, you can include the interest on the loan in your total expenses. The interest amount you may include is limited to $300 per month for vehicles purchased after the year 2009.

If you lease the car you use for work, the lease payments also form part of your total expenses. However, there are limits here as well. The formula for determining the limits basically restricts you to deducting only the portion of the lease payments that relates to the first $30,000 (plus GST, PST, or HST) of the cost of the car (for leases entered into after the year 2009).

If you track all car expenses throughout the year, as noted above, you'll have the information you need to determine your tax deduction when the time comes to prepare your tax return. And remember: keep receipts and other documentation to back up your claims.

At the end of the year you can summarize your information. Because your car is used for both business and personal purposes, your total expenses must be allocated between the two uses on some reasonable basis, with only the business portion being deductible. The allocation is usually done on the basis of the distance traveled; that is, the portion of total expenses that is deductible is determined by dividing the number of kilometres driven for business purposes by the total kilometres driven.

There are some expenses that do not have to be pro-rated. Parking charges incurred while on business trips are fully deductible, as are car repairs resulting from accidents that occurred while the car was being used for business.

Generally, the CRA requires that you record your automobile's odometer reading at the beginning and end of each year in order to determine the number of kilometres driven. In addition, your log should include the details of each trip taken for work or business by date, purpose, and number of kilometers driven.

At times it can be difficult to determine whether a particular trip is business or personal. The CRA's long-held position is that driving from your home to your place of work is personal travel. On the other hand, the CRA has stated that the following trips will be considered to be business travel:

- a trip from your home to see a patient not at your office and back to your home

- a trip from your home to see a patient not at your office and then to your regular place of work
- a trip from your regular place of work to see a patient and then home.

It would therefore appear that you could maximize your business travel by scheduling business appointments on the way to and from your office, but keep in mind the "purpose test[29]."

The automobile standby charge reflects the benefit of having an employer-provided vehicle available for personal use. The regular standby charge is set at 2 per cent per month of the original cost of the vehicle (or two-thirds of the lease payment).

A reduced standby charge can be applied to the extent by which annual personal driving does not exceed 20,000 kilometres, and where the automobile is used primarily – that is more than 50 per cent – for business purposes. For example, if a vehicle is driven 25,000 kilometres a year for business and 15,000 kilometres a year for commuting and other personal driving, the standby charge will be 75 per cent (15,000 divided by 20,000) of the regular standby charge.

Whether you should buy a vehicle or lease it, and whether you do it personally or corporately, is determined by a number of factors. You should always discuss vehicle acquisition with your financial advisor before you proceed.

There are very few things in the *income tax act* (ITA) that can result in double tax, but owning a company vehicle is one of them.

So, let's look at an example: suppose you have a company vehicle and claim 80 per cent of the use for business. If the CRA challenges the percentage, and is successful in having the percentage reduced to 40 per cent, what is the result?

Well, first you have to take the 40 per cent that you lost into personal income. This will result in you having to pay personal tax and interest, because your taxes are now late.

---

29 Purpose test refers to the primary reason you did something or went somewhere. In the example, if you stopped by the hospital each morning on your way to your clinic, to check on patients, then the trip would be deductible because the "purpose" was business related. If you stopped by the hospital each morning to drop your spouse off because they worked there, you would fail the "purpose" test because it's not business related.

The second thing that happens is that the company loses the 40 per cent deduction and has to take it back into income, and it too has to pay tax and interest.

What would happen if the same situation occurred with a personally owned vehicle?

You would have to pay personal tax on the 40 per cent deduction that you lost, and you would have to pay some interest, end of pain - no double tax. So, unless you can clearly demonstrate you will use your vehicle over 90% for business it's best to buy vehicles personally.

Recreational Property

Many people ask me, "Can I buy a vacation home in my professional corporation?" The answer is yes you can, but a better question is, "Does it make sense for me to buy a vacation property inside my professional corporation?"

In theory, if you own a vacation property in a company and personally pay fair market value rent for the use of that property, you shouldn't have a tax problem. However, the CRA can look at fair market value in a number of different ways. The "economic loss" method, for example, can cause trouble. Economic loss refers to the amount of money that the company has lost as a result of buying that vacation property.

Let's suppose that the company purchased a $750,000 condo in Whistler. When fair market value isn't easily determinable, the calculation in the past has been to take the prescribed rate multiplied by whatever the company spent on the property and make that the benefit that is added to your tax return. There's no problem in doing this – you just have to consider the cost. For instance, if the prescribed rate is 5 per cent the "economic benefit" would be $750,000 x 5 per cent = $37,500. That would be the amount you would have to include on your personal tax return – every year. As the prescribed rate increases so does the economic benefit.

If you rent your condo out through a rental pool for $400 per night, then the fair market value is probably $400 per night. If each night you stay in the condo, you pay the corporation $400 you shouldn't have a problem. However, if you decide that because your professional corporation owns the condo you should only pay $100 per night, you could find yourself having to pay tax on the $300 per night as a taxable benefit. The CRA could even go so far as to disallow certain deductions being made against the condo, thereby subjecting you to double taxation. The reason for this is that there is no deduction to the corporation, but there is a taxable benefit to you.

Some people rent the condo out for two months, claim two months of rental income, and say it's available for rent the rest of the year but no one wanted to rent it. They then have the corporation write off the property costs. The CRA will see through this scenario and say that the property is really only there for the use of the shareholder and look at it from an economic rent perspective.

There is nothing preventing you from owning property in a professional corporation; the real issue is the personal use you get from that property. If you're going to use the property personally and you are going to own it for a long time, you should probably own it personally. This is particularly true if there is a chance that the value of the vacation property could increase substantially, and because you could always elect that vacation property as your principal residence.

I've seen motor homes, yachts, as well as foreign vacation property inside professional corporations. If they're investments, great, if they generate revenue, even better; but if you use them yourself, be very careful how you pay for them. You may end up paying much more in taxes than if you had bought it personally in the first place.

You can also run into HST/GST problems when dealing with corporately owned properties, but that's covered in my new book The Financial Navigator. You can also have deemed disposition problems (see glossary) when you change the use of your vacation property, or the percentage of ownership. The CRA can be quite aggressive in their review of properties that have risen significantly in value.

A physician I know was reassessed because he was renting his condo out 50 per cent of the time and then stopped doing so. The CRA said there was a deemed disposition due to change of use, and the only argument became the fair market value of the property. The issue of value became a nightmare. Because the property wasn't actually being sold, what was it really worth? The client said one thing and the CRA said something else. I tell you, that's a place you'd rather not go.

I believe that over time most things increase in value, whether it is stocks, real estate, or art. If you use the asset personally, you're usually better off in the long run to pay the tax on the down payment when you withdraw the money from the corporation.

If you have a property in your professional corporation that you want to take out, make sure you get a third-party valuation of the asset. I've seen the CRA challenge the value of assets being removed from companies. The more you are able to prove that you removed it at fair market value, the better.

I sometimes recommend that clients purchase revenue properties in professional corporations for a variety of reasons, but I have never advocated purchasing vacation property inside a professional corporation. More often than not, the risks don't justify the potential savings.

Conventions

The *Income Tax Act* states that you are allowed to deduct the costs of two conventions a year; however, it doesn't define what a convention is. What about meetings, or courses for continuing education?

For expenses to be deductible, the convention must be held at a location that can reasonably be considered to be within the scope of the host organization. For example, a provincial organization must host the convention within the province. National organizations are allowed to hold conventions anywhere in Canada and the US (this does not include conventions held on ocean cruises).

A portion of the expenses may be subject to limitations, such as meals and entertainment; deductible expenses do not include those related to your spouse or significant other.

The CRA seem to be reasonable when examining meetings and courses. If you need to travel to a meeting or course, they haven't often queried the deduction of related expenses. And even if they do, it doesn't discount that you needed to be there anyway. But if your intention is to have more than two vacations a year and deduct the expenses as convention-related, I would suggest that you reconsider this strategy. It really isn't worth the risk.

Home Offices – What Is Deductible?

A self-employed person can deduct all reasonable expenses associated with maintaining a home office. Such expenses can include property taxes, utilities, insurance, mortgage interest or rent, upkeep and maintenance, and capital cost allowance.

The calculation to determine the reasonable portion of the expenses pertaining to the workspace in the home is generally based on the portion of the area devoted to the home office. For example, 240 square feet out of 2,400 square feet represents 10 per cent of the expenses. Note that when making this calculation you can usually exclude common areas, such as hallways, kitchens and washrooms. Where the workspace is not used exclusively for that purpose, the above calculations are adjusted to reflect the percentage of time devoted to the employment or business activity. Say you use your home office 60 per cent for business and 40 per cent for personal matters; you should reduce your 10 per cent to 6 per cent before calculating the eligible deductible amount.

Another method used to determine the percentage of use is by calculating the number of rooms in your house and converting it to a percentage, including common areas used to get to the office. For example, if your house has eight rooms, your office is one-eighth of the house or 12.5 per cent. Although some people use this method, accountants do not prefer it.

It should be noted that the deduction is based on a reasonable portion of the actual expenses incurred and not the value of the office space. This means that you must track all the home expenses and allocate a reasonable portion as home office expenses.

CHAPTER EIGHT

Saving For Retirement

When you are in business, you are responsible for taking care of yourself; one of the most important considerations is your retirement plan. You probably don't have a pension or stock option plan, so how comfortable you are going to be in retirement is entirely up to you. There are many ways for you to fund your retirement and in this chapter I explore the various options you have as an employee, and shareholder, of your professional corporation.

Retirement Compensation Arrangements

A lesser-known retirement plan is the retirement compensation arrangement (RCA). This plan was introduced in 1986 as a way of dealing with deferred income schemes. An RCA is a plan whereby the employer agrees to make contributions on behalf of an employee to an RCA trust in lieu of salary. Unlike an individual pension plan (IPP) or a retirement savings plan (RRSP), the total plan contributions are not tax sheltered. When the employer deposits money into an RCA trust, 50 per cent goes to an investment plan and 50 per cent goes to the CRA. The difference between this tax account and your basic tax account is that the taxes paid to the CRA from an RCA trust are kept in a refundable tax account. At retirement, the refundable tax account is refunded to the employee as part of their pension income. This plan is often misunderstood and underutilized.

There is no rule of thumb to decide if, and when, to use an RCA. Each situation has to be individually assessed. One obvious deterrent is the 50 per cent refundable tax. If your personal tax rate is less then 50 per cent, there would appear to be little or no benefit; however, you may be surprised to find that there could be a benefit if you use an exempt life insurance contract, or a tax-efficient investment like Berkshire Hathaway common shares. An exempt life insurance policy is usually a universal life insurance policy, which is not subject to annual tax reporting. If the policy is subject to annual tax reporting it is not exempt and therefore undermines the investment return of the RCA. A "tax-efficient" investment is one that does not generate income on an annual basis.

The investment vehicle used to fund the account can determine the benefits of an RCA. Each year the trustee has to file a trust return that includes declaring the investment earnings of the trust. Then 50 per cent of the investment earnings is remitted to the CRA and is added to the refundable tax account. There is no interest paid on the refundable tax account so only half of your money is working at one time. One way around this is to use a tax-sheltered life insurance policy. There is no taxable income to declare each year; therefore, you do not have to remit investment tax to the CRA. I believe that, given the right situation, setting up an RCA funded by an exempt life insurance contract, or tax-efficient investment, can be a powerful planning tool. You should be aware, however, that I have seen situations in which life insurance sales people have sold RCAs inappropriately. The purpose of the plan is to supplement your retirement income, not just to buy a life insurance policy. Approach using an exempt life insurance policy to fund an RCA in the same way you would when purchasing life insurance inside a professional corporation – with caution. Also, remember that the death benefit of a life insurance policy becomes taxable if held inside an RCA account.

Occasionally, people are shown what is referred to as "split-dollar" life insurance contracts. These are life insurance policies that are divided into two separate parts – the insurance part and the cash value part – with the individual or company owning the life insurance portion and the RCA trust owning the cash value. I've heard different opinions as to whether this works. If you decide to proceed with a split-dollar contract, ensure that all documentation is provided by the issuing company and filed with the RCA trustee.

When comparing various investment options you get a different view, depending on what you focus on. The table below shows three RCAs with three different investment vehicles. The first investment is an exempt life insurance policy based on a female non-smoker age 50, with annual deposits of $25,000. The second investment is a non-tax sheltered investment and the third is a tax-efficient investment. All examples were generated using a 5 per cent compound annual rate of return. Let's look at the results:

Life Insurance/RCA	Refundable Tax Account	RCA Total Value
Cash surrender value at age 60 $294,779	$250,000	$544,779
Cash surrender value at age 65 $526,217	$375,000	$901,217
Non-Sheltered Investment/RCA		
Accumulated value at age 60 $280,084	$280,084	$560,168
Accumulated value at age 65 $448,298	$448,298	$896,596
Tax-Efficient Investment/RCA		
Accumulated value at age 60 $314,447	$250,000	$564,447
Accumulated value at age 65 $539,464	$375,000	$914,464

If you live to retirement, the best option would appear to be the tax-efficient investment because it resulted in the biggest pool of capital. This is a result of not having to pay for insurance costs as in the case of the life insurance policy. However, if you die prior to retirement, the life insurance policy has the added advantage of paying out a death benefit much greater than the cash surrender value. At age 60 the death benefit of the life insurance policy would be $950,000, leaving your estate with an RCA account balance of $1,200,000 ($950,000 + $250,000). If you died at age 65, that number would increase to $1,389,004.

In this particular example, using a female non-smoker, age 50, who is probably a good insurance risk, I created a scenario using a $950,000 exempt life insurance policy. Each RCA has to be designed to maximize the individual circumstances. However, if you analyze the same RCA using a male, age 46, who's a smoker, you would get a very different picture because the insurance costs would be that much higher. That would seriously undermine the effectiveness of the life insurance option.

Before setting up an RCA you need to have the actuarial calculations. Not all actuaries will do RCA calculations. The numbers are different from IPP calculations because they are not limited in the same way as regular pension calculations. Ask your financial advisor to provide you with the name of someone who can make these calculations. You can usually get these initial calculations done free of charge.

Unlike IPP contributions, the amount of money you deposit into an RCA does not affect your RRSP deposits. You can take full advantage of RRSPs when using an RCA. You can also defer taking a pension from an RCA beyond age 71. This can be beneficial if you have sufficient income at retirement.

As with IPPs, RCA accounts are normally protected from creditors. Both IPPs and RCAs can be used to reduce the amount of taxable income the professional corporation has. The necessity to bonus down is sometimes eliminated when these programs are used. It is also interesting to note that interest paid on money borrowed to fund both IPPs and RCAs is deductible to the company. This is not the case with money borrowed to purchase RRSPs.

Individual Pension Plans

An IPP is a private pension plan that is designed for small groups or even a single member. An actuary, who tells you how much you can contribute each year, does the pension calculations. An investment advisor, chosen by you or your financial advisor, then invests the pension funds.

In order to be eligible to set up an IPP, you must be incorporated and receiving a salary. The amount you can contribute each year will depend on your income and years of service with the company. The benefit of an IPP can be examined by comparing it to other tax sheltered plans, such as RRSPs. Like RRSPs, IPPs allow a 100 per cent tax deduction of all contributions, and all investment gains in both plans are tax sheltered. You can determine whether it is beneficial to you by comparing the benefits of each program, when you consider your age and the allowable contributions. If you are over age 50 and have had your professional corporation for a number of years, and you are drawing a salary, you are a candidate for an IPP.

The first step is to talk to your financial advisor. Setting up an IPP is not like buying an RRSP. You know each year what you are allowed to contribute to your RRSP based on your previous year's income. When you get your tax assessment notice back from the CRA each year, your RRSP limit is calculated for you. When dealing with an IPP, to determine your legal contribution limit, you must have an actuary calculate the amount for you based on your specific details. After you have determined that an IPP is right for you, you have to choose an investment advisor. The actuary and the investment advisor are usually two separate people. Alternatively, insurance companies offer both actuarial and investment planning services.

Another option is to hire an independent actuary to do the calculations. Again, once you've decided that an IPP is right for you, you can then hire an independent investment advisor. Neither way is better than the other; some people like to deal with one company or person and others like to deal with more than one. My advice in either case is to review this option with your accountant prior to set-up. In terms of cost, you should not have to pay anyone to carry out these initial calculations. Actuaries are banking on you hiring them to implement the plan and to provide you with ongoing actuarial services. For this potential opportunity they will usually forgo any fee.

The actuarial calculations should highlight the advantages of the different plans (for example, the amount you can currently deposit and deduct). The estimated value of the plan at retirement is based on a number of assumptions, including deposit amounts, rates of return, salary, and number of years to retirement. Actual values will fluctuate; for instance, the more aggressive your investment, the greater the potential benefit and corresponding risk.

It is interesting to note that investment losses in an IPP can be replaced, but this cannot be done in an RRSP. Let's look at an example. Suppose you have an RRSP and have invested in a security that you purchased for $60.00 per share, but upon retirement it is worth $20.00 per share. If you sell it you will have a loss of $40.00 per share. That money is gone forever and there is nothing you can do about it. For this reason, I encourage people to be more conservative with their retirement investments because of the permanent loss. If you are going to expose yourself to a potential capital loss you are best to do it outside your retirement plan, so that if you do lose money you can at least write it off against capital gains.

Let's look at what would happen if you had the same stock in your IPP, and at retirement you didn't have enough money in your plan to pay your pension. In this case, you would be allowed to put more money into your plan to make up the difference. You can replace losses because the IPP is calculated to pay out a pension amount at a certain age. If at age 65 you are entitled to a monthly pension of $2,500 per month, the actuary will calculate how much money should be in your IPP account at that time. If the amount is determined to be $417,000 and you don't have that much money in your account because of investment losses, you are allowed to make up the difference to ensure that the $417,000 is available.

When comparing the potential benefits of an IPP, make sure you include the set-up and maintenance costs. Set-up costs are about $2,500 and annual maintenance costs are about $700. In addition, every three years there are actuarial calculations made that cost about $1,800; these are carried out to determine if there is sufficient money in the plan to support the pension payments. If there is a deficiency, more money is required into the plan; if there is a surplus, contributions are reduced or money is refunded to the employer.

If you set up an IPP, remember that you are setting up a trust. You are required to have trustees and file a trust return each year. Failing to file a trust return will lead to severe penalties. Your trustee or your actuary can file the return but ultimately it is your responsibility to make sure that it's filed.

Another benefit of an IPP is that it is creditor-proof because it is a trust account. Money can be moved out of your professional corporation this way, and not normally be exposed to creditors.

Like most things in life there are pros and cons.

Unlike an RRSP, which allows you to withdraw as much as you like whenever you like, there are restrictions with IPPs.

First, you can't take your money out whenever you want. You also can't take whatever amount you want. When taking money out of an IPP there is a minimum limit and a maximum limit. The minimum may be 4 per cent but the maximum could be 5.25 per cent.

IPPs should be analyzed very carefully before they are put into place. Once you have one, in one way or another, it's going to be with you the rest of your life.

```
Re: Pensions: Yes/No?
From: Lange Zhu
To: tim@tpcfinancial.com

Hi Tim - I received a newsletter today talking about
Individual Pension Plans. Is this something I should
have?
```

Re: Re: Pensions: Yes/No?
From: tim@tpcfinancial.com
To: Lange Zhu

Hi Lange

There can be situations where an IPP make sense, but for you I say no.

IPP's aren't for everyone. Although the manufacturers of these programs would like you to think they are, the fact is they are not the end all and be all.

IPP's, like everything else, have a good side and a bad side. It seems that whenever you read something, or talk to someone who sells them, they appear to have little or no downside.

Just so that we are on the same page, IPP's are not some sort of super RRSP. They are government regulated plans that, once put into place, will be with you for the rest of your life.

It's true that you can take money out of your professional corporation to fund an IPP, and that in certain circumstances you can make past service contributions, but my question to you is why take money out of your professional corporation when you can leave it in there and invest it however you want? Furthermore, if you leave it in your PC, you can decide how and when to take the money out; the amount and the timing isn't regulated.

Another thing to consider is that when you take money from an IPP in retirement, it's all taxed as regular income. When you accumulate money inside your PC we have the option to remove it as: eligible dividends, other then eligible dividends, capital dividends, interest, or capital gains depending on what types of investments you have. Accumulating money in your PC gives you significantly more flexibility.

I'll continue to monitor the rules relating to IPP's and may change my position on them in the future, but for now, Lange, I advise you to pass.

Tim

Registered Retirement Savings Plans

Since 1957, RRSPs have been used by Canadians to accumulate retirement funds. Most advisors have not taken the time to explore alternative methods and as a result have defaulted to making maximum contributions. As an incorporated professional, you have more opportunities to accumulate wealth in a controlled, tax-efficient manner. Consider the new maximum limits for RRSP contributions.

In 2010 you were allowed contribute $22,000; these limits are based on 18 per cent of earned income. In order to take advantage of these higher limits you are required to earn more income, or remove more money from your professional corporation. To reach the maximum amounts you would have to earn about $122,222 (in 2010).

If you subtract the RRSP contributions from the earned income you would end up with the following situation: $122,222 - $22,000 = $100,222

Current federal income tax is calculated based on four thresholds.

Tax Brackets	Marginal Tax Rate
$0 – 40,970	15 per cent
$40,971 - $81,941	22 per cent
$81,942 - $127,021	26 per cent
$127,022 and over	29 per cent

Provincial and territorial tax thresholds (for the second tax bracket) vary from 7 per cent in Nunavut to 13.8 per cent in PEI. In all jurisdictions there is a break at $81,941. This means that in every province and territory, if you can keep your personal taxable income below $81,942, you will not be taxed above 22 per cent federally. You can check the tax tables in the back of this book to see the combined federal and provincial or territorial tax rates. These calculations determine at what point it makes sense not to make maximum RRSP contributions. If you do not require the extra income, or if you can split income with family members, you may be better off to reduce your RRSP contributions or stop them altogether.

Consider the following example. Dr. Powell has a lifestyle requiring $108,000 per year, net after tax. For the last 15 years, she and her spouse have been making maximum RRSP contributions. In order to contribute the maximum, they will each require an annual income of $122,222. After they buy their RRSP, their taxable incomes are $100,222. On an after-tax basis, their cash flow will each be about $74,533 for an annual cash flow of $149,066. If you look at the difference between what they need – $108,000 – and what they have – $149,066 – it means that they have exposed excess money to higher tax rates. The total amount of taxes and CPP contributions will be about $51,378. The excess amount available to invest personally would be $41,066 ($149,066 - $108,000). How does this affect wealth accumulation? Let's give them what they need and see what happens.

In order to net $108,000 per year, their individual incomes would have to be about $83,000. In this case, their RRSP contributions would drop to $14,940 ($83,000 x 18 per cent) and their tax and CPP contributions would total about $14,415. This would give them a net annual income of $53,645 each or $107,290 combined. Because they don't need the extra income, they can leave it in their professional corporation and remove it later. Instead of taking $122,222 to maximize their RRSP, they take what they need, which is $83,000. They are then able to leave $78,444 in the professional corporation.

In our example we are paying both spouses from the professional corporation; therefore the amount that can be left in the professional corporation is $78,444. Using a corporate tax rate of 16 per cent, the taxes payable would be $12,551 leaving $65,893 to invest. The tax deferral would therefore be $24,827 ($65,893 - $41,066). If they are 45 years of age and project this through to age 65 it would mean having an extra $759,879 available to them, at retirement, assuming an average return of 4 per cent (I am not accounting for annual accrual tax because there are a number of ways to invest money without having to pay tax annually).

Now, before we leave this example, you might be questioning my math. Remember you took $122,222 to make an RRSP contribution of $22,000 and then in the second scenario you took $83,000 and made an RRSP contribution of $14,940. Won't you have an extra $7,060 in your RRSP each year? Yes, but there is something different about accumulating money in your RRSP, instead of in your professional corporation. If both spouses invested the extra $7,060 until age 65 at 4 per cent, they would have another $230,010. Assuming they are both in the top tax bracket in retirement, they would pay about $102,204 in taxes, leaving them an extra $127,806 each or

$255,612 combined. If they really wanted to, they could totally withdraw the $759,879 from the professional corporation and pay tax of $243,161 and have a net/net amount of $516,718. That's a 100 per cent increase in after-tax money. Why is there such a difference, other than the amount invested? The answer is: taxes on withdrawal. When you remove money from your RRSP, it is taxed as regular income. When you remove money from your professional corporation after retirement, it is normally taxed as dividend income, which is tax-preferred. If you are in the top tax bracket living in Nova Scotia, for example, and remove $10,000 from your RRSP, you would pay about $5,000 in income tax. If the $10,000 were in dividends removed from your professional corporation, the taxes would be about $3,357 for eligible dividends, and $3,621 for other than eligible dividends.

You are required by law to start to withdraw money from your RRSP in the year you turn age 72. Most people will convert their RRSPs to a retirement income fund (RRIF – see glossary) in the year they turn age 71 and then start to receive income the following year. This income is fully taxable and forced upon you whether you want it or not. Money left in a professional corporation can stay there beyond death. There is no requirement to remove it at any age or at any time. If you don't require additional income when you retire, you can leave the money invested in your professional corporation – forever.

If you do need money, you can remove it at any time and pay tax on it as a dividend – not salary income. In 2010, tax on income at the top marginal rate in BC is 43.70 per cent, on eligible dividends it's 21.45 per cent and on other than eligible dividends it's 33.71 per cent. In the Yukon, the top marginal rate on income is 42.40 per cent, on eligible dividends it's 18.8 per cent and on other than eligible dividends it's 30.49 per cent. In 2010, Alberta had the best tax rates for dividends; the highest you would pay on eligible dividends would be 15.88 per cent and on other than eligible dividends 27.71 per cent.

All of these figures are based on annual taxable incomes above $127,021. In retirement, if your taxable income is, say, $60,000 and you live in Alberta, you would pay tax on eligible dividends at a rate of zero per cent. This is pretty significant when you consider that if you took the same taxable income from your RRSP, and lived in Alberta, you would be paying 32 per cent marginal income tax. Taking money from your professional corporation in retirement can literally cut your tax liability by more than half (or in this case by 100 per cent). You also have complete control over when and how you take it out.

If you're a tax practitioner, you are probably saying $60,000 of taxable income is only $41,380 of eligible dividends (remember the 1.45 gross-up). That's true, but if you and your spouse are both receiving $41,380 in eligible dividends that's a retirement income of $82,760 without paying personal income tax.

Many people today are finding themselves being affected by what is referred to as Old Age Security (OAS) "claw backs". When you reach age 65, you are entitled to apply for OAS. This is a social benefit that is income-tested. Currently, if your total personal income is above $66,733, you have to start paying back your OAS pension.

More and more people are being subjected to claw backs when they start taking money out of their RRSPs. They have no ability to reduce their income and, in most cases, they are required to take more from their RRIFs each year. By having the money in your professional corporation, you have more control over when and how you take it out and if you want to, you can reduce the amount you remove when your OAS starts.

Rule of thumb buster: You should always maximize your RRSPs.

No. Sometimes you are better off not buying RRSPs.

Should I Buy RRSPs?

There is no hard and fast answer here. Everyone should have this evaluated on a case-by-case basis. In British Columbia, in the case of physicians, I usually say yes because of the RRSP matching program. With dentists I usually say no unless they have to bonus down (see page 174). In Nunavit, I usually say no to the physician or dentist and yes to their spouses. In the Yukon my answer is usually no. Each jurisdiction is different because of the different share structures allowed. Every situation is unique because of different income levels and cash flow requirements. Before making any calculations you first have to know if you have a choice. If you are the professional, you don't have to take a wage, or salary from your professional corporation and it can be taxed as corporate income and removed as dividends. If the only income you receive is dividend income, you are not eligible to make RRSP contributions (unless you have carry-forward room from previous years). If you are paying your spouse a wage, or you are taking a wage yourself, you have the option to purchase an RRSP. If this is the case, it would probably make sense to make maximum RRSP contributions.

So, when shouldn't you buy an RRSP? The answer is when you can leave the money in your professional corporation. If we refer to our previous example of making maximum RRSP deposits each year, you would need to take $122,222 in income to make a maximum RRSP contribution of $22,000. If a couple only needs $108,000 net annually to live on, why take the extra money in income? On a combined basis they would have to take $244,444 in personal income to deposit $44,000 into their combined RRSPs.

If both contributed $22,000 to their RRSPs for 20 years at 4 per cent they would accumulate $1,446,870. Because they took the extra income, they would have $41,066 left to invest personally. If this amount were invested for the same 20 years at 4 per cent, they would accumulate, outside of their RRSP, another $1,350,559. This makes a total of $2,797,429 available for retirement. If all taxes due were paid at one time, the net amount would be only about $1,566,560 (assume a 44 per cent tax rate). This example assumes no annual accrual tax and that all investments are cashed in at one time.

Instead of buying RRSPs and investing personally, let's take enough money out to support a lifestyle of $108,000 per year and leave the balance in the professional corporation. To net $108,000 they will each have to take $68,000 gross income. That will leave $108,444 to be taxed in the professional corporation. Assuming 16 per cent corporate tax ($17,351) there will be $91,093 left to invest. At 4 per cent over 20 years they would accumulate $2,995,928. If all taxes due were paid at one time the net would be about $2,037,231 (assuming a 32 per cent dividend tax rate).

Your total pre-tax income and the net household income you require will determine whether or not you should buy RRSPs. This example shows about 30 per cent difference. If your spouse has an income below $35,000, it probably doesn't make sense to buy RRSPs because the tax savings are minimal. Furthermore, at retirement your total income could be higher than your work income, resulting in higher taxes after retirement. If you know this is going to be the case, you can buy an RRSP in the current year and then deduct it in future years.

If you know you are going to have a higher income year in the future and your current taxable income is not above $81,941, you should probably defer buying an RRSP. You can carry forward the unused amount to be used in that future year. You should carefully review your current and future cash flows with your financial advisor before deciding whether or not to purchase RRSPs.

Tax Shelters In RRSPs You Can't Get At

A word of warning about RRSPs, never have assets trapped inside them that you can't use. The best way for me to explain this is through an example. A group of people invested in a company (I can't mention the actual name). They were told that the company was going to grow fast and eventually go public. The investors were given the option of using personal money, corporate money from their professional corporations, or they could transfer money from their RRSP. Most chose the last option and used their RRSP funds. As fate would have it the company ran into financial difficulty and the investments became worthless. Nothing happened until one of the investors turned age 71. At that time he wanted to convert his RRSP to a registered retirement income fund (RRIF), so the entire RRSP account was transferred, including the bad investment. The problem was the investment was still showing the initial value of $50,000. This meant he was going to have to take money out of his RRIF based on the total value of his account including the $50,000. He had no way of writing off the loss and now has to take income from an asset that has no value and therein lies the problem. The last time I spoke to him there was a lawyer involved trying to figure out how he can get the CRA to acknowledge that the asset is worthless. It's a huge mess caused by what I would consider very bad advice.

I'm not a big believer in taking unnecessary risks. I believe that the *Income Tax Act* is fair, if you use all the opportunities that are available to you. Always remember that the hardest dollar to make is the one you earn. Protect it.

That reminds me of a meeting I had recently. One of my clients, who is a very successful businessman, told me he had a dinner party at his house last month. At the dinner were two dentists and a physician (I know this is beginning to sound like a joke, but it isn't, honestly); at one point in the evening they started discussing investments. My client told me he was amazed at how these professionals talked about losing money. He said they mentioned, on more than one occasion, that it was acceptable if they lost only a little money, instead of a lot. Not once did they talk about making money – only how much they could have lost. My client said that he couldn't imagine, as a businessman, repeatedly accepting losses. He stated that he would never go into a business venture if the primary feature were tax benefits. He believed, without exception, that the primary objective of any business venture or investment should be making a profit. He found it intriguing that these three professionals thought otherwise.

The Canada Pension Plan

If you've been paying into the Canada Pension Plan (CPP), you should know what it is. If you are going to stop contributing to the CPP, you should know what you're giving up.

The CPP provides contributors and their families with a basic level of protection against loss of earnings due to retirement, disability, or death of a contributor to the plan. CPP benefits were designed to provide a basic level of earnings replacement in retirement, to be supplemented by income from other sources. The specific objective was to replace gross earnings equal to 25 per cent of average career earnings up to a ceiling, the yearly maximum pensionable earnings (YMPE[30]), which approximates the average industrial wage. The CPP is part of a package of federal programs that also includes Old Age Security (OAS), the Guaranteed Income Supplement (GIS), and Spousal Allowance (SPA), an age-related tax credit and pension credit, as well as provincial and territorial income support programs targeted at the elderly. The CPP, and the Quebec Pension Plan (QPP) which is similar to the CPP, are earnings related, contributory, mandatory, publicly administered programs. The CPP was designed to be self-supporting, with all CPP benefits paid from the contributions of employees and employers and from the investment earnings of the CPP fund.

A CPP retirement pension is a monthly benefit paid to people who have contributed to the plan, who live outside of Quebec and are at least 60 years old. The amount of pension you receive is based on your total contributions. The amount you pay is based on your employment earnings. You do not make contributions on any other type of income, such as investment earnings. The amount you receive is determined by how long and how much you contribute over your contributory period. In 2010, the maximum pension per month was $934.17.The age at which you choose to retire also affects the amount you receive. The retirement pension is indexed to the Consumer Price Index annually.

---

30 Yearly Maximum Pensionable Earnings (YMPE) for 2010 is $47,200

The contributory period is based on a starting date based on age 18 or 1966 (whichever is later) and age 70 or death. You do not contribute while you are receiving a CPP disability benefit and this time is excluded from your contributory period, which increases your future benefits.

To keep your pension as high as possible, the CPP omits some parts of your contributory period from the calculations such as:

- periods when you stop working, or your earnings are lower while you raise your children (under the age of seven)
- months after the age 65 (which can be used to replace any low-earning months before age 65)
- any months when you were eligible for a CPP disability benefit
- 15 per cent of your lowest earnings years during your contribution period.

You pay contributions only on your annual earnings between the minimum and maximum level (called "pensionable" earnings). The minimum level is $3,500. The maximum level is adjusted each January, based on increases in the average wage. In 2010, the maximum level is $47,200.

Disability Benefits

The CPP pays a monthly benefit to people who have contributed to the plan and who are disabled according to CPP legislation. The CPP also pays monthly benefits for dependent children. Your disability condition can be either physical or mental. Under CPP legislation, your disability must be "severe and prolonged". "Severe" means your condition prevents you from working regularly at any job, and "prolonged" means your condition is long term, and/or may result in your death.

In addition, you must have contributed for a minimum number of years, and contributed to the CPP for four of the last six years. During that period, you must have earned at least 10 per cent of each YMPE.

If your contributions fall short, you will not normally be eligible; however, under certain CPP provisions, you may still qualify:

- if you delayed applying (that is, you had enough years of contributions when you first became disabled, but don't have enough now)
- if your CPP contributions stopped or were reduced while raising your children under age seven
- if you acquired CPP credits from your separated or former spouse or your former common-law partner
- if you worked in another country with which Canada has an agreement, and contributed to its plan
- if you were medically incapable of applying
- if you are no longer receiving CPP disability benefits, and you have made the required contributions each year since they stopped.

Benefits start four months after the date the CPP judges you to be disabled. Benefits stop when you are no longer disabled according to CPP legislation, at age 65 when your CPP retirement pension begins (or between ages 60 to 64, if you take early retirement), or at your death.

The benefit is made up of two parts: the first is a flat-rate amount, and the second is based on how much, and for how long, you paid into the CPP. There is a maximum amount that can be paid. If there is any increase in the cost of living, your payments will be increased. The maximum disability benefit in 2010 was $1,126.76 per month.

CPP disability benefits are not permanent. From time to time, the CPP may check to see if you are now able to work. The CPP provides assistance to help you get back to work. You may:

- attend school or do volunteer work without fear of losing your benefits as long as you have not regained the capacity to work (you must report successful completion of a school program)
- continue to receive benefits for three months after returning to work
- have your application reinstated quickly if the same disability again prevents you from working.

The CPP pays for vocational rehabilitation, if it determines that:

- with a vocational rehabilitation program, you would likely be able to return to work, and

- you are receiving CPP disability benefits, and
- you are willing and able to undergo a vocational rehabilitation program, and
- your medical condition is stable, and your doctor approves.

While receiving CPP disability benefits you can also receive child benefits. A dependent child is:

- your natural or adopted child, or a child in your care and control, and
- either under age 18, or between the ages of 18 and 25 and in full-time attendance at a recognized educational institution.

A dependent child's benefit is a fixed amount. In 2010, the benefit was $214.85 per month, per child. If there is any increase in the cost of living, the benefit will be increased. A child may get up to two benefits, when both parents paid into the CPP and each parent is either disabled (as defined by the CPP) or deceased. Your child's benefits stop and start at the same time as your disability benefits.

Survivor Benefits

There are three types of benefits:

- The death benefit is a one-time payment to, or on behalf of, the estate of a deceased CPP contributor.
- The survivor's pension is a monthly benefit paid to the surviving spouse or common-law partner of a deceased contributor.
- The children's benefit is a monthly benefit for dependent children of a deceased contributor.

CPP survivor benefits are paid to the deceased contributor's estate (or the person who is responsible for funeral expenses), the surviving spouse or common-law partner, or the dependent children.

To be eligible for survivor benefits you must have contributed to the CPP for at least three years. If your CPP "contributory period" is longer than nine years, you must have contributed in one-third of the calendar years in your contributory period, or 10 calendar years, whichever is the lesser.

The CPP death benefit is a one-time, lump-sum payment made to the deceased contributor's estate. If there is no estate, the person responsible for the funeral expenses, the surviving spouse or common-law partner, or the next of kin may be eligible. The CPP survivor's pension is paid to the person who, at the time of death, is the legal spouse or common-law partner of the deceased contributor. Separated legal spouses may be eligible if the deceased had no cohabiting common-law partner for at least the year before death.

The amount of the death benefit depends on how much, and for how long, you paid into the CPP. The death benefit is equal to six months of retirement pension, up to a maximum of $2,500. The amount of the survivor benefit depends on:

- how much, and for how long, you have paid into the plan, and

- your spouse's or common-law partner's age when you, the contributor, die, and

- whether your spouse or common-law partner is also receiving a CPP disability benefit or retirement pension.

The maximum monthly survivor's benefit in 2010, for someone who dies before age 65, is $516.57, and the maximum monthly survivor's benefit for someone who dies at the age 65 or later is $560.50.

The CPP child benefit is paid to natural or adopted children of the deceased contributor, or children in the care and control of the deceased contributor at the time of death. A child who has lost at least one parent who was a CPP contributor may[31] qualify. The monthly benefit is a flat rate adjusted annually. In 2010, the children's benefit was $214.85 per month.

- CPP benefits are taxable in all cases in the following manner:

- CPP benefits are taxable to the recipient.

- CPP disability benefits are taxable to the individual.

- The CPP lump-sum death benefit is taxable to the estate of the deceased.

- CPP survivor's benefits are taxable to the spouse or common-law partner.

- CPP children's (both disability and survivor's) benefits are taxable to the child.

---

31 For benefits to be paid, the deceased parent must have met the contributory requirements.

Paying For CPP You Can't Collect

Here is an interesting question: when is it possible to pay for CPP and never collect? The answer is, when you're incorporated and have a spouse earning income from more than one source. Suppose you were paying yourself $100,000 and your spouse $24,000; you will be responsible for making CPP contributions for both yourself and your spouse. Based on current CPP contribution amounts, you (as the employer) and your spouse (as the employee) are required to pay $4,326.30 for you and $2,029.50 for your spouse, a total of $6,355.80 in CPP contributions.

Now, suppose your spouse also works part-time somewhere else and earns another $36,000 per year. The total income for the year would be $60,000. On that $36,000 income he or she would pay $1,608.75 in CPP contributions and the employer would be responsible for an additional $1,608.75. CPP limits contributions to individuals at $47,200 (YMPE) or $2,163.15 per year. But this only applies to companies on a company-to-company basis. The over-contribution rules do not take into consideration contributions from multiple employers. As an individual, you would apply for a refund of over-contributions on the amount you paid over $2,163.15. As a corporation you could only apply for a refund if you happen to pay more than $2,163.15 for an individual employee. In this example you would be making total contributions of $5,247 ($2,029.50 for your professional corporation on their $24,000 of income and $3,217.50 in contributions from the other job), even though you would only get credit for $4,326.30. This is another thing to take into consideration when hiring family members.

In order to prevent an employer over-contribution to CPP you should give dividends to your spouse, or family members, or limit the total wages and salaries they receive from all employers to the YMPE limit of $47,200.

Spouse's Income			
Professional Corporation		Second Employer	
$24,000		$36,000	
CPP Employee	$1014.75	CPP Employee	$1608.75
CPP Employer	$1014.75	CPP Employer	$1608.75
Total CPP Employee: $1014.75 +$1608.75 = $2623.50			
Over contribution amount: $460.35 Tax refund: $460.35			
On the corporate side, both employers are less than the maximum of $2163.15 therefore no over-contribution because corporate contributions are not pooled.			

There are a number of changes to CPP that are due to come into effect in 2011 that I will deal with, as well as the economics of the CPP, in my new book, "The Financial Navigator – A Professional's Guide to Keeping More of What You Earn", to be published in 2011.

In the meantime consider this; in 2004 when I first wrote Professional Corporations – The Secret to Success, the CPP contribution maximum for self employed individuals was $3,663.00. In 2010 the maximum is $4,326.30. That's an increase of 18 per cent.

In 2004 the maximum benefit amount was $814.17 per month whereas in 2010 the maximum benefit amount is $934.17, or an increase of 14.75 per cent.

As demands on government pensions become greater, and if investment returns continue to falter, where do you think the extra money is going to come from?

CHAPTER NINE

Planning Your Professional Corporation

Planning your professional corporation begins with the first meeting between you and your financial advisor. Every effort should be made to create a corporate structure that allows for maximum flexibility. Coordinating the planning of your professional corporation with your personal planning is the secret to success.

Holding Companies

Holding companies are sometimes known as investment companies. When dealing with lawyers and accountants they are referred to generically as Holdco or Investco. They differ from your professional corporation in that they usually do not have "earned income." In the simplest terms, holding companies hold things. In order to move money out of your professional corporation you might set up a holding company that will hold, amongst other things, shares in your professional corporation. By moving the money inter-corporately, you are not subject to corporate tax a second time. This opportunity is not allowed in those jurisdictions that only allow a registered member of the college or association to be shareholders, or do not allow other companies to own shares.

Earlier in the book, we discussed the most common types of share structures. One diagram illustrated the use of a holding company (Holdco) an operating company (Opco) and a trust (see page 233). The operating company represents your professional corporation. The purpose of this particular structure is to allow the professional to earn money in the operating company and pay tax on the first $500,000 of net income at the small business rate of about 16 per cent. The net income from the operating company can then be moved to either the holding company or the trust because both entities own shares in the operating company.

If you are legally allowed to have a holding company own shares in your professional corporation, this structure provides many opportunities to split income and reduce overall tax. If your professional activities generated $200,000 of income and you paid tax on that amount personally (say, $70,000), you would be left with about $130,000. Conversely, if the $200,000 was earned by you and the money was left in your professional corporation, and then taxed at a corporate rate of 16 per cent ($32,000) and subsequently moved into a holding company, the overall tax liability would be reduced by as much as $38,000. Of course, leaving all your income in your company is not realistic for most people.

This movement of money can take place via dividends on the shares owned by the holding company. If you want to split income, you can move the money to the holding company and then distribute it to the shareholders of the holding company. Throughout the whole process, the income retains its form as a dividend.

If you want to accumulate assets for distribution at a later date, you can move the money from your operating company to the holding company. There are a variety of reasons to do this; for instance, you might want to keep your investment assets separate from your practice assets. This is important if you want to sell your practice. You wouldn't want to try to sell the shares of your practice when you have other non-business assets inside it. Also, a holding company can provide you with an added level of creditor protection, in that the investment assets are held in a separate legal entity. Holding companies are particularly helpful when doing an estate freeze (see pages 46-49). You can also use a holding company to split income in the future and to hold assets beyond your lifetime.

What Is The Difference Between Active Income And Passive Income?

Active income is money made as a result of earning professional income. As a physician, you earn income practicing medicine. As a dentist you earn income practicing dentistry. This definition extends to related work such as lecturing, training and consulting.

Unearned or "passive" income is money that is made as a result of investment. When you have money in the bank that earns interest, the interest is passive. Capital gains are usually unearned, as are dividends and net-rental income.

The importance of knowing the difference between active and passive income lies in the tax treatment of the two. Active income is eligible for the small business tax rate, passive income is not. Normally, interest, taxable capital gains, and net rental income are subject to big business tax rates of about 48 per cent; dividends from a public company, on the other hand, are subject to a 33.33 per cent tax, and dividends from a related company are tax-free, assuming no dividend refund to the payor corporation. Depending on the individual company and circumstances, some of these forms of income can be classified as active instead of passive but generally this is the way they are taxed.

```
Re: Moving Tax Rates?
From: Sven Hansen
To: tim@tpcfinancial.com

Hi Tim

I was reviewing my corporate tax return and I
calculated that my tax rate last year was 18.6%. I
thought the tax rate was only 16%. Why is there a
difference?

Sven
```

```
Re: Re: Moving Tax Rates?
From: tim@tpcfinancial.com
To: Sven Hansen

Good question Sven, the variation is because various
types of income are being taxed at different rates.
The 16% small business tax rate only applies to earned
income. This is income generated by you. Investment
income is taxed at various rates depending on the type
of income. Investment income is also referred to as
passive income.
```

When your accountant is calculating your corporate
taxes he or she will separate the various types of
income. In BC, interest and net rental income are taxed
at 48%. Capital gains are taxed at 24% and eligible
dividends are taxed at 33.3%.

When you're looking at your tax bill from last year
it's made up of all these different tax rates. The more
interest income you have, the higher your total tax
payable because, as I just mentioned, interest income
is taxed at the highest rate. If you had no investment
income at all, your tax payable would be 16% of your
taxable income, but because you had investment income
it pushed up your overall tax rate.

Kudos to you for noticing Sven, I'm really pleased
that you are running your practice like a business.

Tim

How Do I Deal With Passive Income?

A key advantage of a professional corporation is the ability to accumulate equity faster than through a sole proprietorship. You can earn money, pay tax at the low corporate rate, and then accumulate all those extra dollars inside the company. This works incredibly well if you don't have to pay tax on your passive income at 48 per cent. Unlike active income that is taxed at lower corporate rates on the first $500,000, investment income is taxed at higher corporate rates beginning with dollar one. The tables in appendices A and B (pages 333 to 339) show the tax rates on various forms of investment income in each province or territory. This is where the services of a qualified financial coordinator can be worth his, or her, weight in gold. They can help you decide where to draw income from and when and where to use eligible and other than eligible dividends.

I have often heard people claim that they don't pay tax at the high corporate rate, and that their accountant would have told them if they were. The reality is that you are probably paying tax at the high corporate rate on your investment income and if you were to look closely at your T-2 you would see it there. Check out line 440 that asks about aggregated investment income. This amount is deducted from the income amount eligible for the small business deduction. If your total pre-tax income, from all sources, for the year was $220,000 and it was derived as $190,000 earned income and $30,000 interest income, the $190,000 would be taxed at the small business rate (say, 16 per cent) and the remaining $30,000 would show up on line 440 of your T-2 and be taxed at the big business tax rate (say, 48 per cent).

If you live in a jurisdiction that doesn't allow the use of holding companies, it's more difficult to reduce the tax you pay on passive income.

Suppose you're the only shareholder of your professional corporation and your PC has net rental income. When your accountant files your corporate tax return, they will separate the net rental income from your earned income and the two types of income will be taxed at different rates (check the schedule on page 333 to see what the tax rates are in your jurisdiction).

If you are fortunate enough to live in a jurisdiction that allows the use of a holding company, you may be able to reduce the taxable income of the holding company down to zero. This can be accomplished by paying out a management salary equal to the net rental income. Here's how it works.

Suppose you have a PC with earned income of $200,000 and net rental income of $10,000. If you pay out a bonus or salary of $10,000 it will be deducted from the $200,000 and leave the net rental income to be taxed at the higher investment tax rate.

If you had the use of a holding company and the $10,000 net rental income was the only income of the holding company, you could pay out a management salary of $10,000 from the holding company and reduce it's income to zero. In this case, the salary paid to you would be deducted from the net rental income. However, ensure that when you pay out management salaries from a holding company that sufficient work is being carried out to justify the amount being paid. If this is not the case, the CRA can deny the deduction.

Where you live will dictate the opportunities and limitations you have when dealing with passive income. Later in the book we'll look at the different types of passive income and their related tax issues. For now let's leave this section with a heads-up: just because something works in British Columbia doesn't mean it works in Ontario.

Trusts

In general terms, a trust may be defined as an obligation imposed on a person (trustee) to hold and administer property for the benefit of another person (beneficiary). A trust is not a distinct legal entity like a corporation. There are normally three participants in the trust.

The settlor is the person who establishes, or creates, the trust by transferring the property to one or more trustees. The settlor sets out the objectives of the trust and determines the elements of the trust.

The trustee is the person, or persons, to whom the trust property is transferred. The trustee is the legal owner of the trust property and holds and administers it in accordance with the terms of the trust document. Although the trustee has legal title to the trust property, creditors of the trustee cannot claim against the trust property.

The beneficiary is the person, or persons, for whom the benefit of the trust is established. The beneficiary is not the legal owner of the trust property but merely has beneficial ownership. A beneficiary does not necessarily have a direct claim to the trust property, but can require the trustee to carry out the terms of the trust.

A beneficiary can be a capital beneficiary, an income beneficiary, or both. The assets put into trust form part of the capital. Other amounts can be added to the capital depending on the terms and conditions of the trust. This capital can be paid out only to the **capital beneficiary.** The **income beneficiary** is entitled to the income earned by the assets being held in trust. Normally, if all the income is not paid out to the income beneficiary, the net amount is added to the capital of the trust for later distribution.

Suppose your parents decide to give your children $50,000, the normal set-up would be as follows: your parents (the settlors) would put the money into trust with you (the trustee) in control of the funds. The income beneficiaries would be your children and the capital beneficiaries would be your children and you (if your children die before receiving all the trust capital). As the trustee, you would take the money and invest it as allowed by the terms of the trust. You should carefully examine and understand what is allowed in your province or territory, as every jurisdiction in Canada has rules that govern the investment of trust assets.

A trust is created as a result of three certainties.

Certainty of intention. The settlor must use language that clearly indicates an intention to create a trust. It must be clear that the settlor intends that the property be held for the benefit of the beneficiary and not for the absolute benefit of the trustee. Usually, the use of the words "as trustee for" or "in trust" is sufficient to establish a trust. However, these words are not necessarily conclusive of a trust relationship.

Certainty of subject matter. The trust property must be clearly identified. In addition, the interests of the beneficiary in that property must be clearly set out.

Certainty of objects. The objects of the trust, including who the beneficiaries are, should be clear. The beneficiaries should be named, or at least identified as a class (e.g., all my grandchildren).

If any one of these three essential elements is not established, then a trust does not exist.

Types of trusts

There are two basic types of trust: inter vivos trusts and testamentary trusts. An inter vivos trust is created while the donor is still living. It holds property for the benefit of someone else and can be revoked. It is sometimes called a living trust. The person who establishes the inter vivos trust is called the settlor. The trust is usually established by way of a written trust deed or agreement, which is executed, by the settlor and trustee. Testamentary trusts are trusts that arise under the terms of a will and do not take effect until after the death of the grantor.

Under these two general categories of trusts there can be found a number of various forms. Here is a sample of some of the more common types:

- spousal trusts
- family trusts
- spendthrift trusts
- trusts for handicapped persons
- blind trusts
- life insurance trusts

- alter ego trusts (charitable remainder trust)
- bare trust
- health and welfare trust
- immigration trust
- non-resident trust
- real estate investment trust

A trust can be "discretionary" or "non-discretionary." It can also be "revocable" or "irrevocable."

A **discretionary trust** is one in which the power to pay out income or capital of the trust to the beneficiaries is completely within the discretion of the trustee.

A **non-discretionary** trust is normally one that is considered to be not fully discretionary, such as a trust that states that the income must be paid out to the income beneficiary each year.

A **revocable trust** is one in which the settlor reserves the right to terminate the trust or change its terms and recover the trust property.

An **irrevocable trust** cannot be revoked or changed by the settlor after its creation. If a settlor wants to shift the tax liability to a trust or its beneficiaries, then an irrevocable trust must be used.

Taxation of trusts

Inter vivos trusts are taxed at the highest federal tax rate and therefore are taxed at the highest marginal rate. Income is not usually left to be taxed within inter vivos trusts for this reason.

Testamentary trusts are taxed as individuals and are subject to progressive tax rates. You are not allowed a personal exemption but are allowed to deduct trust-related expenses, like accounting fees. Net income is taxed using the normal personal tax brackets.

One has to be aware of the attribution rules when dealing with trusts. The attribution rules simply state that if the trust property has not been given away, then the income from that property is "attributed" back to the settlor.

Kiddie tax

"Kiddie tax" is a term used to describe the tax rule that prevents the transfer of income from high-income individuals to their children under the age of 18. Rather than redirecting income and taxing it in the hands of the high-income family member, the rules provide for a tax on minors who receive income under an income splitting arrangement.

Since 2000, minor children have been taxed at the top federal personal tax rate on dividends or business income received from a family business. Specifically, the tax applies to the following sources of income:

- Taxable dividends received directly by a minor, or indirectly through a trust or partnership. Dividends from publicly traded corporations are excluded.

- Income inclusions required under the *Income Tax Act*, in respect of the ownership by any person of shares of the capital stock of a corporation (shares of a class listed on a prescribed stock exchange are excluded).

- Business income from a partnership or trust, where the income is from property (prior to 2003, this reference was to goods) or services provided to, or in support of, a business carried on by:

  - a person related to the minor, including a relative who is a partner of the partnership earning business income,

  - a corporation where a relative of the minor owns 10 per cent or more of the corporation's shares, or

  - a professional corporation where a relative of the minor is a shareholder.

The "kiddie tax" rules have effectively cut off the tax benefits that were available by using the distribution of dividends from a professional corporation, through an inter vivos trust.

How long can I keep my trust?

Assets held in a trust can be kept there in perpetuity; however, there could be tax consequences if assets are kept in a trust beyond 21 years. Under certain situations, trusts are deemed to have disposed of all their assets at fair-market value on the twenty-first anniversary of the trust. This means that, as far as the CRA is concerned, the assets were all sold and any and all taxes as a result of the sale are due. This can create a very serious problem if the trust has to come up with large amounts of cash to pay taxes. To avoid the 21-year rule, the *Income Tax Act*, in most cases will allow the assets to be distributed by the trustee to one or more of the capital beneficiaries of the trust. This transfer would take place at the tax cost (i.e. cost base) of the assets and will defer the tax.

Depending on the type of trust, there may or may not be a taxable event twenty-one years after the trust is established.

If you have a spousal trust that is holding assets with a cost base of $1,000,000, there is no tax owing on any gains unless the assets are sold or when the spousal beneficiary dies.

If you establish a family trust, the assets of that trust have to be dealt with no later than twenty-one years after the trust was established. Suppose you established the trust in 2010 to hold shares of your professional corporation. At the time the trust was established, it purchased 100 shares of your professional corporation for $0.10 per share ($10.00). If you live in a jurisdiction that allows the trust to hold shares for a spouse, parent or child, the shares will sit in the family trust until 2031 at which time the CRA will force you to make a decision. Do you leave the shares in the family trust, or do you give them outright to one or more of the beneficiaries.

If the shares have increased in value to say $200,010 and you leave them in the trust, the CRA will deem the shares sold, thus triggering a capital gain of $200,000. This would result in a taxable capital gain of $100,000 or about $45,000 of tax owing by the trust.

If you don't want the tax to be triggered you have to remove the shares from the trust and give them outright to one or more of the beneficiaries. If you give all 100 shares to your spouse or divide them amongst the beneficiaries, they would assume the cost base of those shares ($0.10 each) and would not have to pay tax on the gain until the shares are subsequently sold or they die (unless they leave them to their spouse).

The downside of leaving them in the trust is the deemed disposition of the shares, if they've increased in value.

The downside of giving them to the beneficiaries outright is that they would then own them, leaving them exposed to creditors and potentially family property claims.

Certain trusts, like spousal trusts and alter-ego (see glossary) trusts, are not subject to the 21-year rule. In all cases, you should consult a trust lawyer in your jurisdiction to get a complete understanding of the rules relating to trusts.

Probate planning with trusts

One of the many uses of trusts is to reduce or eliminate probate fees by removing assets from the estate. When an asset is placed into trust it is owned by the trust and therefore is not the property of the individual on death. The trust document will normally specify what the distribution of the trust capital will be and therefore not be dealt with in the person's will. All provinces and territories have estate and probate rules and costs; however, these can be eliminated by placing the assets into a trust prior to the death of the individual.

The added benefit of a trust from an estate-planning point of view is that the terms of the trust are not known to anyone other than the trustees and the beneficiaries. This can be very important because probated wills are public information and trusts are not.

The reasons why a will may be probated are too numerous to mention, but suffice it to say that if it is probated, anyone can obtain a copy of your will. The probate documents will not only include a copy of the will itself but also a list of assets and liabilities as well as correspondence between the various parties. The point here is that everyone can look at your personal affairs after you are dead, if your will is probated.

If assets are moved into a trust prior to death, they do not form part of the deceased's estate and therefore are not part of the probate procedure. If all assets are moved into a trust prior to death, there effectively isn't an estate and therefore nothing is subject to probate. And no one will have access to your personal information after death (remember, these are the assets that you are leaving to your family, charity or others).

Let me give you an example. A few years ago I was asked to look at a situation by Randy, whose father had died. Randy and his brother Brian had been running the family business for 10 years. Mom and Dad had started the business 40 years before and had retired. When the father died, his will left his shares of the company to his wife. It also stated that Gail, the office manager who was still working at the company with the sons, was to receive a specified house or a cash bequest of $500,000. Apparently Dad had been having an affair with her and wanted to make provisions for her in his will – not a good idea! The immediate problem was that the specified house had been sold and the estate now owed Gail $500,000 cash (after-tax). The estate didn't have the money and so the wife was forced to pay off Gail personally.

Now, just so that you can really shake your head, the brothers had to get Gail to agree to quit after she got the money, because they couldn't fire her without repercussions.

Of course, all of this was completely preventable had the father received the right advice. If he had set up a trust and put the house he wanted to give Gail into it, it would have never been mentioned in Dad's will. If the house was sold prior to his death, the proceeds could have stayed in the trust and he could have left that to Gail. No one would have been privy to the trust or the house or the money except Dad, his lawyer, and Gail. This family and Gail could have been spared a lot of embarrassment, heartache and headache if Dad had used a trust.

Residency of trusts

One last thought on trusts. It's important to know where the residency of the trust is, so that you can plan properly. Trust assets can be anywhere. They can be a bank account in Whitehorse, or a vacation home in Peggy's Cove. The beneficiaries of the trust might live in Toronto or Vegerville, Alberta. These locations have no bearing on the residency of the trust. The location of the trustee, or the majority of trustees, determines the residency of a trust. The residency of the trust is important because the trust is subject to the tax rates in that jurisdiction, as well as local trust laws.

I have seen countless situations where a trust was established to accomplish good things and only resulted in difficulty and hardship. For example, I was asked to review the wills of some new clients (a husband and wife). They had made provisions for their children, ages two and four, to live with the wife's sister if they both died. The sister lived in Montreal. The trustee of their wills was their 64-year-old lawyer in Prince Rupert, British Columbia. I asked them what they envisioned the situation would look like if their children were living with her sister, and the children's money was under the control of a trustee in northern British Columbia. How difficult would it be for the guardians to access the funds and have a working relationship with the trustee? What would happen if the trustee was not available (he was planning on retiring the following year)? The moral of this story is that you should always try to consider the situation you are creating when you name the trustees of any trust.

Using a trust

Over the years there have been many different set-ups with trusts but the most common ones that I see when dealing with professional corporations are family trusts and spousal trusts.

A family trust is usually set up to hold shares in the professional corporation and has family members as beneficiaries. The purpose of this structure is to allow for income splitting without having your spouse and children as direct shareholders of your professional corporation. Paying dividends on the shares held by the family trust and then subsequently paying those dividends out to the various beneficiaries achieves this. By using a discretionary family trust you can pay out different amounts to each beneficiary.

When you initially set up a family trust you should consider all family members with whom you might want to split income, including, for example, you, your spouse, children, grandchildren, parents, siblings or nieces and nephews. You may not split income with them now but you may want that opportunity in the future. If the trust is constructed in the right way, you may be able to add beneficiaries later; however, this is usually more costly.

Let's look at an example. A husband and wife have two children, aged 16 and 19, who attend school full-time. The professional is drawing a salary of $80,000 and his spouse has a part-time job that pays $20,000 per year. A dividend is declared on the shares of the professional corporation owned by the family trust in the amount of $60,000. Due to the 'kiddie' tax rules, no dividends are distributed to the 16-year-old. The 19-year-old has no income so the trust pays out $25,000 that can be used to pay for school (there is no requirement to use it for school; it can be used for anything the 19-year-old wants because it's his money). There should be little or no tax on this amount if this is his only source of income.

The balance in the trust ($60,000 – $25,000 = $35,000) can be paid out to the spouse. When added to the employment income of $20,000, their total taxable income would be $63,750. This is the calculation: $20,000 + $43,750 ($35,000 + 25 per cent gross-up). This would bring them to the top of the middle tax bracket, thereby effectively splitting income with the higher income spouse. The same income-splitting can take place with other dependents who require your financial assistance.

Another advantage of using a family trust to hold the shares of your professional corporation is that, if properly constructed, no one individual can lay claim to the shares. This can become very important if you want to split income with your children. Normally, if your children own shares directly in your company, these shares can be subject to the child's creditors, including ex-spouses. Having the shares held by a family trust, of which your children are beneficiaries, allows you to split income without this exposure.

A **spousal trust** is one set up for the benefit of your spouse. The difference between this trust and any other trust is that a spousal trust, for tax purposes, works the same way as if the assets were left directly to the spouse and is eligible for the same roll-over provisions.

On death, all assets are deemed disposed of and, as a result, all deferred taxes are due. If you have an eligible spouse at that time who is the beneficiary of your assets, those assets can be transferred on a tax-deferred basis. This same deferral is available to a qualifying spousal trust.

The principle conditions that must be met for a trust to qualify as a spousal trust are:

- all income of the trust must be paid to the spouse during the spouse's lifetime, and
- none of the capital can be distributed to anyone other than the spouse during the spouse's lifetime.

One immediate benefit of these trusts is the continuation of income splitting after death. Most of my clients split income with their spouse. On first death, normally their wills, however, leave all their assets to the surviving spouse. This eliminates the income splitting by giving all the assets directly to the surviving spouse.

As an example, suppose your gross estate value is $1,500,000. On your death this amount is left to your spouse. If they took this money and invested it at 5 per cent it would generate $75,000 in income. This income would be taxed in addition to any other income they might have such as employment income or CPP survivor's benefits.

If you were to leave your estate to your spouse in a spousal trust, this would result in the creation of a testamentary trust that has its own tax brackets. The same money invested inside the trust would be taxed as a separate person (the first $40,970 taxed at the low federal rate of 15 per cent, the next $40,970 taxed at the next federal rate of 22 per cent, the next $45,080 taxed at the next federal rate of 26 per cent and then anything above $127,021 taxed at the highest federal rate of 29 per cent); provincial taxes will also apply. The only real difference between the taxation of a testamentary trust and an individual is that the trust cannot claim personal tax credits.

The surviving spouse's personal income would be taxed separately from the trust income, not in addition to it. This would result in continued income splitting. But, how do you get money out of the trust after it's taxed? That's the best part – tax-free! Capital distributions from a trust are tax-free. Once the trust has paid tax on the income, the after-tax balance becomes capital and can be removed tax-free.

Spousal trusts can also help protect your spouse and your children from future problems. Let's discuss some examples; have you ever known anyone who has been widowed and then subsequently remarried? Have you ever thought about the consequences of that situation? What happens if you leave your estate to your spouse who remarries someone with children and then dies? What happens to your children? What happens if you leave your estate to your spouse who remarries and then subsequently gets divorced?

A spousal trust can help in all these situations. As the settlor of the trust, you can dictate the ultimate distribution of the trust. After your spouse's death, you can indicate that the residual value will be divided among your children, or however else you would like.

If your spouse remarries, he or she still has access to all the income of the trust as well as the capital, as required; however, at the spouse's death you determine the distribution of the balance. It will not form part of your spouse's estate; therefore it will not pass to the new spouse. Furthermore, if your spouse divorces the new partner, the spouse and your children's interests are protected because the trust assets should not form part of the family assets. At the time of writing I am not aware of any cases that allow a spousal trust to be declared a family asset for property division purposes.

Corporate Planning

Corporate planning begins with the decision to incorporate. Once you find out who can be shareholders of your professional corporation you have to decide if and when to introduce a holding company, and or trust. If the only person who can be a shareholder of your professional corporation is you, then you have to decide if you should hire various family members as staff.

If you are fortunate enough to live in a jurisdiction that allows for non-professional shareholders, then I would strongly recommend that you take advantage of this income-splitting opportunity. It may not be in your best interests to have your children as direct shareholders; however, you can have your spouse as a shareholder, or better yet consider putting a family trust in place. Name as many family members as you can, including yourself, and then distribute income as appropriate.

The reason to consider using a family trust instead of allowing your children to be direct shareholders is really to protect you and your children. Let me give you an example of this. I have a client who owns a number of medical laboratories. He was told that if his two children were shareholders of his business, he could pay dividends every year to them and have those dividends taxed in their hands. Furthermore, they would be eligible for the enhanced capital gains deduction if the value of their shares increased and the shares were sold at some time in the future. Lastly, he was told that, from an estate planning point of view, the value of the children's shares would not be included in his, or his wife's, estate values because they belonged to the children. This all made sense, so they set up the company so that he and his wife owned all the voting shares and his two children owned all the non-voting shares. As set out in the rights and restrictions on the shares, the company value was effectively split four ways.

Everything worked well for a number of years. The two children went through university, funded by the dividend payments, and went on to their own careers. They both got married and had children of their own. One day their daughter announced that she was getting a divorce; things weren't good at home and she wanted out. That's all well and good, but what about her shares? Ouch! Dad ended up in court with the unhappy couple arguing about the value of the shares. Eventually he had to buy the shares back and then buy out his ex-son-in-law. Now as fate would have it, his son also ended up getting a divorce. Same story – same ending. Dad had to pay off his ex-daughter-in-law as well.

When I reviewed this situation, it became clear that a family trust would have been such an easy solution. Mom, Dad and the two kids could have all been beneficiaries of the trust, both for capital and income. They could have had all the benefits of the kids owning shares in the company without having them as direct shareholders.

The other area to deal with in corporate planning is developing a corporate investment plan. Because investments in corporations are taxed differently, you should integrate your corporate investment plan into an overall investment plan. As was described earlier, capital losses suffered inside an RRSP do not get tax relief. You shouldn't have risky investments inside your RRSP. You can, however, get tax relief if you suffer a loss inside your professional corporation the same way you can personally.

Working with your financial planner or accountant, figure out what your overall investment strategy should look like. Where should you hold liquid assets like cash and T-bills? Where should you hold bonds and GICs? Where should you hold equities and real estate? Once you've looked at this macro view, you can then set up a micro plan for personal (RRSP and non-RRSP) and corporate investments.

Try to get interest-bearing investments in your RRSP and capital appreciation investments in your non-RRSP and corporate accounts. This should reduce your overall tax liability and allow you to accumulate equity faster.

I'll give you one more example, just to make things clear. Last month I was introduced to a new client; when I got all his information together, I reviewed his corporate investments. He had been incorporated for 16 years and had accumulated a very large investment pool. Initially, I thought he was doing pretty well, that was until I reviewed his T-2 and noticed that he was paying an enormous amount in taxes. I went back to his investment statements and studied them more closely. There I found the root of his high tax bill. His broker had invested the majority of his money in debt. My question was, why does he have interest-bearing investments inside his professional corporation when he is still working? I couldn't figure it out but I do know that his broker couldn't explain it either. The tax liability each year was undermining the efficiency of the investment. If he had been invested in investments that were not subject to tax (at the high rate) each year, he would have probably been able to retire 10 years earlier than he can now.

Setting Up Another Company

> **Rule of thumb buster:** You can't split income through another company if your spouse can't be a shareholder of your professional corporation.
> **Not true.** Often you can set up a separate company through which you can split income.

As a professional, you are allowed to have share ownership in non-professional corporations. This can be helpful in jurisdictions that do not allow non-college or association shareholders. Suppose you are a physician who is paid periodically for things like teaching or lecturing. These activities can be included in the income of your professional corporation, or can be directed to another company because they are not directly related to your practice. By setting up a second company, you can effectively split income with a spouse or other family members because there is no restriction on who owns shares of a non-professional corporation. This income is classified as earned income and therefore eligible for the small business deduction. If you have these or other sources of income, you should check to see if the employing party would be willing to pay your non-professional company instead of you or your professional company. As a dentist, you can direct the revenue derived from hygiene services, x-ray services, and equipment sterilization to a separate company. A proper allocation of income must be made of the services charged to patients and billed by the new company. A similar allocation must be made of the expense incurred in providing these services (such as wages, equipment costs and rent). By using this second company, you can then split income between your spouse, holding company, or family trust. You will incur additional costs associated with having an additional company; however, your accountant can help you to determine if this is a worthwhile income-splitting opportunity.

Agreements

Agreements come in many forms, but I would like to limit my comments to three that are relevant to professional corporations:

- associate agreements
- cost-sharing agreements
- shareholder agreements.

An associate agreement is a legal document between a principal and an associate. These agreements are usually found between dentists. An established dentist will bring on an associate to help take over part of the practice and to help build the overall practice. Often it is the associate that ultimately buys the practice from the principal.

There are many different types of associate arrangements. In some cases, the associate is an employee of the practice, receiving a salary or wage from the owner. In other cases, the associate enters into a contract to perform services for the owner's patients and is compensated on the basis of billings. An associate agreement is very important for both parties in that it can help avoid misunderstanding by having things in writing.

An associate agreement should cover the following points:

- who the parties are
- days and hours of work
- emergencies – who is responsible for emergency patient coverage
- facilities and supplies – who is responsible for providing and maintaining premises, equipment, staff and costs associated with running the practice
- billings, accounting and collection – who is responsible for charging and setting fees, bookkeeping, collection of accounts, defining accounts receivable and what to do about uncollected accounts, and what will happen to accounts receivable in the event of death of the associate
- compensation – how will the income be split, when will it be paid, definitions of 'payment period', 'gross billing', 'net fees', how to deal with family members who have work done, and a review schedule of the compensation

- records – who is responsible for keeping records and how those records will be kept
- income tax, licence fees, insurance – who is responsible for paying these costs
- term of agreement – should state when the agreement starts and when it should be renewed
- termination of agreement – should describe under what circumstances the agreement will terminate and how it will terminate, what will happen to the patients, equipment and other assets of the practice.

A cost-sharing arrangement normally provides for both parties to maintain separate patient lists and charts and bill their own patients. The cost of the facilities, shared equipment and shared staff are divided on an agreed basis. The cost-sharing agreement should describe in detail the respective obligations of the parties who are participating in the cost-sharing arrangement. It should also cover how the arrangement will be terminated if a participant dies, becomes unable to continue to practice due to disability, or wishes to withdraw from the arrangement.

A cost-sharing agreement should cover the following points:

- who the parties are
- that the practices are run separately
- billing for services – who is responsible for billings
- trade style – if the clinic is run under a separate name, that each party has the right to use that name, and if the agreement is terminated which party has the right to the name
- receptionist allocation of patients – that each party agrees to establish a predetermined text to be used by the clinic receptionist in order to enable the patients of the clinic to determine which clinic doctor will provide the services to them
- allocation of new patients – how new patients are distributed between doctors
- hygiene patients (if a dental practice) – how all hygiene patients and revenue is split

- ownership of charts – who owns the clinic's charts and how they will be dealt with if the agreement is terminated
- use of premises – what the lease agreement is, the hours of work, what, if any, additional hours of operation there may be
- common equipment – who has title to the equipment, use of the equipment, and the allocation of individual equipment and individually leased equipment
- employee matters – who is responsible for dealing with employees
- sharing expenses – who is responsible for various expenses including individual expenses like professional fees, liability insurance, education costs, entertainment costs, specialized supplies, malpractice insurance, interest and bank charges as well as any other costs attributed solely to one party; and joint expenses, like equipment fees paid pursuant to the equipment lease agreement, wages, common insurances, expenses that benefit both parties (i.e. buy/sell life insurance, rent, utilities, advertising, receptionist, additional support staff required and supplies)
- right of first refusal – if either party wants to sell, the other has first right of refusal
- miscellaneous provisions, like effective date and term of agreement.

A shareholder agreement (buy/sell agreement) should cover the following points:

- who the parties are
- the procedures and circumstances for issuing more shares
- loans and advances to officers or shareholders
- the declaration of dividends
- the encumbering of assets of the corporation
- hiring of family members
- transfer of shares
- major contracts
- right of first refusal
- what happens when a principal retires
- what happens if a principal becomes insolvent

- what happens if a principal dies
- what happens if a principal becomes disabled
- how to deal with disagreements between principals
- the use of life insurance to fund the agreement
- how to value the shares of the business
- non-competition clauses.

Each of these agreements has a specific purpose and should be designed by your lawyer so that your individual circumstances can be addressed. The more detailed the agreement, the less chance of misunderstanding. It is always easier to discuss these things in advance of any disagreement.

I always tell my clients that these agreements are simply rulebooks. You write the rules out so that if, at some time in the future, you can't reach a consensus about a specific issue, you can refer to it. You can change the rules whenever you like as long as all parties agree. These agreements are designed to deal with situations where agreement can't be easily reached, or where one party cannot represent themselves (for instance due to death or disability).

Before I leave this section I want to make one point. Do not draw up agreements that talk about schedule A or B and then omit a schedule A or B. I see this all the time; references are made in the documents about schedules that are never completed. If you are reviewing your agreement and it makes reference to a schedule, do not sign the agreement until the schedule is complete. That way you can be sure that it gets done.

Divorce and Separation

When my book was first published, I sent a copy of it to the Dean of Dentistry at UBC. His only question was, "Where's the section on divorce?" Well I took this to heart and have added it in this new edition.

His question, of course, was completely valid. The reality is that a high percentage of you will get divorced at least once in your lifetime, so forewarned is forearmed.

To the best of my knowledge, pre-nuptial or cohabitation agreements are valid all across Canada. There are, however, differences so I encourage you to seek legal advice in your own jurisdiction; in all cases I recommend that you get such an agreement long before you need it. I know that sounds strange, as you might think that you can't get such an agreement once you're married, but in fact it is possible to get a post-nuptial agreement.

A pre-nuptial agreement is made prior to marriage and should define:

- ownership in, or division of, any property or business
- support obligations
- the right to direct the education and moral training of children, but not the right to custody of, or access to, them
- any other issues in the settlement of the couple's affairs.

A co-habitation agreement should define the same things, if the parties are living together without the immediate intention to marry.

Before I talk about the emotional aspect of these agreements, I want you to understand a very important point. Regardless of where you live, you should understand the meaning of the word "spouse".

The CRA (Canada Revenue Agency) has its definition of spouse for tax purposes, but each jurisdiction has its own definition of spouse for Family Law purposes, which can be a little different.

There is also another commonplace term that's important to know: "common-law spouse". What defines a common law spouse and what rights, if any, they have depends on where you live.

Before you move in with someone, have a child or get married, it is in everyone's best interest to have a written agreement. If you're just starting out and you have nothing but debt, you may not see the need to have an agreement. Nothing can be further from the truth. If you're 25 years old and have just graduated from medical or dental school, your earning potential to age 65 is in excess of $11.5 million, assuming $250,000 of gross income annually indexed at 2%. Let's face it; you're a walking, talking, winning lottery ticket!

Now, I've heard all the arguments about pre-nuptial agreements being unromantic. I don't believe that's the case. If you're going to be in a relationship with someone, you should be able to sit down together and have a forthright discussion about your financial plans and expectations. Love is a beautiful thing but it will only take you so far. Like it or not, money is a major factor in everyone's lives. If you can't talk about money with your partner before you get married or move in together, how do you expect to talk about it after the fact?

Here's the way I look at a pre-nuptial or cohabitation agreement (and yes I do have one myself); it's a rulebook that gets pulled out when all else fails. In other words, if you have a successful relationship with someone, you're never going to use it. However, if you're relationship fails and you can't agree on the terms, that agreement can save both you and your partner a lot of time, pain and money.

I have an equal number of male and female physicians and dentists as clients. This means I have male clients paying female ex-partners and female clients paying male ex-partners. I have females raising kids and males raising kids. So, gender is also irrelevant to the issue of whether you should have an agreement.

In preparation for a discussion on these types of agreements, be clear about the following: that if you have an agreement and nothing happens (your relationship is successful) then the agreement is irrelevant; if you have an agreement and your relationship doesn't succeed, and both of you want to alter the terms of the agreement, you can. The agreement only comes into force when your relationship fails and you're not talking. Then you pull out the agreement, abide by what it says, and get on with your life.

If you, or your spouse, are still unconvinced about the value or importance of a pre-nuptial, ask someone you know who's divorced if they had an agreement in place when their relationship hit the rocks. Now here's the interesting thing - if you're talking to a professional who did have a pre-nuptial in place, they undoubtedly will tell you that they were relieved to have it in place. On the other hand if you're talking to the spouse of the professional, they may say they wish there had been no pre-nuptial agreement in place. As a professional, which camp would you want to be in?

I saw this recently on a law firm's website and I think sums it up well, "… it is when the parties are still enamoured of each other that generosity and fairness will most likely be felt. It is, in fact, the best time to negotiate a fair agreement on how the relationship might end. Each party will know where they will stand in the event that the relationship terminates."

The way to look at these agreements is that they are really inexpensive insurance – that could save you millions!

Let me give you a real life example. About fifteen years ago I was meeting a young couple for the first time. I asked them if they had a pre-nuptial agreement and they politely smiled and said no, they didn't need one.

The next day I had to stop by the clinic to pick up some information. When I saw the doctor he asked me, based on what I knew from our meeting the night before, if they were they in good financial shape.

I'm often asked that by clients, "How are we doing in relation to other people our age?" My answer to that specific question isn't relevant because keeping up with the Joneses shouldn't be the objective. The relevant questions are: how are you doing in relationship to your current and future needs; how's your cash flow; how's your debt load; what's your tax position; what's your current non-work income; and finally, what unnecessary or excess costs are you paying?

I told the doctor that, based on what I knew, I thought they'd be fine. I said the only thing that could derail them would be something unforeseen. "Like what?" he asked. "You mean like a death?" I told him that that he appeared to have sufficient insurance for that, but that I was thinking more along the lines of a divorce.

The last thing I said to him that day was, "Being financially successful is really quite easy, just never get divorced".

A few years later the good doctor's marriage ended and his wife took the customary half his assets with her (plus a little more for good measure). Now every time we meet he recites my now famous words – "Never get divorced".

If you get married and everything works out, that's wonderful. You will always be together and you will willingly contribute or take care of your loved one financially. However, in the event of a marital breakdown, and in the absence of a pre-nuptial agreement, you could end up financially supporting someone you no longer love for the rest of your (or their) life.

Well, sometimes you don't have a choice about divorce, but you certainly do have a choice to get a pre-nuptial agreement. As I said earlier, I have a pre-nuptial agreement and my wife and I are totally in love. Would I give it up? No, and neither would she. Why? Because we know we don't need it.

If after reading this section, you go out and get a pre-nuptial, or even post-nuptial agreement and later get divorced, remember to send me a thank you card!

Why Would I Need A Buy/Sell Or Shareholder Agreement?

One of the most disturbing situations I have ever come across happened in a dental clinic. There were three dentists sharing space and some common costs, but they were running separate and distinct practices. One day they were approached by a life insurance agent who suggested that they should insure one another in case one of them died. The idea was that if one of them predeceased the others, the survivors would have the funds to buy the deceased dentist's practice. Taking this advice, they personally insured each other and the years passed. When one of them eventually died, the two surviving dentists collected the proceeds and waited. When the widow showed up to discuss the transfer of the practice, they informed her that she could do whatever she wanted with the practice, but they were going to keep the money. She tried a few times to sell the practice but each time the prospective purchaser was shunned by the two remaining partners. Last time I checked the case was still in litigation. The problem was created because they failed to get an agreement that legally bound them to use the insurance proceeds to purchase the practice. Remember: wills are wish lists; buy/sell agreements are contracts.

Not everyone needs an agreement but most could use one. If your practice has no value, it won't be sold. However, you may want an agreement simply to provide continuity of service for your patients.

Most business people perceive a buy/sell agreement to be between partners or associates. You may want to set up an agreement with a peer who may or may not work with you. A typical agreement could be one that provides coverage in case of disability. One example that comes to mind was an agreement set up by six dentists. The agreement read that if one of them became disabled, the remaining five would each spend one day a week covering the practice of the disabled member. The disabled member's practice would be open four days a week, which allowed for one dentist to be off each week.

Another agreement was set up between two physicians who worked in the same area of town. Instead of leaving it to family members to deal with their respective practices in case of death, they decided to enter into a buy/sell agreement. The agreement stated that if one physician predeceased the other, the surviving physician would purchase the practice of the deceased from the estate. The agreement was funded by life insurance that cost them about $30.00 per month. This is inexpensive insurance to take care of such a difficult situation.

Owning Your Own Building

Owning your own building is an individual choice. You need to look at it both from an investment perspective and also from a "headache" perspective. Once you've decided that you want to own your own building, you can decide whether you are going to own it personally or corporately. There is also an issue of liability to be considered. I believe one important factor is whether you will be able to sell the building independent of your practice. Owning your own building should be looked at in the context of your overall financial plan. Being totally invested in real estate is probably no better than being totally invested in stocks or bonds. Diversification is still important.

Pros	Cons
build up equity over time	fluctuation in real estate prices
paying "rent" to yourself	maintenance and upkeep
control of rent	liquidity – what happens if you can't sell it or rent it out at retirement
access to enhanced capital gains deduction	liability issues

I have a client who used to own his own building. He had a medical practice and decided that he was tired of paying rent. He was sharing office space with another physician and the two of them agreed to buy a building to house their practices. Things worked well for a number of years until one of them decided to expand. There wasn't enough room in the current building, so my client approached his partner and asked if he would be interested in expanding the building. The answer was no, so my client decided that he would move. He asked his partner if he would buy out his interest in the building. Once again the answer was no, so my client decided to find someone else to buy his interest in the building.

It was very difficult to find someone who wanted to buy half of a medical building. Furthermore, that person had to be acceptable to the remaining physician. The process took months, and even though he eventually found someone, he barely got his money back. This situation resulted primarily from the lack of a written agreement and owning a single-use building. If the two partners had signed the agreement I had recommended when they purchased the building, there would have been a mechanism in place if one of them wanted to get out. Moreover, if the only use for your space is a medical or dental practice, it reduces your options significantly. If you own a building that has a number of different tenants, or you own a building that is part commercial and part residential, you can always rent out the space you vacate and hold the property as an investment.

Accumulation Of Equity

The greatest benefit of a professional corporation is the ability to rapidly accumulate equity. Because you have significantly more after-tax money inside a professional corporation than you would if you took everything in personal income, you can pay off debt and accumulate assets faster.

For instance, if you are a dentist in Ontario who is not incorporated and you purchase a practice for $500,000, you have to earn $932,835 to pay off the debt (assuming a top marginal personal tax rate of 46.4 per cent). If we look at the same dentist with the same practice and the same loan who is now incorporated, he will only have to earn $610,500 to pay off the debt (assuming a corporate tax rate of 18.1 per cent). This difference represents a 74.47 per cent savings. The extra $322,335 he didn't use to pay off the loan can now be used to accumulate even more equity.

This same principle applies to investment loans. Suppose you borrowed $250,000 to invest. The interest on the loan would be deductible, but the principle would have to be paid back with after-tax dollars. Regardless of whether the loan is personal or corporate, the interest is deductible; however, the amount required to repay the loan is vastly different. It would take $466,417 of personal earnings to repay the loan, whereas it would take $305,250 of corporate earnings (assuming the same tax rates used in the example above). I normally recommend aggressively paying off the practice debt of the company before starting an investment program. After the practice is paid off, then you can look at investing.

When deciding on investments, tax is a consideration. Consider the following example.

Suppose you have a $25,000 investment earning 8 per cent; now look at the difference between not having to pay accrual tax and having to pay it at 48 per cent.

Year	At 8 per cent	After accrual tax 48 per cent
1	$25,000	$25,000
5	36,733	30,651
10	53,973	37,579
15	79,304	46,073
20	116, 523	56,488
25	171,211	69,257
30	252,566	84,911
35	369,633	104,105
40	543,112	127,637

After 20 years you have twice as much money available because you haven't been sending money to Ottawa each year. After 40 years you have almost four times as much. Imagine what these numbers would look like if you added $25,000 per year to your investment pool. Remember, this example shows a one-time $25,000 investment only. When you add this deferral of taxes to the previous example of cost savings on debt repayments, you can see how professional corporations offer an exceptional opportunity for rapidly accumulating equity.

Charitable Donations: Personal Or Corporate?

I'm often asked if it's better to make donations personally or through the corporation. What I normally tell people is that their income and the amount they want to donate will dictate which way is better. Clearly, if you're in the low tax bracket (your taxable income is below $40,970) and you want to donate $5,000, you are better to do it personally. That's right, I did say personally. The reason is in the difference between the way that individuals are taxed and the way that corporations are taxed. Charitable donations made personally are converted to tax credits. The federal tax credit on the first $200 is 15 per cent, which is the federal tax rate in the low tax bracket. Donations above $200 are converted to tax credits at a rate of 29 per cent. This is the federal tax rate at the top bracket. If your income is in the low bracket and you are getting tax credits in the high bracket, you are saving money.

Donations made from a corporation are not converted to tax credits but are simply deductions. If you make a corporate donation you simply write it off.

A $5,000 corporate donation would save the company about $900 (assuming small business tax rates) in income tax.

If the same $5,000 were donated personally, the federal tax credits would be 15 per cent on the first $200 and 29 per cent on the next $4,800. That would give you a $1,422 federal tax credit. If you lived in Manitoba and your taxable income was $60,000, the total tax saving would be $2,279 (when you add the provincial tax reduction).

Another consideration is whether the donation is going to a registered charity or a non-registered organization. Suppose you wanted to make a donation to the Canadian Red Cross. It is a registered charity and will issue you a tax receipt for your contribution. Each charity registered with the CRA is assigned a charitable registration number. When the charity issues a receipt it should have that registration number on it. If you are concerned that a charity is not legitimate you can contact your local CRA office and have them check. Not all charities are registered. If it's not a registered charity, you cannot write off the contribution as a charitable donation. However, with a professional corporation you have options. You can make a contribution to a charity or you can make a promotional donation in support of an organization. As a professional corporation you are allowed to promote your business. If you want to support a local baseball team you can do so as a promotional expense. If you want to make a donation to the Canadian Olympic team you can do that. One is a promotional expense and the other is a charitable donation but both can be written off in the same way. One more thing to consider is that promotional expenses are not personally deductible.

The last issue is one of money. If you want to make a donation personally you have to have the money. If you have to take the money out of your professional corporation, it's going to have to come out as salary or dividends. If it comes out as salary you have to worry about source deductions. If it comes out as a dividend you should be fine.

Registered Retirement Savings Plans – Other Uses

Using Your RRSP To Fund Your Education

The CRA allows you to finance your education through the Lifelong Learning Plan (LLP). The program allows you to withdraw funds from your RRSP to finance education or training for you or your spouse. You can withdraw funds under the LLP for up to four years as long as you qualify for the LLP each year. The maximum you can withdraw in one year is $10,000, and the maximum you can withdraw over the life of your program is $20,000. Furthermore, funds from the LLP must be repaid to your RRSP over a period of no more than 10 years.

Certain conditions must exist before you can withdraw RRSP funds under the LLP. For instance, you can withdraw funds only from RRSPs in which you are the annuitant, and when you withdraw funds using the LLP you have to be a resident of Canada. Furthermore, the LLP does not allow you to withdraw funds from plans that are considered inaccessible (such as locked-in RRSPs).

Before you withdraw funds from your RRSP under the LLP, one of the following conditions must apply:

- The LLP student must be enrolled in a qualifying program at a designated educational institution.
- The LLP student must have received a written offer to enrol before March of the following year in a qualifying educational program at a designated educational institution.

In order for an educational program to qualify under the LLP, the student must spend at least 10 hours a week on courses, or course work, in the program for at least three consecutive months. Designated educational institutes include universities, colleges, and other educational institutes that qualify for the education tax credit. Enrolment must be on a full-time basis unless the student meets one of the disability conditions.

To repay the LLP, an RRSP contribution must be made to an RRSP in which you are the annuitant. Contributions to a spousal RRSP are not considered repayments to the LLP. The minimum repayment is a tenth of the total amount withdrawn, and the first payment is 60 days after the following year your payment period begins. Your repayment begins (whichever is the earlier):

- the second year after the last LLP student was entitled to claim the education amount on line 323 of the students tax return, or
- the fifth year after your first withdrawal under the LLP.

Once you begin repaying the LLP, you can no longer make further withdrawals. Furthermore, you must file a tax return every year until you have either repaid all your LLP withdrawals or included them in your income.

There are many benefits to using the LLP. If you do not have any other sources of income to fund your education, then it may be appropriate to use the LLP. You should, however, consider the opportunity cost outlined in the following example. You withdraw $20,000 over the next two years to pay for a specialty program that ends in 2010. You are allowed to claim a tax deduction in 2010 so your repayment year begins in 2012. You then decide to repay your LLP over the next 10 years.

At a rate of 6 per cent, once you have repaid your LLP, the original $20,000 that you borrowed and paid back would be worth just over $26,000. If you never used the LLP, your $20,000 could have grown in an RRSP for over 14 years. If you had left $20,000 in a RRSP to accumulate at 6 per cent you would have $45,000 in 14 years. If you remove the $20,000 and use it for four years you will be required to pay it back over the next 10 years at a rate of $2,000 a year. In this case, you wouldn't have earned anything on your $20,000 for four years. Then, you will only earn (for example) 6 per cent on the money you put back, starting in year five. After putting back the $20,000 over 10 years you would have about $26,000 in your RRSP once it's paid back at the end of year 14.

Using the LLP in this example cost you about $19,000 over 14 years. However, the education you completed and the opportunities you now have may outweigh that cost. Before considering the LLP, be sure that the benefit potential of using the program outweighs the cost.

RRSP Home Buyer's Plan

The RRSP Home Buyer's Plan allows participants to withdraw $25,000 from their RRSP to purchase or build a house. No income tax is deducted from these funds, as long as they are repaid to an RRSP according to the government repayment schedule. You may participate in the plan if you (or your spouse) have not owned a home that you occupied as your principal place of residence in any of the past five calendar years. Generally, you can only participate in the RRSP Home Buyers' Plan once.

Once you enter into an agreement to buy, or build, a qualifying home, you may withdraw funds from your RRSPs under the plan. You must acquire the home before October of the year following the year of withdrawal. Under certain circumstances you may be granted an additional year to acquire a qualifying home. To do this you must complete a form that is then submitted to your RRSP issuer.

Once approved, the form gives you permission to withdraw funds from your RRSP with no taxes being withheld. You may withdraw money from multiple plans as long as you do not exceed the overall $25,000 limit. If you have a spouse who is also eligible, you can each withdraw up to $25,000 towards the down payment, for a total of $50,000. You may withdraw money from your RRSP tax-free if that money was deposited at least 90 days prior to withdrawal.

To participate in the plan, you must enter into an agreement to purchase or construct a home, which falls into the following categories:

- It is located in Canada.
- It was acquired not more than 30 days before receiving the withdrawal under the RRSP Home Buyer's Plan.
- It is intended to be occupied as a principal residence within one year after buying or building it.

Both existing and newly built homes are eligible (this includes detached or semi-detached homes, townhouses, condominiums, mobile homes or apartments in a duplex, triplex, fourplex or apartment building. Shares in co-operative housing corporations also qualify).

The money you withdraw from your RRSP must be repaid over a period of not more than 15 years to retain your tax-deferred status. If you choose to pay less than your scheduled annual payment, the amount that you don't repay must be reported as income on your tax return for that year.

Let's say, in October 2010, you withdraw $15,000 from your RRSP to finance the purchase of your home. Your annual repayment for 2012 is $1,000 ($15,000 divided by 15 years) and is due by December 31, 2012.

If you decide to repay only $800 to your RRSP in 2012, then the $200 shortfall from your scheduled annual repayment of $1,000 will be included in your income for 2012. Your outstanding balance will still be reduced by $1,000 from $15,000 to $14,000 and your scheduled annual repayment for 2013 will again be $1,000 ($14,000 divided by 14 years).

Your RRSP repayments have to be made on or before December 31 of each year. The repayment period begins the second year following the year in which the withdrawal is made. These repayments do not have to be made to the same RRSP from which you withdrew the funds.

You do not receive a second tax break when you make an annual payment. So, you must inform your RRSP issuer that it is not a regular contribution and complete an RRSP repayment form.

If you have RRSPs and have not owned a home in the last five years, this may be an alternative way for you to purchase a home without pulling the down payment out of your professional corporation.

When you've taken a Home Buyer's Loan from your RRSP, you are responsible for remembering to ensure the loan gets repaid, or to include the equivalent amount of income when filing your tax return.

When you're repaying your loan, it has no effect on your current year's contribution limit and you can repay it in full whenever you want. There is no special form to complete, or indication that it's a loan repayment. What happens is that when you are doing your personal tax return you have to indicate how much of your current RRSP deposits should be credited toward the Home Buyer's Loan.

If you and your spouse both took $25,000 from your RRSP and either of you are in the low tax bracket then you should probably just take the $1,666.66 ($25,000 / 15 years) into income.

Registered Disability Savings Plans

A Registered Disability Savings Plan (RDSP) was introduced to help those with disabilities, and their families, save for the future. A Canadian resident who is under age 60 and eligible for the Disability Tax Credit is eligible for an RDSP. Earnings accumulate tax-free until the beneficiary takes money out of their RDSP. Parents or guardians may open an RDSP for a minor. With written permission from the holder, anyone can contribute to the RDSP.

Like the RESP, the RDSP has a grant program. Through the Canada Disability Savings Grant, the Government deposits money into a RDSP. The Government provides matching grants of up to 300%, depending on the amount contributed, and the beneficiary's family income. The maximum grant is $3,500 each year, with a lifetime limit of $70,000.

If you have a child or spouse who is eligible for the Disability Tax Credit you should look into the RDSP. More information can be obtained from the CRA, just Google the term 'Registered Disability Savings Plans'.

What Can You Source Deduct From Your Taxes Automatically?

Some clinics make a group RRSP available for their employees. A typical arrangement requires employees to make a minimum contribution to a RRSP in their name through a group RRSP program (for example, 3 per cent of gross salary). This is deducted by their employer from their regular payroll and remitted directly to the fund manager. This also permits the employee to immediately receive a tax benefit for the amount of the deduction, reducing the source deductions taken from the paycheque. The employer can then match the employee's contributions, to a maximum percentage (e.g., 3 per cent of gross pay). The employer gets an immediate tax deduction as an expense, and the taxable benefit to the employee is tax-deferred because it counts as an RRSP contribution. The group RRSP is administered and managed through a trustee (a bank, insurance company or mutual fund company, for example). Some plans provide that the employer contributions are "locked-in" for a minimum period of time to give a retirement planning element to the program. This kind of arrangement can be a win-win for the employer and the employee, and can allow smaller practices an opportunity to provide a retirement plan.

One of the main differences between a group RRSP and a pension is that the employer contributions to a group RRSP are optional. However, even without employer contributions, a group RRSP can be a great benefit for employees. Consider the following example. If an employee is earning $36,000 per year (living in Manitoba) and wants to purchase an RRSP, they would normally have to use after-tax money. Their employer would deduct the taxes from the wage and then they would use this after-tax money to purchase their RRSP. After deductions they would have about $28,500 available for living expenses. Suppose their annual living expenses were $27,900. That would mean that they would have $600 left to make an RRSP contribution. The estimated refund from their RRSP contribution would be about $222. If they participated in a source-deducted group RRSP program (their contributions automatically taken off their paycheques), they could afford to contribute about $1,000 to their RRSP with no significant change to their take-home pay. This is the result of using pre-tax income to purchase the RRSP. Now, granted, the employee wouldn't get a tax refund and they would still have to make CPP contributions on the $1,000, but they are still further ahead because they have an extra $400 in their RRSP.

Tax Free Savings Accounts

When you have a professional corporation, you have more choices than a normal salaried employee. You can choose to take money out, or you can choose to leave it in. This is the same with all corporations.

A tax-free savings account allows an individual to take after-tax money and invest it on a tax-free basis. That is to say that any income or gain made on those investments is tax free when removed. For example, if you earn $500 in interest you don't have to declare it, or if you had a $10,000 capital gain, you pay no tax on that gain. Sounds great, and it is if you have money sitting around outside your professional corporation or RRSP.

But what if you don't? What if you have to take the money out of your professional corporation in order to put the money into your Tax Free Savings Account (TFSA)?

Regardless of whether you remove the money from your professional corporation as an extra wage or as a dividend, the overall tax rate is the same (the taxes you would pay personally as an extra wage would equal the combined taxes you and the company would pay if you took it out as a dividend).

Assuming a tax rate of 46.41 per cent you would have to take $9,330.09 from your professional corporation to net $5,000.

Instead of taking $9,330.09 as an extra wage to put $5,000 into your TFSA, why not leave it in the company and invest it? If your professional corporation were in Ontario, for instance, this would leave you with $7,837.27 (Ontario corporate tax in 2010 is 16 per cent).

You can fool around with the calculations but I'm sure you'll find that investing $7,837.27 per year is better than investing $5,000 per year even when you take the ultimate tax liability of the corporate investment into account. Remember eligible dividends?

Family Education

There are a number of ways to finance your family's education. You can set up a family trust, pay your children wages, or loan them money. If you are in a jurisdiction that allows a trust to own shares of your professional corporation, this can be a preferred method of funding educational expenses. There is no limit to the amount of money that can be paid out, and the dividend amount does not have to be justified. The only caution here is that the child must be at least the age of majority in the year you start paying dividends out.

If you decide to pay your children wages, make sure that there is some relationship between what you are paying them and the job they are performing. I remember a situation where a company was paying a wage of $42,000 per year to a child of the owner of the company. What's wrong with that? Nothing by itself, except that the child was going to school in Montreal, the company was in Vancouver, the child hadn't set foot in British Columbia in three years, and the company was a dental office.

The third option is loan your kids money (as was described on page 191). If you can't have additional shareholders in your professional corporation, this may be a very viable alternative. Loan your adult children money for school from your professional corporation and have it ultimately taxed in their hands when they don't pay it back.

Registered Education Savings Plans

Like other government programs, Registered Education Savings Plans (RESP) have benefits and shortcomings. As with most financial products the focus is usually on the benefits and not on the shortcomings or any alternatives. Before looking at the shortcomings and alternatives, let's take a look at what the common stated benefits are:

- Tax deferred income: the income from (non-deductible) contributions made to an RESP plan are not subject to tax as earned (this, of course, assumes that you actually earn income, which has been a challenge for a lot of people over the last two years).

- Income splitting: amounts paid out of an RESP are taxed in the hands of the beneficiary who are usually in a lower tax bracket than the contributor.

- Canada Education Savings Grant: the federal government provides a grant covering a specific amount each year to a lifetime maximum.

The basics of the RESP program are:

The total RESP lifetime contribution limit for each child named in one or more RESPs is $50,000. Part-time students are also eligible for RESP assistance.

Although there are no annual limits on contributions made to an RESP, the Canada Education Savings Grant will only be paid on the first $2,500 of contributions made every year. If the child has accumulated grant room, then the Canada Education Savings Grant will be paid on the first $5,000 of contributions made per year. The lifetime maximum Canada Education Savings Grant is $7,200.

If you have a child and want to contribute to an RESP, you have to take money out of your professional corporation to invest. This will result in paying additional tax now, in order to gain a potential benefit later. It also restricts you in that if one or more on your children doesn't attend post secondary school the benefits are all but eliminated.

As the owner of a business (your professional corporation) you can use a number of alternative strategies, rather than investing in a RESP, to fund your children's education, in most cases far more cost-effectively.

From the moment your children can push a broom you are allowed to pay them to work for your company, as long as you are paying them fair market value for their work. In this case, fair market value for wages is defined as the amount you would pay a stranger to do the same job.

You can also give them dividends, as long as they are shareholders or beneficiaries of your family trust and are over the age of 17.

Or, you can give them shareholder loans as I detailed on page 188.

There are a lot more rules and regulations involved with RESPs, but this should give you an idea of a few alternative ways to fund your child's education. In my second book *The Financial Navigator* A Professional Guide to Keeping More of What you Earn, I go into greater detail about RESPs and alternative education funding.

Tax Shelters And Off-Shore Investing

Over the years I have been asked to review hundreds of tax shelters and investment opportunities that have been presented to my clients. On many of these occasions I was asked to review these prospectuses after they had been purchased. A common selling feature of these investments is that they are RRSP-eligible and that you can use your existing RRSP to purchase these investments. In many cases the additional carrot is a tax credit for investing in venture capital.

I recently reviewed a prospectus for a winery. They were offering investors an opportunity to purchase debentures, which paid 10 per cent interest for 18 months and were then converted to preferred shares. The deal included a 30 per cent tax credit on your investment. The debentures were being sold in $25,000 units and could be purchased using RRSPs. The prospectus went on to state that there was no immediate market for the preferred shares and that the company had no intention of going public, and that there was no guaranteed dividend rate on those shares.

This investment was definitely suffering from a liquidity issue. How do you sell your investment in the future and get your money out? I'm currently dealing with a number of situations where individuals have purchased investments like this inside their RRSPs.

On paper the investment is worth, say, $25,000 because that's what you paid for it, but what happens when you are age 71 and you have to convert these investments into a RRIF or annuity? How do you get income from a non-liquid investment? The CRA says you have to take a percentage of your RRIF each year starting at age 72. If the amount required is 5 per cent, how do you get 5 per cent out when you have no way of selling your units? These situations can cause enormous problems for people, and I have yet to see this problem resolved.

These tax shelters and investment opportunities come in many forms. I remember a real estate tax shelter in which individuals were told they could invest in a development project in Arizona. The actual cost would be very minimal because of the tax savings generated by leveraging – the projects were totally funded with borrowed money – and write-offs, including CCA[32] and maintenance. There would be a net loss each year for the first 10 years; therefore you would save on taxes. They were told that the only thing they had to do was sign a personal guarantee for the amount being borrowed. These tax shelters were being sold in $50,000 US units. The investors were also told that the idea was to sell the real estate in 10 years and everyone would make a lot of money because real estate prices would certainly go up in 10 years.

As it turned out, the real estate development itself was never fully occupied. As a matter of fact, the occupancy rate never got above 60 per cent. The management costs were higher than projected and interest rates increased more often over the 10 years than decreased. All these factors resulted in the guarantees being called in. Investors had to put in money and were unable to sell their units. Eventually an offer was made by the initial developer to take the units off the hands of the investors for 10 per cent of their face amount. Many took the offer just to get out of it with something.

Another example that comes to mind is an ice cream company that had a recipe for low-fat ice cream and was looking for investors. The promoter of this tax shelter convinced a number of individuals to take advantage of this

---

32 Capital Cost Allowance (see glossary)

opportunity by transferring their existing RRSPs to this investment. They were given shares in the company and issued tax receipts for deductions created by the set-up costs. I saw at least one case of an individual who moved an entire RRSP portfolio into this investment.

After about two years the company went bankrupt. Every investor who put money into the venture lost, but the biggest losers were the ones who used their RRSPs. Not only were they not allowed to write off the loss, but as it turned out, the CRA re-assessed every one of them and notified them that the investment they had made in the ice cream company was not an eligible RRSP investment (as was defined by the rules at that time). Income tax was due on what the CRA was deeming a de-registration of their RRSPs. Last time I checked there was still correspondence going back and forth between the CRA and a lawyer the investors hired.

My advice is keep these illiquid investments out of your RRSP. As was mentioned earlier, if you lose your money on this type of investment outside of your RRSP, at least you can write it off as a loss. Not so from inside your RRSP. Always examine these investment opportunities on their investment merits first, not their "tax advantages."

A client once told me that it was a good deal because they got a 30 per cent tax credit. So what? If you are going to lose your money anyway, does it really matter? Why do you have to lose anything? If the investment is no good, avoid it! My advice to clients is that you've worked hard to make a dollar, invest it in such a way that you should make a profit, or at least break even.

The CRA has done quite a thorough job of catching the income, or capital gains, from just about every kind of offshore or foreign investment that Canadian residents can get involved in. Taxes are either applied as gains are made, or they are applied when an investment is realized, with taxes being calculated back over the period of the investment and compounded forward to the time of payment.

Almost all foreign source income held in straightforward individual ownership is taxed under the FAPI rules (Foreign Accrual Property Income), and it is normal for income to be taxed as it arises and not when distributed. It's evident that any increased returns that may be possible from offshore investments may be eaten away by greater costs of capital, and possibly by higher tax rates. Canadians therefore have to be very careful before making offshore investments.

Although Canadian citizens may still choose to set up offshore trusts, the rationale will be asset protection rather than tax minimization. Trusts are caught by the legislation as much as other types of investment structure, and should be considered as tax-neutral at best.

As far as investment income is concerned, international tax planning for Canadian residents is therefore concerned with providing investment structures that are fiscally transparent, so that the gains from higher-yielding international or offshore investments can be taxed in the investor's hands on the same basis as domestic investments. Other than for mutual fund investments, this usually means employing limited partnership or limited liability company structures, which are provided by many offshore jurisdictions, and are usually un-taxed in the offshore jurisdiction, and treated as fiscally transparent by the CRA.

Offshore trusts are not much use for permanent Canadian residents (the funds invested off shore must be after-tax and the annual income must be declared). There have been a number of situations where individuals have set up off shore accounts only to find the tax haven they've chosen isn't a tax haven any longer. In 2009 the IRS was successful in forcing the Swiss Banking giant UBS to provide them the names of up to 4,450 individuals who had accounts and were suspected of using Switzerland's vaunted banking secrecy rules to avoid paying billions of dollars in US taxes.

Rewarding Employees – Profit Sharing Plans

Employers use profit sharing plans as a way of rewarding good performance by their employees and to instill a sense of partnership with them, which will lead to increased profits. Although these plans are rarely seen in professional corporations, they provide you with another way of rewarding your staff. As a limited company, you have the same access to these plans as other corporations.

The four types of profit sharing plans are: the cash profit sharing plan; the employee profit sharing plan; the deferred profit sharing plan; and the registered profit sharing pension plan. The plans vary from immediate compensation and taxation to having both compensation and taxation deferred until the monies are withdrawn.

Cash or current distribution profit sharing plans are designed to provide periodic cash distribution to plan members based on the profits of the employer. The employer determines the distribution schedule. As the distribution is made periodically rather than held until the participant leaves employment, this plan is a form of direct compensation. This is the simplest form of a profit sharing plan. It does not require registration with the CRA, as all profit sharing payments are made directly to the employee in cash. Taxation is not deferred and occurs in the year that these monies are paid.

Like all profit sharing plans, the payment of these monies is linked to the services provided by employees in their daily work that assist the company in earning profits. As their share of the profits arise from the performance of services, these earnings will be allocated to the week or weeks in which the services were performed.

Employee Profit Sharing Plans

In employee profit sharing plans (EPSPs), a share of the profits each year is placed in a trust fund and is allocated to participating employees along with their share of the accumulated interest in the fund for that year. The allocation may be in proportion to the employee's earnings, length of service, or some other formula.

These monies generally remain in the trust account until the participant's employment is terminated; however, some plans may allow cash withdrawals by the employee while still employed. Employees may also make contributions to this fund, although these contributions are not tax deductible.

Vesting[33] of the EPSP contributions can vary from immediate to vesting only on death, termination of employment or retirement. In cases where vesting is not immediate, cash withdrawals cannot be made while employed, as the employee has no right to these payments.

---

33 Non-forfeitable ownership (or partial ownership) by an employee of the retirement account balance, or benefits, contributed on the employee's behalf by an employer.

Although a participant may not normally receive a distribution from this trust fund until retirement or until employment is terminated, the employee is taxed each year on his or her share of the profits, the interest accruing in the trust, and any realized capital gains, as if he or she was in immediate receipt of such money. There is no income tax payable on any employee contributions made to this fund as these monies come from the employee's after-tax income.

These monies are earnings that arise out of employment. However, these earnings are not considered payable until the actual distribution of them is made to the employee. Like all profit sharing plans, the payment of these earnings is linked to the services provided by the employees in their daily work that assists the company in earning the profits. These earnings will be allocated to the week or weeks in which the services were performed, because the share in the profits arose from the performance of services. If the amount of the interest is known, this amount is deducted.

Employer (sponsor) advantages:

- control over plan design – the plan sponsor retains control and flexibility over eligibility and vesting requirements as well as contribution levels
- hassle-free administration – less time spent on daily plan administration compared to a pension plan arrangement; less time and fewer regulatory requirements mean lower costs
- reduced government reporting – an EPSP does not need to be registered with the CRA; the EPSP trust is, however, subject to annual income tax reporting
- tax deduction – plan sponsor contributions and any administration expenses are tax deductible.

Employee (member) advantages:

- plan sponsor contributions – members benefit from value added plan sponsor contributions
- dollar cost averaging – regular deposits of a fixed dollar amount over a prolonged period of time reduce investment risk by averaging out the purchase price of investments

- flexibility at termination and retirement – no locking-in rules apply; various options are available to members at employment termination and retirement.

In a deferred profit sharing plan (DPSP), the employer allocates a share of the profits to all participating employees each year and places it in a trust account. These monies remain in the trust account until the participant's employment is terminated. Employee contributions to these plans are no longer allowed except for direct transfers from other registered tax-assisted plans.

Taxation of the employee's share of the profits and the interest accrued in the trust fund is deferred until the employee is in receipt of these monies. These plans are registered with the CRA, and are subject to greater regulation and control than EPSPs. To qualify for registration, the DPSP must:

- provide for full vesting within two years, or immediately at retirement on account of age or disability
- define a normal retirement age, with annuity or instalment payments to begin no later than age 71
- follow strict investment rules comparable to those for pension plans; and
- provide for significant employer contributions when profits are realized.

Although a DPSP may have some of the same characteristics of a pension plan, it has some important differences. A DPSP may allow for withdrawal of all or part of an employee's account (including the vested employer share) while still in active employment. This is not allowed under a pension plan. The entire withdrawal amount, above the employee's own contributions, is then taxed as income. At termination, or retirement, lump-sum payments from a DPSP are similarly taxed as income but may be taxed-sheltered by the purchase of an annuity or a transfer to an individual RRSP. This payment in a lump sum is not normally available at termination or retirement under a pension plan.

These monies are earnings that arise out of employment. However, these earnings are not considered as payable until the actual distribution of them is made to the employee. Like all profit sharing plans, the payment of these earnings is linked to the services provided by the employees in their daily work that assists the professional corporation in earning these profits. As the share in the profits arose from the performance of services, these earnings will be allocated to the week in which the services were performed.

A registered profit sharing pension plan (RPSPP) is a type of money purchase pension plan in which employer contributions are related in some way to profits. The provisions under which these plans operate are the same as for other pension plans and they are subject to the same pension legislation as are all other plans. The profit sharing aspect of the pension plan is solely a method of funding. Any monies placed in the fund must remain there until retirement or termination of employment.

Employee and employer contributions are tax deductible and the investment income of the trust fund is free from tax; however, all benefits are taxable when paid out. These benefits must normally be paid in the form of annuities and only on retirement, with lump-sum payments available only in exceptional circumstances. Lump-sum payments on retirement or termination of employment are only allowed in the following circumstances: if the contributions have not been locked in, the annuity amount due is below a set limit, or there is a shorter-than-normal life expectancy. These are just a few of the exceptional circumstances they may be applicable. The maximum amounts (i.e. contributions) that are deductible from taxable income are the same as for other pension plans.

Payments made from an RPSPP are earnings, as they have all the characteristics of a pension that arises out of employment. Payment from these plans will be handled in the same manner as any payment out of a pension fund: as a periodic pension, as a lump-sum pension benefit and as a return of contributions. If the employee should terminate his or her employment prior to retirement age, any locked-in pension credits transferred directly to a locked-in vehicle are not considered to be payable until they are paid to the claimant.

The table below shows the primary differences between each option.

	Cash or Current Distribution Plan	Employee Profit Sharing Plan	Deferred Profit Sharing Plan	Registered Profit Sharing Pension Plan
Distribution	Cash periodically distributed	Accumulates in a trust fund along with interest	Accumulates in a trust fund along with interest	Accumulates in a trust fund along with interest
Taxation	Taxed with wages and other benefits when paid	Taxed each year on share of profits and accumulated investment income in the trust fund	Taxed only when money is paid out	Taxed only when money is paid out
Registration	Not registered	Registered	Registered	Registered
Access	Immediately as paid out to employee	On termination or retirement, or sometimes during employment	On termination or retirement, or sometimes during employment	Only on termination or retirement as there is no access while employed

CHAPTER TEN

Moving From One Jurisdiction To Another

The catalyst for me to write this book was the story I told at the beginning of the book, of the physician who moved from Alberta to British Columbia. There are many circumstances where professionals move from one jurisdiction to another and there is much they need to take into consideration. Let's discuss the differences between relocating temporarily versus permanently.

Temporary Absence From A Jurisdiction

If you are incorporated and temporarily move somewhere else, you will need to consider whether this is going to cause any legal or tax issues. As an example, suppose you are an incorporated physician from Nova Scotia who wants to switch practices with a physician in Alberta. You leave Nova Scotia in July and are planning to return in June of the following year. Let's further suppose that your professional corporation year-end is December 31. In this case, the two jurisdictions have different rules about who can be shareholders of professional corporations; with Nova Scotia being more flexible, you probably wouldn't want to change your existing share structure to meet the Alberta rules.

If you were to be paid personally in Alberta, instead of trying to have the money paid to your professional corporation, there would be no need to register your professional corporation in Alberta. Your professional corporation would still reside in Nova Scotia because the company never left, and you would file a corporate tax return for your professional corporation as if you never left the province. Your personal income would include all income earned in Alberta. When you return the following year you can have the income earned in Nova Scotia directed to your professional corporation and you're back in business.

If you know you are going to be making such a move, you can tax plan in advance to ensure it is handled in the best possible way. For instance, if we use the previous example, we know that Nova Scotia allows for family members to be shareholders. We also know that income earned in Alberta from, say, August to May, will be taxed personally. If you know in advance that you are going to have income earned in another jurisdiction from August to December in one year and January to May in the next year, you can calculate what you expect to earn and then adjust your income from the professional corporation accordingly, as shown in the example below.

Let's look at how this might work. Suppose you were going to make the trip described above, starting July 2010. If your professional corporation was earning $168,000 per year and you were paying out dividends to you and your spouse at a rate of $4,000 each per month, your annual individual incomes would be $48,000. Total household income would be $96,000. When you move to Alberta, suppose you expect to earn the same monthly income your professional corporation was making, $14,000 ($168,000 ÷ 12). Because the income will be paid to you directly, you can expect to earn $70,000 ($14,000 x 5) in the first year (August-December) and $70,000 ($14,000 x 5) in the second calendar year (January-May). Knowing that your personal income is going to be higher than the normal $48,000, you should stop the income you are taking from your professional corporation as of January 2010 and not start it again until January 2012. This way you will restrict your personal income to the amount you earn in Alberta. If you need additional income between January and July, you can double your spouse's dividend between January and June and then reduce it to zero between July and December. If you want to continue to pay your spouse the same amount from your professional corporation, you can, or you can reduce their income to reflect your higher income.

If you don't plan these things in advance, you can end up pushing yourself into the high tax bracket. To complete our example, if you didn't stop your income on January 1, 2010, you would have dividends from January to July of $28,000 (7 x $4,000) plus your earnings in Alberta of $70,000. When you gross up the dividend to $35,000 ($28,000 x 1.25), your total income would be $105,000 (35,000 + 70,000). If you compare this to your pre-trip income of $60,000 (48,000 x 1.25) you would be exposing a lot of income to the higher tax brackets.

This method of planning also works well when you're planning an extended trip. I've had clients leave the country for months or years and in each case we've been able to reduce their tax liability before and after their return. If you're leaving the country for more than two years, you could be a non-resident and not subject to Canadian tax; however, there are a number of requirements that have to be met for this to occur. If you are planning such a trip, review your situation with your accountant.

If, however, you are planning a shorter trip, say, one year, you can spread income over a couple of years. Remember, your professional corporation is like a valve. You can stop and start income. I am always asking my clients what their plans are. If I know they want to take a year off to travel, we can plan for it. Why take a lot of money out of your professional corporation the year before you're going away when you won't have income while you're away? You can spread the tax liability over at least two years. If you know you're not going to have income next year, you should make sure there is sufficient money in the professional corporation for you to take out during your year's absence. This way you will be able to take advantage of the low and middle tax brackets in the year you're away.

This is all a function of good tax planning. You can still take dividends from your professional corporation even while you're away. If you need extra money before you go away, you might be better off using a personal line of credit and then paying it off from your professional corporation while you're away.

As an example, suppose you plan on going to Europe for eight months leaving February and returning September next year. It's now September and year to date you've taken $110,000 from your professional corporation. If you continue to take more from your professional corporation in the current year it will be added to the $110,000. If you were to stop taking money from your PC immediately and use a personal line of credit to live on for the balance of the year your gross income would stay at $110,000.

When January rolls around you can take a lump sum dividend or salary to pay back the line of credit and that income will be taxable to you next year.

Instead of taking a lot of money out of your professional corporation before or after you return from your trip, if you know you're going to be traveling for extended periods of time, simply continue taking dividends.

Permanent Absence From Jurisdiction

If you are moving permanently to a new jurisdiction you should check with the local college or governing body before you move. Where you are moving to and where you are moving from will determine whether it will be, from a professional corporation's point of view, a benefit or a detriment.

If you are currently living in a jurisdiction that does not allow non-professional shareholders and going to one that does, you may want to reorganize your professional corporation to take advantage of this opportunity. Conversely, if you have your spouse as a shareholder or you are using a family trust as a shareholder and are moving to a jurisdiction that does not allow these practices, you will be forced to change the share structure of your professional corporation.

This is the primary reason I wrote this book. Most people don't realize the consequences of these moves. If you are moving from British Columbia to Ontario and are incorporated, you may be forced to change your share structure to conform to different rules, depending on what your current share structure is. However, if you are moving from Ontario to British Columbia and are already incorporated, you can keep your existing share structure because it's compliant in British Columbia. The problem is that you can change the share structure to make it more tax friendly but you have to take the initiative. You may, or may not, be told you can do this depending on whether your accountant and/or lawyer know about these different rules.

You are allowed to have more than one professional corporation if you're working in multiple jurisdictions. For example, if you work in Saskatchewan part of the time and Alberta part of the time, you can have separate professional corporations and you are allowed to set them up in accordance with each province's specific rules. What you're not allowed to do is earn income in Alberta and have it taxed in your Saskatchewan company. Income earned in Alberta would be taxed in the Alberta company and Saskatchewan income would be taxed in the Saskatchewan company.

Re: A possible future move
From:
To: tim@tpcfinancial.com

Hi Tim

Although we haven't been here that long we're pretty
sure we won't be staying here forever. In a few years
we'll probably be looking to move to a bigger city.
I was talking to a colleague of mine who said if we
left the Province I'd have to shut down my PC here and
start a new one there. Is that true?

Sven

Re: Re: A possible future move
From: tim@tpcfinancial.com
To: Sven Hansen

Hi Sven

Finding winter a little too cold? I was wondering when
the novelty of minus 19° temperatures like last Sunday
was going to wear off. I should warn you that the all-
time low for Dawson Creek in December was a staggering
-49.2° back in 1992.

Anyway, your colleague may be right depending on where
you move. If you move from one province to another that
has the same incorporation rules, you can transfer your
PC to the new province of residence. If you move to
a province that has more restrictive rules you would
have to set up a new PC there, but you could keep your
existing PC as well. The two main reasons to keep a
second PC would be if you're planning to practice in
both jurisdictions, or you have significant investment
assets in your existing PC.

If you do have significant assets in your existing PC,
and you're not going to practice in the province you
left, you can change your existing PC to a simple
investment company and keep it there.

If you happen to move somewhere where the rules are
more flexible you can transfer your existing PC to
the new province and then keep it "as is" or, after

the transfer, change it to better suit your needs. However, if you are going to look at changing it, it may be cheaper to start a brand new PC, and just let the other one go.

Regardless of what you decide about moving, let me know before you make any final decisions and I'll explain more fully what needs to be done.

From a positively balmy Victoria - over and out.

Tim

CHAPTER ELEVEN

Estate Planning

Estate planning to me has always been everything you do prior to the time your heart stops beating. You can be prepared or not prepared. Not being prepared is asking for trouble. If you don't have the following documents, get them – it's as simple as that. Life is difficult enough without adding trouble for no reason. Let's take a look at why.

Powers Of Attorney And Wills

Are powers of attorney and wills necessary? The simple answer is yes. When you have a professional corporation, they are critical. I like to think of a will as something you do for someone else, and a power of attorney as something you do for yourself. If you die or become incapacitated while owning shares of a professional corporation, you have a special problem in that you own all the voting shares and are the only director (this is the most typical form of professional incorporation). Decisions made on behalf of the company are solely up to you. Certain jurisdictions, like Alberta, allow for more than one professional to be in the same professional corporation as long as the other shareholders are also members of the College of Physicians and Surgeons of Alberta. Let's look at both situations.

If you became an angel last night, the shares of your professional corporation will form part of your estate. If you die without a will, you are said to have died intestate. Wills and estates legislation varies depending on which province or territory you are in. Thus, the actual distribution of your estate will depend on where you live at the time of death. From an estate distribution aspect, if you die intestate in Quebec, your assets will be distributed differently than if you die intestate in Alberta with the same assets.

When you die owning shares of a professional corporation, the decision has to be made as to whether or not to keep it as a regular company. With a will you can direct your executor to make the decision based on circumstances at that time. If it makes sense for your heirs to keep the company, they could; or if it's in their best interest to sell it they can choose to do so. Without a will, there may be little or no opportunity to do this.

A professional corporation can continue to exist as a regular corporation without having to shut down the existing company. You can also continue to keep your corporate assets inside the company after retirement (see page 284) or death.

By having a valid will, you give your executor directions about what to do with your professional corporation. A will should instruct the executor on how to distribute the assets of your estate. This is very important from a tax point of view. If you leave the shares of your professional corporation to your spouse, there is a full tax deferral available. This means that your spouse can defer paying any tax owing on the shares of your professional corporation until the shares are sold or their death. If you don't have a valid will or leave the shares to anyone other than your spouse, you could trigger capital gains tax on those shares.

Each province and territory has a pre-defined distribution of assets between the surviving spouse and children if someone dies without a valid will. If the shares of the company were partially given to your children, then the deferral available to your spouse on that amount would be lost. This is one more reason to have a proper will.

It's truly amazing what can happen if you don't take the time to make proper provisions; take the case of Bill Dyer. His wife Bobbi left him and married another man. Her second husband died a number of years later and she inherited his estate. A number of years after that, Bill passed away. He did not make a will and therefore he did not make any provisions as to who would inherit his estate. Amazingly, Bobbi made a claim, even though she had left him 20 years earlier. She claimed that she was still legally married to Bill and, therefore, under applicable law, she should inherit his estate in her capacity as his wife. In making this claim she, of course, had to admit her illegal marriage to her second husband. The court found that she never legally divorced Bill and, even though she had committed bigamy by marrying her second husband while still married to the first, she was in fact still legally married to Bill at the time of his death. The courts applied the laws governing in that province that stated that the estate would go to Bill's spouse. This seems like an unjust result considering that she left him over 20 years before and married another man, but the court was bound to apply the statute governing those who leave no wills.

This case points out two things: first, just how far people will go if there is money in it for them, and second, if Bill had made a proper legal will, none of this would have happened.

Rule of thumb buster. I have my power of attorney in my will.

Not so! A power of attorney is a separate document.

It is also important to have a power of attorney (POA). If you are unable to deal with your own affairs, someone will have to make application to the courts to get control of your assets. This provision is not in your will. Many people believe that their POA is contained inside their will; it isn't. Wills work well when you die but provide no assistance to your family if you are alive.

The process of getting approval from the courts to administer someone else's affairs while they are still alive is very expensive and laborious. Your professional corporation is in limbo because you are the controlling shareholder and director, and no legal decisions can be made until someone has legal authority to act. A POA is a document that designates, in advance, the person who is going to have legal control of your affairs if you are unable to act on your own behalf.[34]

The most common type of POA is an enduring power of attorney. It may or may not be in effect at the time of execution. A basic enduring POA gives the attorney complete power to act on your behalf as soon as the document is signed by the appropriate parties, mainly the person giving and the one accepting the POA. The POA allows the attorney to do anything you are legally allowed to do, including, but not limited to, voting your shares, entering into contracts on behalf of the company, selling your assets, banking,

---

34 The person you name is known as your "attorney".

and dealing with the CRA. You must have a great deal of trust in the person to whom you give that much control over your affairs.

Often a triggering event is stipulated in an enduring power of attorney, such as "upon determination of mental incapacity." In this case, it's a good idea if you decide on some predetermined method of determining when you are mentally incapacitated. Mine reads, "…as determined by my family physician Dr.…". This additional clause effectively blocks the use of the POA unless it is accompanied by the medical determination of my family physician. Another way is to say, "…as determined by two physicians licensed in my province or territory of residence." In either case a POA is a very inexpensive document that can ultimately save your family a lot of heartache and time, time that would be better spent looking after you.

I remember a case many years ago involving the parents of a client. I had just starting working with this client and asked if they had a POA. They asked what it was and I explained it to them. After the explanation they said no, but they wished that their parents did. Apparently one of their mothers had recently had an accident and was in a coma. They were told to expect the worst and so prepared for her death. During that time a number of investments came up for renewal and no one had authority to deal with them. They thought about getting her certified but decided against it because of the cost and stress involved. As it turned out she ended up living for fifteen months during which time most of her investments were reinvested and locked in for 5 years at low interest rates. They had matured after being invested for 5 years and no one had legal authority to change the investments so they were automatically reinvested for another 5-year term.

A POA would have ultimately saved the family thousands of dollars and removed all the frustration of deciding when to get letters of administration. The other caution here is if you don't take it upon yourself to decide, the courts may appoint someone you would rather not have. Most people, for instance, aren't thrilled about having a government agency controlling their affairs.

In Ontario they use Power of Attorney for property, and Power of Attorney for Personal Care, documents.

In British Columbia they have Representation Agreements. A Representation Agreement is a relatively new concept in British Columbia; it arises out of the Representation Agreement Act, which came into affect in early 2000. There are two levels of Representation Agreement. A basic Section 7 agreement that gives limited powers to a representative to deal with certain aspects of a person's estate and their personal needs. The Section 7 agreement can be granted by a person having diminished capacity.[35]

A Representation Agreement made under Section 9 can go into great detail as to how you want both your financial affairs and your person cared for during any incapacity or other event occurring which prevents you from making those decisions yourself. The Agreement can spell out under what circumstances your representative is empowered to act, and what input he or she must seek from yourself and others in making those decisions. We can provide for a monitor to make sure that your representative is carrying out the terms of your Representation Agreement. The Representation Agreement Act provides for the very specific manner in which Representation Agreements must be executed and we would encourage you to seek legal advice if you are contemplating a Representation Agreement.

These various documents do the same job in different ways. The message here is that when you die you want your own will. If you become incapacitated you want to have someone take care of your stuff and if you're on life support you may want someone to have your authorization to "pull the plug".

What Happens When I Die?

When you die all your assets are deemed to be sold at fair market value; this is called a deemed disposition. The assets are not really sold; the CRA, for tax purposes, pretends that they were sold. This includes the shares of your professional corporation. They do this to prevent gains from accruing indefinitely without ever being taxed.

If you were married at the time of death, or had a spouse as defined by the CRA, taxes owing at that time, as a result of the deemed disposition, can be deferred as long as the assets are left to them. The CRA allows your spouse and the executor to select which assets they want to defer taxes on, on an asset-by-asset basis. This means they can defer taxes on certain assets and elect to pay taxes on other assets.

Why would they want to pay taxes on certain assets now? Well, one reason may be the actual date of death. If you died at the beginning of the year,

---

35 http://www.mcbop.com/publications/wepp5.html

you might not have any income. If your spouse elects to declare $100,000 of capital gains on your final tax return, the taxes owing would be based on only $50,000 because only half the gain is included in income.

To fully understand this let's look at the following example. Joan dies on January 2, 2010, owning shares of a professional corporation worth $925,100. She also owns a stock and mutual fund portfolio worth $300,000. Her principal residence is owned jointly with her husband Ron. Ron is also the named beneficiary of her RRSPs.

When Joan first set up her professional corporation, she bought her shares for $100 (which is the cost base of the shares). Her stock and mutual funds have an adjusted cost base of $200,000. If there were no tax deferral available, the deemed disposition rules would require that the capital gain on her professional corporation shares and the capital gain on her stock and mutual funds would have to be declared on her final tax return. Because capital gains are only taxed on 50 percent, the actual amount that would be added to her final return would be $512,500: ($925,100 - $100 = $925,000) + ($300,000 - $200,000 = $100,000) divided by two. If no deferral were available, Joan's estate would have to pay tax on $512,500.

If Ron was to opt out of the spousal roll-over provisions, when he receives the assets from the estate his cost base on those assets would be $925,000 for the shares of the professional corporation, and $300,000 for the stocks and mutual funds. In this situation, the estate would be responsible for paying the tax on the $512,500. If there were insufficient cash in the estate, assets would have to be sold by the executor to meet the obligation. It's the deemed disposition rule that causes most spouses to opt for the deferral.

The CRA allows you to look at each asset individually when deciding whether or not to defer the taxes. This goes so far as allowing you to look at shares of a company on a share-by-share basis. If you own 100 shares you can elect to have the deferral apply to 60 of them and not to the other 40. This is very important if you are going to use the enhanced capital gains deduction.

In this example, Joan's shares are worth $925,000 on her terminal tax return. She paid $100 for them and, as a result, has a capital gain of $925,000. If her shares qualify for the enhanced capital gains deduction, it will only cover the first $750,000, assuming that Joan has never used any of her capital gains deduction in the past.

If Joan owned 100 shares in her professional corporation, they would each have a value of $9,251 ($925,100 ÷ 100). The cost base for each share would be $1.00; therefore, the capital gain attributed to each share would be $9,250. In order to access the enhanced capital gains deduction, the executor of Joan's estate could decide to have 20 shares deferred and elect to have the tax on the 80 shares not deferred. Not deferring the tax on the 80 shares would trigger a capital gain of $740,000 (80 x $9,250) and then the enhanced capital gains election could be used to offset this gain.

Electing out of the rollover[36] allowed access to the enhanced capital gains election and increased the cost base on the shares that Ron now owns by $740,000. It may also be to Ron's benefit to elect out of the rollover on the stocks and mutual funds.

Because Joan died at the beginning of the year she had no income. If Ron decided to defer the taxes on the portfolio, he would assume Joan's adjusted cost base of $200,000. When Ron sells the assets he would have to pay tax at his marginal rate. Knowing that each calendar year brings a new set of marginal rates into play for everyone, Ron can take advantage of Joan's zero income year. If Ron doesn't defer the taxes, Joan's estate would pay tax on half the capital gain of $50,000 and it would be the only income. Ron would be able to use Joan's personal exemption and may be able to make a spousal RRSP deposit if she has room from the previous year.

After filing her final return in this manner, Ron would assume the portfolio with a bumped-up cost base of $300,000. Therefore, when he sells the investments some time in the future, he would only have to pay on gains above $300,000.

---

36 Rollover – see glossary

Re: What happens when I die?
From: Lange Zhu
To: tim@tpcfinancial.com

Hi Tim

I know we talked about this before but I can't remember
the answer. What happens to my PC when I die? Can it
still be used or does it die with me?

I went to a great conference in Toronto last week, I
was surprised that you weren't one of the speakers;
you seem to do so many these days.

Lange

Re: Re: Pensions: What happens when I die?
From: tim@tpcfinancial.com
To: Lange Zhu

Hi Lange

Yes, I knew about that conference, but I can only do so
many of them and in any case Patti and I had already
planned to go to Seattle for a few days.

What's with the morbid thinking? I'm joking, you're
right to consider all the potential issues that you and
your PC might face in the future, and we all have to
think of those we leave behind. The thing that makes
a professional corporation different from a normal
corporation is the fact that a "professional" owns it.
When the professional dies the corporation still exists
but it's no longer a "professional" corporation.

What happens on death is the shares of the corporation
are deemed sold, for tax purposes, and any increase in
value is taxable, unless those shares are left to a
spouse.

Regardless of who inherits the shares the option is
there to keep the company going, unless you specifically
state in your will that the company is to be wound-up.

Any questions – call me.

Tim

When A Professional Corporation Stops Being A Professional Corporation, It Becomes A Regular Corporation

When you die or retire from practice (assuming you don't sell your shares), your professional corporation has to change its status. This does not mean that you have to sell all your assets and wind up your company. What it does mean is that you are effectively removing the "professional" from the corporation and are left with a limited company. This is something that can be done with the help of your lawyer and accountant. After you are no longer a professional corporation, you can change the share structure to whatever you want. This may or may not be a benefit depending on what assets are in the company, you and your spouse's ages at the time, and your long-term plans.

If you are holding a lot of growth assets in your corporation, such as real estate or equities, you may want to freeze the value of your shares and issue new growth shares to your spouse or other family members, including a family trust. The idea behind freezing the value of your shares is to transfer future growth to other family members.

One example that comes to mind is a client of mine who retired at age 50 (I'll call him Brian). Brian had accumulated sufficient assets to generate enough income to focus on the other things he wanted to do in life, so he sold his practice. At the time, his professional corporation was worth about $1,600,000. The assets were primarily an apartment building and some equity mutual funds. His wife (whom I'll call Shari) also retired and was going to receive a small pension from teaching.

After he retired, his professional corporation was changed to a regular corporation from which he was taking a small management salary of $18,000 per year. The income from the apartments, after expenses, was about $150,000 per year.

Because he was only 50 years old and his wife was the same age, he felt that there was a very good chance that the value of his investments would increase over time. Brian's wife had not been allowed to own shares in his professional corporation because of jurisdictional regulations. Now that it was a regular corporation, she was able to own shares so we froze the value of his shares at $1,600,000 and then sold 100 new growth shares to his wife for $100.

Initially, the only way to get money out of the company was to pay dividends to Brian. However, because Shari now owned shares in the company, we could start to shift equity over to her by reducing the number of shares that Brian owned and also allow the assets to appreciate.

The way we reduced Brian's shares was by way of share redemption. Brian originally owned 100 Class A common shares in Brian Professional Corporation. When we froze his shares, we exchanged them for 1000 Class A preferred shares with a fixed value of $1,600 per share. Instead of simply paying a dividend to Brian every year, we redeemed some of his shares. We started out by redeeming 50 shares a year. This resulted in a deemed dividend of $80,000 (50 x $1,600). Brian also received dividends on the balance of his preferred shares. This simple act results in a transfer of equity from Brian to Shari each year of $80,000. How does it happen? When a company redeems (buys) its own shares it is not treated as a capital gain but rather a dividend.

Brian's 1000 frozen shares were worth $1,600,000. Shari's 100 growth shares were worth $100. The total value of the company was $1,600,100. Brian's shares will never increase in value and therefore are frozen at $1,600 each. When Brian sells 50 shares to the company for $80,000, he is left with 950 shares worth $1,600 each or $1,520,000. Because the value of the company is still $1,600,100 (assuming no change in the value of the real estate or mutual funds), Shari's shares represent the difference in value which would be $1,600,100 − 1,520,000 = $80,100.

By doing this, over time we are able to transfer equity to Shari, which can be used by her at some time in the future and taxed in her hands, not Brian's. It should also allow us to eventually pay dividends to Shari as long as Brian receives sufficient dividends on his preferred shares.

Continued Existence

Corporations, unlike people, don't die. They may be wound up or go out of business, but they don't die. When you first set up your professional corporation, you're probably not thinking about what's going to happen 50 years in the future. But the reality is that your corporation could still be active 50 or 100 years into the future. It is important to keep this in mind when you are estate planning. Depending on your particular circumstances, your family may want to continue to benefit from your company after your death and they can because corporations never die.

Multi-Generational Tax Planning

Multi-generational planning can affect both you and your heirs. If you consider your current situation and then project it into the future, you may well find two very different outcomes.

Suppose you are currently working and inherit $600,000 from a relative. You could use the tax-free money you inherited to pay off any debt you might have and then use the money you were using to make payments for investment purposes. As your investment pool grows you would probably have an ever-increasing amount of investment income. This investment income would be added to your employment income and taxed at higher rates. For example, if your employment income was $130,000 and your investment income was $30,000, you would pay tax at the high rate on the entire $30,000. If you lived in Ontario the tax on the $30,000 would be about $13,923.

If you didn't have debt and invested the $600,000 you would still end up with the same situation, with investment income added on top of your employment income. But what if you were to split income with yourself by having your relatives change their will?

Instead of having your inheritance paid directly to you, you have the money paid into a trust. The trust would be defined in your relative's will and would name you as the trustee of your own trust. As previously mentioned, trusts are separate legal entities and as such are subject to tax. The major difference between the taxation of these trusts versus an inter vivos trust is that a trust created in a will is defined as a testamentary trust and is taxed using marginal tax rates. One difference between the taxation of testamentary trusts and an individual's is that testamentary trusts are not eligible for personal exemptions. However, approximately the first $40,970 is taxed federally at the low tax rate of 15 per cent.

In our previous example, your employment income was $130,000 and your investment income was $30,000. Using a testamentary trust to receive an inheritance would result in an annual tax savings of about $7,923. Instead of the money coming directly to you, it is paid to the trust. The money is invested in the trust and the income is declared by the trust. The trust will pay tax of about $6,000. The net trust income will be $24,000 ($30,000 – $6,000). The $24,000 is added to the capital of the trust and can be removed by the capital beneficiary tax-free. This means that every year you could have the trust declare the investment income, pay the tax at its own marginal rates and then remove the after-tax amount as tax-free capital.

Multi-generational planning can also involve your children. In a typical case, a couple with children will have their wills drawn up to read something like this: "If my spouse Patti survives me by 30 days then I leave everything to her and if something happens to both Patti and me, or she does not survive me by 30 days, then I leave everything "in trust" for my children Justin and Brittany."

Why not generation plan with your spouse and children? Instead of leaving all your estate to your spouse and asking them to use the money to raise the children, why not leave some money "in trust" to your children with your spouse as the trustee? If you have two children you could save over $20,000 per year in income tax. How?

Suppose you died last night and left your spouse $2,000,000. If they invested this money at 7 per cent it would generate $140,000 of taxable income. If they happened to work and continued to earn $40,000 per year their gross income would be $180,000. Personal income tax on this amount would be $67,000. That would leave them $113,000 to maintain the family's lifestyle.

Instead of leaving everything directly to your spouse, suppose you left $900,000 in a spousal trust, $400,000 in a trust for each of your two children and gave your spouse the remaining $300,000 as a direct gift. Assuming the same 7 per cent rate of return the tax situation would now look like this:

	Income	Tax	Net Income
Spousal trust	$63,000	$16,240	$46,760
First child's trust	$28,000	$5,700	$22,300
Second child's trust	$28,000	$5,700	$22,300
Spouse's personal gift	$21,000	$6,300	$14,700
	$140,000	$33,940	$106,060

The surviving spouse can have the after-tax income from the children's trusts available to raise the children along with the capital. These trusts can be kept throughout the lifetime of the children but are subject to the

21-year deemed disposition rules. The money could be used for anything during the child's lifetime and would be protected later in life from possible greedy ex-spouses.

You may look at this situation and say, "If my spouse has $2 million, she's not going to work." Maybe she wouldn't, but to me it's about choices. I think it's better to let the surviving spouse choose what to do at the time, rather than not giving them the choice at all. The set-up work for these trusts is carried out prior to death but the trust itself does not come into being until after your death.

I'm often asked about the cost associated with these trusts. First of all, the trusts do not exist until death. They are simply clauses in a person's will; they can be changed at any time, by simply changing the will. On death, the trusts are created. If the trustee is a family member, there is usually no trustee fees (although any trustee can charge a fee up to the maximum allowed in your jurisdiction). The only costs normally associated with these trusts are an annual tax return (one for each trust, known as a T-3 return) and perhaps some bookkeeping. Annual costs may be $750 per trust.

This use of trusts can also be applied to grandchildren. I have two clients who are both professionals and are very wealthy. The thought of inheriting money from their parents was troubling them because of the potential tax consequences. They had concluded that they had already amassed sufficient assets to take care of themselves for the rest of their lives and had no need for their parent's money. After discussing the situation with them and their parents, we decided to rewrite their parent's wills to skip a generation and leave their inheritance directly to their children in trust. As a result of this change, my client's children are now set up with trust accounts under the complete control of their parents. They can use the tax savings for all kinds of things for the children, including education and travel. It also provides benefits in that my clients don't feel frustrated by working and paying more tax than they need to. If they had inherited the money directly from their parents, they would have unwanted investment income on top of their earned income. Granted, it's a nice position to be in, but why pay additional tax when you don't have to?

CHAPTER TWELVE

I'm Retiring – What Now?

When you are preparing to retire, there are a number of considerations. It is to your advantage to think about these things at least three years prior to the actual date. The earlier you understand the options available to you the better your chances of a smooth transition from practitioner to retiree. When I first take on a new client I want to know approximately when they would like to have the opportunity to stop working. I can then work toward that objective without having to change our strategy when we get to that point.

Asset Accumulation And Income-Splitting At Retirement

Depending on where you live, the ability to split income may be easy or may require a little more creativity. It's imperative, to your long-term financial success, to coordinate the accumulation of your personal and corporate assets. If you are working with one individual who handles your RRSP portfolio and with someone else who deals with your corporate assets, you may be working against yourself. If neither party knows what the other is doing, the distribution of your assets could end up unbalanced. Remember, the best-case scenario when you are married or have a common-law spouse, is to split your income equally.

Another consideration is the taxability of the assets. Remember that different investments are taxed differently. If your spouse has all their assets in RRSPs, then their entire retirement income will be taxed as income. If you, on the other hand, have all your assets inside your professional corporation, your retirement income would be taxed (at worst) as dividends. If you both had a gross income of $50,000 per year in retirement, your spouse will pay more tax than you.

There are many strategies to deal with the disproportionate accumulation of assets. One example is to make one spouse the saver and the other one the spender. For example, say that you live in a jurisdiction that only allows the professional to be a shareholder. Your spouse is on the payroll of your professional corporation or has employment elsewhere. You've probably been advised that it would be in your best interests to make your RRSP contributions into a spousal RRSP, or at least make part of your RRSP a spousal contribution.

The theory behind this is that you will be building up equity inside your professional corporation and your spouse will not be able to access this equity in retirement. Their equity is going to be in their RRSP. If you project these numbers out to retirement you may find that your spouse is going to have fewer assets, and their income is going to be totally taxable. So, to avoid this, your spouse should use their after-tax income to save while you use your net income to live on. The actual amounts can be worked out with your accountant or financial planner, but this strategy will create a situation where your spouse will end up in retirement with three pools of money, one in their personal RRSP, one in their spousal RRSP, and one in a non-RRSP investment account.

If we put some basic numbers to our example at retirement, it would look like this.

Value of assets in your professional corporation at retirement	$1,500,000
Value of spouse's individual RRSP at retirement	$ 500,000
Value of spousal RRSP at retirement	$ 500,000
On your $50,000 dividend the taxes would be	$ 3,300
On your spouse's $50,000 RRIF income the taxes would be	$ 11,000

If your spouse was able to accumulate a non-RRSP investment pool of, say, $250,000 the tax situation in retirement could be more favourable. You would be able to take less taxable income from the RRIF and supplement this income with non-taxable capital.

To create the same after-tax cash flow you would reduce your spouse's RRIF income to $25,000 and use $25,000 of the non-RRSP assets as a supplement. The result would look like this:

On your $50,000 dividend the taxes would be	$ 3,300
On your spouse's $25,000 RRIF income the taxes would be	$ 3,700
On your spouse $25,000 non-RRSP income supplement the taxes would be	Nil

Making the spouse the saver ensures there is a clear record of whose money is being saved. If you both add money to an investment account outside of your professional corporation, the CRA could say that the funds belong to you and therefore the income is yours and not your spouse's as a result of the attribution rules.

The attribution rules for spouses provide that where property, including money, is transferred or loaned directly or indirectly by you to your spouse, then all income or loss from the property, and any capital gain or loss on the disposition of the property, will be attributed to you. If, however, you can prove that the money was in fact your spouse's or loaned to them with an appropriate amount of interest, then the attribution rules do not apply.

Since I wrote the first edition of this book the federal tax rules have changed regarding the splitting of retirement income. As of January 1, 2007 individuals who are 65 years of age or older can allocate, for tax purposes, up to a maximum of 50 per cent of the annual income received from a lifetime annuity, registered pension plan, RRSP annuity, registered retirement income fund (RRIF) or deferred profit sharing plan annuity to a spouse (or common-law partner or same-sex partner). Although the actual income is still received by the individual, the splitting for tax purposes is done via the tax return. The receiving spouse is not required to be 65 years of age or older to receive an allocation, and the amount allocated can be changed each year for the benefit of the couple.

For those individuals under age 65, pension splitting only applies to those who receive lifetime annuity payments from a registered pension plan. RRIF income cannot be split under age 65.

With the new changes to pension splitting, spousal RRSPs are not as beneficial for those over the age of 65. However, they still make sense for income splitting under the age of 65. Spousal RRSPs simply allow a spouse, who is in a higher marginal tax rate, to contribute to a spousal RRSP in the name of the lower income spouse.

Similar to pension splitting, couples can split their CPP retirement benefits. The only reason you would do this is if the spouse with the higher CPP is in a higher tax bracket than the lower CPP earner. Unlike pension splitting, both spouses must be over the age of 60 and both must be collecting CPP. Also, the split between spouses must be 50-50 and no other ratio. For example, if the higher income spouse earns $700 per month and the other spouse earns $300 per month, CPP allows each spouse to take $500 per month ($700 plus $300 divided by 2).

Refundable Dividend Tax On Hand

A refundable dividend tax on hand (RDTOH) is an accounting term that refers to the tax a company can get back from the CRA if it pays out a taxable dividend from after-tax corporate investment income. Sounds confusing? Let me explain.

A company can have active income and passive income. Active income is just that – money you earn, for example, from practicing dentistry. Passive income is money that you don't earn, for example, interest, capital gains, rental income and certain dividends. When you earn income in a professional corporation, it is subject to small or big business tax rates depending on how much you earn and how much you leave in the company (see appendices for current tax rates).

Passive income is usually subject to big business tax rates regardless of how much money is made. Two exceptions to this rule are dividends received from a connected company and dividends received from a publicly traded company. Dividends received from a connected company are not generally subject to tax and dividends received from shares of a publicly traded company are taxed at a special part IV rate of 33.33 percent.

Let's look at an example. Money is placed on deposit and earns interest, say $10,000. In this case the company would pay tax at the big business rate of 48.7 per cent on the $10,000 interest income, leaving $5,130 in the company. When the money is paid out as a taxable dividend the professional would pay (assuming the top personal dividend tax rate of 32.6 per cent) another $1,672 in personal income tax leaving them with $3,458. This doesn't leave a lot left of the original $10,000. However, because the company has already paid tax on the $10,000 (remember the 48.7 per cent?), it can apply for a partial refund. The refundable dividend tax on hand represents the amount of taxes the company gets back from the CRA after it pays out a taxable dividend from investment income. It's another aspect of the integration of taxes between individuals and shareholders. In this example the dividend refund to the company would be about $2,570 (Ontario rates).

As a point of interest, the amount of after-tax cash available to pay dividends including the refund is not sufficient to obtain a full refund of the RDTOH in any of the provinces. Using the figures in the example above, an amount equal to 0.3 per cent of the income will remain in the RDTOH account (as shown in the table below).

Corporate income	$10,000
Corporate tax	($4,870)
After-tax amount	($5,130)
Dividend refund	$2,570
Available for distribution	$7,700
RDTOH	
Refundable tax	$2,570
Dividend refund	($2,567)
RDTOH balance	$3

Furthermore, dividends received from a related company are not generally subject to tax because when you take the money out of the second company it will be taxed in the same manner as if it came out of the first company, that is, dividends can be moved inter-corporately tax-free. When the money is paid out of either company, if it's removed as a dividend it's taxed as a dividend, and if it's removed as salary it's taxed as salary. Therefore, there's no tax advantage to taking the money out of one company or the other.

Dividends received from shares of a publicly traded company are taxed at a special rate because the public company has already paid tax on that money at the top business rate before it is paid out to you as a shareholder. It's important to understand this because it affects how you invest money inside a professional corporation.

What If My Shares Aren't Qualifying?

If your professional corporation shares are not qualifying, you may be able to 'clean them up' by going through a process commonly known as "purification". Purification transfers non-practice assets from your professional corporation to a related investment company (Investco), on a tax-free basis. This process is necessary for two reasons: first, if a purchaser only wishes to acquire the practice assets of the professional corporation; second, when the shares do not qualify for the $750,000 capital gains deduction because more than 10 per cent of the fair market value of assets in the professional corporation are not related to the practice.

In order to keep the professional corporation clean, any practice surplus must be distributed to Investco in the form of tax-free, inter-corporate dividends. Since dividends can only be paid to a shareholder, Investco must then be a shareholder of the professional corporation. Not putting a proper corporate structure in place to keep the professional corporation "clean" can cause a lot of grief, as one of my clients learned.

With the sale of her professional corporation in the final stages, Dr. Poplawski was shocked to find that her shares in the professional corporation did not qualify for the capital gains deduction. Dr. Poplawski thought she had followed her accountant's advice exactly when she incorporated her Investco to transfer cash surpluses from the professional corporation. Investco, however, was not made a shareholder in the professional corporation, so the transfer of funds was accounted for as an inter-corporate debt rather than an inter-corporate dividend. Since a receivable owing from a holding company is not considered a dental asset, the shares are ineligible for the enhanced capital gains deduction.

By not paying careful attention to the purification process, Dr. Poplawski is now in a very undesirable situation. She can conclude the deal and pay the taxes because of the wrong corporate set-up of Investco, or she could abort the sale and start again. If she wants to start again, it will take her at least two years after the mistake is fixed before she can sell without the tax consequences.

Experienced tax lawyers and accountants carry out the purification process all the time. Make sure you work closely with them when you embark on these tax-planning manoeuvres.

The Benefit Of Having Divided Income In Retirement

When you get to retirement you and your spouse should have a number of different investment pots on which to draw. Registered accounts like RRSPs and pensions are common. You may also have non-registered accounts, both personal and joint, along with assets in your professional corporation and perhaps your investment company. There may also be CPP and Old Age Security (OAS).

Some of these assets allow you to control the income flow and others do not. Registered money must be taken out starting no later than age 72. CPP cannot be deferred later than age 70 and OAS begins at age 65.

Non-registered accounts can be drawn on, as you see fit. There is no legal requirement for you to withdraw money from your professional corporation at any age. You can leave it in there in perpetuity if you wish. Thus your professional corporation can act like a valve, controlling your cash flow prior to and after your retirement.

We also know that the income that is coming out of your professional corporation is categorized as either a salary or a dividend. In retirement, the majority, if not all of the income will come out as dividends. As was illustrated on page 290, there is a distinct tax advantage to having a dividend income as opposed to an RRIF income. This is also true for CPP and OAS pensions.

When I'm working with someone who is about to retire, we set up cash flow charts to map out the flow of money from the various sources. If you are 58 years old and have RRSPs and have assets inside your professional corporation, you might be better off to use up your RRSPs before you start to draw money from your professional corporation. You can also start to draw CPP at age 60 and so we encourage people to take advantage of this.

The purpose of doing things in this order is to deal with two different issues. One is to control the current tax liability by drawing on the RRSPs in an amount that you want, not an amount that is required by law. Let's deal with this issue first.

Have you ever heard anyone state that they wished they had never bought RRSPs because in the end they just ended up paying more tax? This is normally a result of people deferring taking money out of RRSPs until the last possible moment. What usually happens is that they have to add the RRIF income on top of all the other sources starting at age seventy-two. Drawing down on your RRSP before age 72, and leaving money in your professional corporation to be removed later, can prevent this. It's the difference between having control of your cash flow and income tax and not.

The second issue has to do with estate costs. On the second death of you or your spouse, or on your death if you're single, your RRSPs are fully taxable in the year of death. From a tax point of view, in an ideal world, you would die with no RRSPs. If you have assets left in your professional corporation upon death, the end result will be a tax on a capital gain or dividend; this is preferable to paying tax on RRSPs (that are taxed as regular income).

```
Re: RSP's versus Dividends
From: Sven Hansen
To: tim@tpcfinancial.com

Hi Tim

You once told me you don't have any RSPs and that you
intend on living on dividends in retirement. I told
my friend about what you said, but couldn't remember
your reasoning. What's so great about dividends in
retirement, and why are they a better retirement plan?

Sven
```

```
Re: Re: RSP's versus Dividends
From: tim@tpcfinancial.com
To: Sven Hansen

Hi Sven

I bet your friend thought I was crazy; not many people
think it's a good idea until I explain it to them.
Anyway, let me go over my thinking again, so you let
your friend know that RRSP's are not the be-all and
end-all of retirement planning.

Since the time I set up my first company, I've worked
to keep money inside my corporation. I've never been
excited about government having control over my future
plans, which is the case with RRSPs.
```

If you take money out of a company to put into an RRSP, the tax is deferred but the income that comes out is fully taxable as regular income.

Over the last thirty years I've seen a lot of RRSP rule changes. One that was particularly disturbing was the government moving the withdrawal age down to 69 from 71. They subsequently moved it back to age 71, but in the meantime it caught a number of people unprepared.

Another time they increased the minimum amount that you have to take out. This changed the plans of many people who were pushed into higher tax brackets.

In addition, when you die owning RRSP's they are fully taxable in the year of death, unless left to your spouse. This can result in a loss of almost half their value. Not a very exciting thing for your heirs.

By accumulating money in my companies I control how and when I'm going to take it out. I do have to pay tax now, but the tax on the first $500,000 of earned income here in BC is only 13.5%.

If I leave $100,000 of after-tax income in my company and invest it in, for example, TransCanada Corporation common shares, my company will receive a dividend of about 4%. That $4,000 is an eligible dividend to my company.

The $4,000 in dividends received is subject to tax at 33.33%, but because I only take dividends from my company the tax is fully refundable to the company. That means the company doesn't pay tax, but I pay tax on the dividend income.

Right now, my wife and I take $120,000 of dividends ($60,000 each) annually and pay a total of about $12,000 in personal income tax.

For now we've been declaring other than eligible dividends, but inside the company we're accumulating a GRIP balance. Remember we spoke about the GRIP balance? If you've forgotten, go to page 181 of my book and re-read that section. This is the sum of the eligible dividends the company's received since 2006.

At any time (now or in retirement) we can choose to classify our dividends as eligible, or other than eligible, to the extent of the GRIP balance. If we have enough of a GRIP balance accumulated at retirement we could continue to take $60,000 in dividends each, and if the tax rates don't change we would pay zero personal tax. This is because eligible dividends are taxed at an even lower rate then other than eligible dividends.

When I started doing this years ago there was no such thing as eligible dividends. The fact that government introduced them only enhances what my choices are. If I want to increase or decrease my cash flow, it's up to me. If I want to invest for dividends, or capital gains, it's up to me. How and when I use the money built up in my companies is up to me. This is not the case with RRSPs.

No matter what you invest in, all income comes out as regular income. Furthermore, the timing of your withdrawals and the amount you have to take out is under the control of the government.

By relying on dividends in retirement, I control my income. To me it's all about control and choices.

By all means, pass my contact information along to your friend if he'd like me to explain all this to him personally.

Tim

Retirement Allowances

If you've been incorporated for some time you may be able to take advantage of an old retirement program. Until 1995, when you retired, you could have your employer pay you out a retirement allowance. The amount was calculated by taking the number of years you worked up to and including 1995, and multiplying it by $2,000. You were also allowed to add an amount equal to the number of years you worked for the company prior to 1989 multiplied by $1,500 if you had no vested interest in any employer's contributions to an RPP or DPSP.

Suppose you set up your professional corporation in 1982. You would have been employed from 1982 to 1995. Upon retirement you could have paid to you a retirement allowance equal to $38,500: $28,000 (14 x 2,000) + $10,500 (7 x 1,500). This money could be transferred directly to your RRSP and deducted by the company. This can be a great way to reduce the cash in your company without having to immediately take it into income.

If you incorporated after 1995 this strategy is not applicable; however, if you incorporated prior to 1996 you should consider making a corporate resolution that states that the company is going to pay out a retirement allowance upon the retirement of the professional. By having this resolution on file you should still be allowed to pay out the retirement allowance in the future, because it is already promised.

CHAPTER THIRTEEN

Selling Your Practice

Capital Gains Deduction

Another important tax opportunity for owners of businesses is the capital gains deduction. Every individual is entitled to a lifetime $750,000 of capital gains deduction on certain small business shares and qualifying farm property.

You may have elected to use some of your capital gains deduction in previous years. Up to February 22, 1994, a general $100,000 capital gains deduction was available on all kinds of property for everyone. An election was available for that year when you filed your 1994 return. Any amounts used previously are deducted from your $750,000 balance.

For the shares of your professional corporation to qualify for the capital gains deduction they have to be "qualified small business shares". The definition of a qualified small business corporation share is as follows:

- Substantially all of the business assets must be used for carrying on an active business in Canada or be shares and debt in other small business corporations. The CRA considers "substantially" to mean 90 per cent or more; this is referred to as the 90/10 rule.

- Nobody but you or a person related to you can have owned the shares for the two years before you sell them.

- Throughout the two-year period, more than 50 per cent of the corporation's assets must have been used principally in an active business operated in Canada. This is referred to as the 50 per cent rule.

Let's look at an example of two dentists, one living in Ontario and the other in British Columbia. Dr. Ontario owns a cottage. He inherited it from his father in 1978. At that time, it was worth $80,000. In 1990 the cottage was valued at $400,000. Dr. Ontario was told by his accountant that he should take advantage of the capital gains deduction. He took his accountant's advice and arranged to crystallize (see page 303) $100,000 of the capital gains. His cost base for tax purposes is now $180,000. The cost base is basically what you pay for something, or the value of the asset at the time you receive it. When you sell a capital asset you pay tax on 50 per cent of the difference between what you sell it for and the cost base. The higher the cost base the better.

When Dr. Ontario sets up his professional corporation, he still has $650,000 of capital gains deduction left. If the practice increases in value by $650,000 and he is able to sell his shares to another dentist, he can use the rest of his lifetime deduction and pay no tax on the sale.

Dr. British Columbia doesn't own a cottage but he does have an antique car collection. He bought the first car in his collection in 1982 for $45,000. Between 1982 and 1992 he bought another eight cars totaling $350,000. In 1994 he elected to use $100,000 of his capital gains deduction on his cars.

In 1996 he decided to incorporate and added his spouse as a shareholder. She had not used any of her capital gains deduction. Dr. British Columbia could sell the shares of his practice for $1,400,000 more than the cost base, and not pay any tax because he would have $650,000 of his capital gains deduction still available and his spouse would have $750,000.

In order for you to use the capital gains deduction you must have qualifying shares and you must sell those shares. If you sell the assets of your professional corporation and keep the company then you can't use the exemption.

> **Rule of thumb buster:** Shares of a professional corporation are never sold.
>
> **Not true.** Shares of professional corporations are sold all the time. What can change is the value between selling shares and selling assets. Sometimes the value of shares is discounted to recognize that the purchaser will have fewer tax deductions.

Crystallization

A fundamental strategy in respect of the ($750,000) lifetime capital gains exemption pertaining to qualifying small business corporation shares is to "crystallize" the capital gains exemption. The purpose of this maneuver is to ensure that the benefits of the capital gains exemption – in the form of an increased cost base of the qualifying small business corporation shares – will be available in the future.

Although the crystallization methodology may differ, all methods involve purposely triggering a capital gain by effecting a disposition of the shares in question. Assuming that the shares qualify for the exemption, the gain would be "covered" by the available exemption. The result of the disposition would be to "bump the cost base" of the shares in question.

When an individual sells shares of a qualified small business corporation, the capital gain may qualify for the $750,000 capital gains deduction. The end result could be a significant reduction or elimination of the tax on the sale of the shares. It is a very powerful tax incentive. However, there are many criteria that need to be met in order for the gain to qualify for the enhanced capital gains deduction.

An individual may hold shares of a professional corporation that have increased in value, and for which the gain may qualify for the enhanced capital gains deduction, if they were to be sold today. However, the individual may not be in a position to sell those shares today and there may be some real concerns that the gain will not qualify for the enhanced capital gains deduction when they are sold at a later date. In this case, it may be a good idea to crystallize the capital gains deduction. The individual undertakes a series of steps that trigger a gain on the shares today without actually giving up ownership of the shares. The resulting gain, that is triggered, is reported on the individual's personal tax return, and is offset by the enhanced capital gains deduction. The series of transactions increases the tax cost of the shares in question by the crystallization amount. When the shares are actually sold at a later date, the gain will not qualify for the enhanced capital gains deduction, but the amount of tax paid at that later date would be substantially reduced, or eliminated, because the tax cost of the shares would have already been increased as a result of the crystallization.

The main reason that individuals crystallize their shares is fear that the enhanced capital gains deduction will be reduced or eliminated. By crystallizing the gain now, you are effectively locking it in so regardless of the rules being changed, you have already taken advantage of this tax-reducing opportunity.

Working After You Have Sold Your Practice

Occasionally, people are asked to stay on after the sale of the practice. This can be beneficial to everyone during the transition period. It also provides a unique planning opportunity depending on which jurisdiction you live in.

If you were able to sell the shares of your professional corporation, the name would have been changed to that of the new doctor. This will allow you to set up a new professional corporation that can be used when you go back as an associate.

If you live in a jurisdiction that allows your spouse to be a shareholder, you can set up the new professional corporation to flow income out to them. Depending on the distribution of assets at retirement you may pay out most of that income to your spouse through the use of dividends.

If you can't have a spouse as a shareholder, it may still be advantageous to set up a new professional corporation because you can have your associate income taxed at the lower corporate rates. This net income could be left in your new professional corporation as long as you want, up to and beyond death. If you have the proceeds from the sale of your practice as well as RRSPs, you can coordinate the movement of money from the new professional corporation to your personal account. If you don't need the money in your professional corporation, you can invest it inside and remove it later.

RRSPs are taxable as income. In the year of death they are fully taxable if left to anyone other than a spouse (there are a few exceptions). This can result in a huge tax liability on death. In an ideal world, people would die with nothing left in their RRSPs. This would result in less tax payable at death.

With the ability to keep money in a new professional corporation, you can draw down on your RRSPs while accumulating money inside this new company. The idea is to maintain this company as an investment after retirement. Working as an associate will create income without building up practice assets. You would never sell the shares of your new professional corporation because the only assets it would have would be investment assets.

Re: Is it worth setting up a PC if you're only doing locums?
From: Lange Zhu
To: tim@tpcfinancial.com

Hi Tim

The dentist I bought my practice from wants to come back and work locums. He was thinking about setting up another PC. Can he do that?

Lange

Re: Re: Is it worth setting up a PC if you're only doing locums?
From: tim@tpcfinancial.com
To: Lange Zhu

Hi Lange

The short answer is that he can, but I'm not sure it makes sense. How many hours is he planning on working?

Oh, and has he started receiving CPP yet?

If he is receiving it and comes back to work he can be paid personally, and doesn't have to contribute. If he isn't yet collecting CPP he will have to pay it on any money he earns, unless the money is paid to a new PC, and he doesn't take it out as a salary.

I think it still comes back to the cost benefit of incorporating a new PC. If he's only working a little I don't think it would justify the costs of setting one up and maintaining it.

If he wants me to look at his particular circumstances have him contact me and I'll see what makes sense in his case.

Tim

CHAPTER FOURTEEN

Working With a Financial Planner

Before you rush out and begin looking for a financial planner, you should first understand what a financial planner is. But, before I tell you what they are, I'll tell you what they're not. A financial planner is not someone whose sole focus is to sell you stuff. A financial planner is someone who uses a very carefully defined series of steps to evaluate and recognize the financial needs of their clients. They are well versed in areas such as estate and will planning, investment planning, risk management, cash flow management and tax. They should not be used independently but to complement the services provided by lawyers, accountants, tax specialists, bankers, insurance agents and investment advisors. Often, they may act as one or more of these individuals.

What if you already have a financial planner? Well, before you skip this section, take the following test. Ask yourself whether your financial planner carries out the six duties listed below. Does he or she:

1. collect data essential to your needs
2. identify your goals and objectives
3. identify your financial needs
4. develop a comprehensive written plan by analyzing your situation and recommending appropriate action
5. help you implement the plan
6. conduct periodic reviews of your plan's progress and results?

Most financial planners don't carry out every step and even if you think that your advisor does, you need to ask yourself whether he or she is doing so in a limited way and focusing purely on your investment and retirement projections. You are not getting your money's worth if your financial planner is not providing you with a comprehensive plan that clearly maps out your financial future in its entirety. You need to be able to chart your future and follow a plan that will keep you on course and which allows for adjustments to be made as time passes and your situation changes.

Working with a financial planner can bring to light financial opportunities that might otherwise go unnoticed. Professionals who were trained through the military, for example, have had their education paid for by the military in exchange for service to the military after graduation. In some cases, the service is sufficient enough to give them a pension immediately upon discharge. When they leave the military they often go into private practice. How they set up their professional corporation can greatly influence the outcome of their ultimate retirement. If you add all their practice income on top of their pension income you can end up with the majority of their total income taxed at the high personal rate.

A professional corporation allows you to control the amount of income you are personally going to pay tax on in the current year. You can supplement the pension you are receiving by taking dividends, or wages, from your professional corporation. In addition (if allowed), you can pay dividends or wages to your spouse or children. Any money not required in the current year can be left in the professional corporation to accumulate. This money can then be paid out at a later date.

You should now be able to determine if you are truly working with a financial planner. If you're not, I would encourage you to go and find one. There are many capable planners in this country and I hope you have the opportunity to work with one. Feel free to take this book with you and ask if they use such a process. Remember, you have a right to this service – demand it.

Working With A Financial Coordinator

In the first edition of Professional Corporations – The Secret to Success I used the section above to explain what you should expect from your financial planner. I've decided to include it again but add a twist. The twist is the use of a professional coordinator.

For the last 20 years I've struggled to describe what I, and my company TPC Financial Group Ltd., does. When asked, I used to reply, "I'm a financial planner" which usually resulted in a response such as, "I already have one."

When you examine the financial services industry almost everyone claims to be a financial planner. It has become such a generic term that it really doesn't mean much.

Years ago I decided to change my occupation classification from financial planner to financial manager. When I started to tell people I was a financial manager they usually asked, "What's a financial manager?" Although there's no such industry classification as financial manager, it did give me an opportunity to explain that we didn't just create financial plans for people, we actually helped with the implementation and follow through of those plans. Financial management I'd explain, results in direct interaction with other professionals and advisors. For example, we don't just tell people they should have their wills revised or written but we actually work with their lawyer to make sure their wills are written the way the client wants. We work directly with the clients' other advisors too. In my mind it's this direct interaction that separates us from those who call themselves financial planners.

Today, when people ask me what I do, or what TPC Financial Group Ltd. does, I tell them we're professional coordinators. It's not a recognized occupation as such, but I do believe it more accurately describes what we do.

As I think about the thousands of people I've met over the last 30 years, all have had one thing in common – they all have multiple professional relationships. That is two or more professional relationships, with the most common ones being: banker, accountant, lawyer, insurance broker and investment advisor. In each case the individual has to decide to what extent they are personally going to be involved in dealing with these people. Our clients are highly educated, so they are capable of learning just about anything. If any of them really wanted to learn how to write a will, or do their own corporate tax return, they could. The question is would it be a good use of their time and energy?

When I started financial planning I followed the six steps as described by the Financial Planning Standards Council. When it got to helping with implementation, I would become very involved with the insurance and investment part of the plan, but was not involved with the banking or legal parts. At that time I thought it was the responsibility of the client or their banker or lawyer to work on those areas. However, what I discovered was that not all lawyers are good at drafting wills, not all accountants know about tax planning and not all bankers are working in their clients' best interest. The reason I started to get involved in these areas was because my clients rarely knew a good will from a bad one, or whether there was a better deal available at another bank.

Today, I have a team of people who are dedicated to providing an integrated planning service. We coordinate our clients' advisors and work on their behalf to make sure they are getting the most complete and objective advice. Think of it as financial planning on steroids.

The TPC Process

I thought it would be helpful if I explained my company's process so you can use it as an example of the type of service you deserve. This process has been developed over 30 years and will continue to be refined for the benefit of our clients.

F.O.O.T. PRINTS TECHNOLOGY ™

We call our method F.O.O.T. Prints Technology, which stands for Financial Outlook Of Tomorrow. Before we take on any new client they must agree to participate in the entire process. Like you, we will not recommend treatment without a thorough examination and history. If a step is missed, or a shortcut taken, the result can be a missed opportunity which can mean lost investment dollars or unnecessary taxation.

The nine processes of F.O.O.T. Prints are:

1. discovery
2. information assimilation
3. clarification
4. integration
5. opportunity maximization
6. turnkey
7. time recovery
8. accountability
9. refinement.

Each process is designed to integrate the personal with the corporate. Let's look at the processes in more detail.

The discovery process

The discovery process is used as an initial introduction to TPC Financial Group Ltd. and our system. We begin by sending out an information package prior to the first meeting; it includes information about what to expect, the types of information we are going to require, and general information about financial planning.

The primary objective of this first meeting is to meet the client and introduce the planning process. If the clients wish to proceed with the planning process we provide them with a confidentiality agreement that outlines exactly what we are going to be doing with the information they provide us with.

The information assimilation process

Clients are asked to fill out a two-part questionnaire that includes a cash flow statement and personal information. They are then asked to provide us with the following information:

- Assets
    - property assessment notices – principal residence, vacation or rental property
    - current statement of all investment holdings, RRSPs, including on-line brokerage accounts
    - bank accounts
    - vehicles, jewellery, and art that would be considered an investment
    - list of any other assets not included above.

- Income
    - current pay stub showing all deductions
    - spouse and children
    - pension statements from any employer pension plan, and most recent CPP statement – client and spouse.

- Liabilities
  - mortgage statement
  - personal loan statement
  - line of credit statement
  - RRSP loans
  - loan guaranteed
  - corporate loan statement and details.

- Legal
  - copy of wills and powers of attorney
  - separation and/or divorce agreements
  - prenuptial and/or cohabitation agreements
  - trust agreements
  - lease agreements.

- Corporate
  - corporate tax returns for two previous years
  - corporate financial statements for two previous years
  - copy of minute book or outline of corporate structure
  - shareholder, cost-sharing, or associate agreement.

- Insurance policies
  - life insurance
  - disability insurance
  - critical illness insurance
  - long-term care insurance
  - overhead insurance
  - general insurance including liability.

Re: Inquiry into your services
From: Dr. Greg Koper
To: tim@tpcfinancial.com

Hi Tim

My name is Greg Koper, I got your name from Sven. He
was telling me some of the things you do for him and
I was wondering if you could tell me a bit more about
what you do?

Specifically, why do you need so much information to
work with someone? My advisors don't ask for everything
Sven tells me he's given you. I may be interested in
working with you but I'm concerned about giving that
much information to one person.

I look forward to hearing from you.

Greg

Re: Re: Inquiry into your services
From: tim@tpcfinancial.com
To: Dr. Greg Koper

Hello Greg

First of all, thank-you for your interest in TPC
Financial Group Ltd.

Before I answer your question specifically, let me ask
you a question.

When you first meet a new patient do you listen to
their reason for being there and prescribe something,
or do you work up a history? I suppose that's a loaded
question because, if it's not an emergency and you're
not working at a walk-in clinic, you'd probably like a
complete history if you were going to treat someone.
For us, it's basically the same thing.

If someone comes to us with an emergency we deal with
the emergency. If someone wants us to look at a specific
problem then we can look at that particular issue, but
if we're going to take on a new client for the long-

term we want to have as complete a picture of their circumstances as we can get.

The reason we work the way we do is because I figured out a long time ago that most people aren't getting the most from their professional corporations because their affairs aren't coordinated. The accountant is only looking at certain things; the lawyer is looking at different things. The investment advisor is focused on the investments they manage and the insurance advisor is looking for opportunities to sell insurance. Add a banker or two into the mix and you have a whole lot of balls in the air at the same time.

Gathering up all the information in these different areas allows us to determine what things are being missed, or perhaps not working as well as they could. If you're only working with one banker you may be getting the best deal, but how do you know for sure? We work with all the various banking institutions, so we know what's out there. This holds true for all the advisors you work with. The $64 million question is - are you getting the best possible advice from all these people?

If you are getting the best advice, and everything is working for you, then we won't advise change for change's sake. All we do initially is gather up all the relevant information and see if everything is working in harmony, and in your best interest; if it is that's great. However, if it's not we'll tell you exactly how we can help you and what the cost will be. You decide at that point whether it makes sense to work with us.

I'd be happy to send you out an information kit, if you'd like some more information. Or, feel free to call me toll free at 1.888.315.0058.

Tim

Clarification process

The clarification process takes place during the second meeting. Any additional information requested is gathered at this time, including:

- draft copies of net worth statements and cash flow statements are reviewed for accuracy
- goals and objectives are developed
- a contract of engagement is reviewed and signed by both the clients and myself
- the contract of engagement details what we are being hired to do and what our fee structure is for performing those services.

Integration process

- We follow up with other advisors, if necessary, for additional information. This will include the client's accountant, lawyer, banker, insurance agent or investment advisor.
- Data input is finished and the financial plan is completed.
- Strategies are identified to help achieve goals.
- A financial plan policy statement is completed that details the necessary steps to achieve financial goals.
- All tax and legal documents are reviewed.
- Draft plans are reviewed with other financial advisors at the client's request.

Opportunity maximization process

The third appointment is for presentation of the completed financial plan. The financial plan will include the following statements:

- net worth
- investment holding statement
- income tax performance
- cash flow
- objectives
- insurance summary
- disability analysis

- estate analysis
- asset allocation
- retirement projection – current scenario
- recommendations for:
    - estate planning
    - bank management
    - corporate planning
    - investment planning
    - tax planning
    - risk management
    - cash flow management
- retirement projection – proposed scenario.

Turnkey process

Think of a franchise. When you buy one, everything is done for you. You don't have to go it alone; you have the franchiser to help you. This is the stage where everything is pulled together; we go through every change with the client and the plan is implemented. We then review and sign a disclosure document with the client that explains exactly how we are going to be paid for the work we do and discloses all sources of revenue. We then set out priorities and timelines, address urgent concerns and establish expectations and frequency of meetings.

Time recovery process

We work in twelve-month cycles. Everything that we are going to do during the next twelve months is scheduled; this is done with our planning schedule. We establish secondary relationships, if necessary, to bring in a tax or trust lawyer or perhaps a banker or tax accountant. We set up electronic files for each client that include all their financial information for easy access.

We also encourage our clients to call us in case of emergency. The whole idea behind time recovery is simple – we do anything we can to free up valuable time for our clients. For example, say you are planning to purchase a car in two years' time. Tomorrow the engine falls out of your car and you need a new car now. Should you buy it, lease it, or finance it? Buy it personally or corporately? Simple – call us. You go find the car you want and let us (and your accountant) work out the best way to buy it. That's time recovery!

Accountability process

Having a financial plan is of little use if you don't implement it and monitor it. Have you ever wondered if a decision you previously made was the right one? What if you had left everything as it was? What if you made other choices? We review the entire financial plan once a year and compare our progress with the previous year. About six weeks prior to the annual review we send out a detailed request for any information that we might not have, as well as changes in cash flow requirements and objectives. This information is then added to our database and a new financial plan is prepared and new strategies are worked out for discussion.

- During the annual review meeting we:
- present an annual report
- review objectives
- evaluate progress
- review cash flow
- review mortgage and loan details
- review risk management issues.

Refinement progress

Living on the Pacific coast allows me the opportunity to watch ships as they sail by. To sail from Canada to Japan is not just a matter of going due west until you see the other side and then hanging a right. Rather it's a series of thousands of minor adjustments. It's the same with a financial plan. You continually need to make a number of small course corrections to deal with what life throws at you. We use the refinement process to make these adjustments. The refinement process includes:

- discussing necessary changes to the financial plan
- implementing necessary changes to the financial plan
- reviewing multi-generational planning
- preparing an annual schedule.

As you can see, this is a very comprehensive approach to financial planning. If you now review the six steps to financial planning we mentioned earlier, you'll see how we covered them using our F.O.O.T. Prints Technology. We:

- collected data essential to the client's needs
- identified the client's goals and objectives
- identified the client's financial needs
- developed a comprehensive written plan by analyzing the client's situation and recommending appropriate action
- implemented the plan
- conducted periodic reviews of the plan's progress and results.

When I work with someone I make it a requirement that they go through each step of the process. Drafting a financial plan is only the beginning. Execution and review are the keys to success.

When I produce a financial plan I take the current situation and set up a model to show the results one can anticipate if you carry on with your current path. Then, after reviewing all the information, I make recommendations that are designed to maximize opportunities, eliminate dangers, and build on the individual's strengths before developing a second model that shows the anticipated outcome, if the recommended changes are made. This sets benchmarks for us to use in the future.

If clients make changes at a later date, we can monitor the outcome by comparing them to the original benchmarks. These plans are constantly reviewed to ensure that adjustments are made to address new circumstances.

The purpose of the entire process is to be proactive by planning. Most people review their financial lives as a history lesson. This year's tax return shows you what you personally did last year. This year's corporate financial statement shows you what your corporation did last year. This month's investment statements show you what you did last month.

Postscript

If you have spent any amount of time with this book, you will have realized a few very important things. First, that incorporating your practice can potentially save you hundreds of thousands of dollars. Second, that the rules and regulations surrounding taxation are as complex and often indecipherable as James Joyce's book Ulysses. Third, but certainly not least, relying on the array of financial advisors you have working on your behalf to always know what they are talking about, and what course of action is in your best interests, may be wishful thinking.

I believe the most significant thing I've discovered over the last 30 years is that most Canadians believe that the people they're working with are the best and that they are being taken good care of by their financial advisors. Unfortunately, for most, this simply isn't the case.

I'd like to leave you with a few thoughts. Did you know:

- most financial advice is being delivered to Canadians by salespeople
- most accountants don't spend time planning with their clients
- most lawyers don't understand tax planning
- most bankers won't refer you somewhere else, even if it's in your best interest to do so
- the very organizations that are charged with the responsibility of protecting you, are more interested in protecting themselves.

These are just some of the issues I discuss in my new book "The Financial Navigator – A Professional's Guide to Keeping More of What you Earn.

Oh, I should also mention that Sven and Lange continue to be successful practitioners in their respective fields. They are both clients, of course, and continue to email me regularly. We chat occasionally on the telephone, although now we more often Skype each other. Since the first edition of this book was published in 2004, social networking has changed the way people connect with each other, and Mike, my collaborator on this book, has encouraged me to set up Facebook and LinkedIn pages and to open a Twitter account. Through these new mediums I'm going to discuss the issues and challenges people put to me, and generally try to be a source of up to date information on all the things we talk about in this book. So, search for me on the social network sites if you'd like to keep ahead of the game when it comes to keeping more of what you earn.

In the meantime, consider my top eleven reasons why you may not be getting the most out of your professional corporation and keeping more of what you earn. These points are discussed in my new book coming in 2011.

11. Not taking advantage of the CDA

10. Putting money into a tax-free savings account when you shouldn't

9. Having your investment opportunities restricted

8. Not using your will effectively

7. Not using eligible dividends

6. Having the wrong type of income

5. Buying RRSPs when you shouldn't

4. Not income-splitting properly

3. Making decisions with partial information

2. Thinking everything is being done properly when you don't really know

1. Not knowing how much things really cost

Glossary

ABIL (Allowable Business Investment Loss)	An ABIL is a capital loss that is incurred on very specific types of assets, namely shares or debt of a small business corporation. Whereas a normal capital loss is of limited use because it can only be deducted against capital gains, an ABIL can be used to offset any type of income.
Accrual	An accrual is done at the end of an accounting period to record costs that have been incurred but not paid for or previously recorded, and to record revenue that has been earned but not received or previously recorded. In contrast to the cash basis of accounting, expenses do not have to be paid to be deductible, nor does income have to be received to be taxable. Unearned income (e.g., prepaid interest and rent) generally is taxed in the year of receipt, regardless of the method of accounting used by the taxpayer.
Accumulated Depreciation	The total of all depreciation that has been written off over the years against fixed assets.
Add-Back	Amounts that are added back to your corporate income when your tax return is filed.
Adjusted Cost Base (ACB)	Adjusted cost base (ACB) includes the original purchase price and all costs related to the purchase of an item. The adjusted cost base of an investment in securities would include the purchase price as well as any commissions paid. The adjusted cost base of a fixed asset such as equipment includes installation costs, customs brokerage and legal fees and any other costs expended to get the asset into operation. The adjusted cost base of a rental property would include any repair or renovations that cannot be expensed for tax purposes, such as a new roof, new appliances, etc. There may be costs related to any fixed asset (for instance, major repairs that extend the life of the asset) that must be added to the adjusted cost base instead of being expensed.

Amortization	Amortization is the gradual expensing of an asset over a number of years instead of expensing it in the year of purchase. Usually relates to intangible assets such as goodwill. Depreciation is the term used for amortization of a fixed asset.
Arm's Length	Two people, or entities, are said to be dealing at arm's length with each other if they are independent, and one does not have undue influence over the other. However, the *Income Tax Act* deems some people NOT to be at arm's length with each other (non-arm's length). This is the case with "related persons," who are individuals connected by blood relationship, marriage or common-law partnership or adoption." Blood relationships do not normally include aunts, uncles, nieces, nephews or cousins for purposes of the *Income Tax Act*.
Articles of Incorporation	Every corporation has articles of incorporation, a document prepared by the people creating the corporation. This document sets out the structure and purpose of the corporation, and specifies rules that the corporation must follow regarding issuing or transferring shares, electing officers, conducting general meetings, voting of members, borrowing funds, paying dividends and other corporate functions.
Assets	Assets are items owned by or owed to a company or individual, such as cash and investments, inventories, prepaid expenses, accounts receivable, fixed assets (land, buildings, machinery and equipment), and intangible assets (goodwill, intellectual property). Assets are generally shown at cost on a balance sheet.
	Fixed assets and intangible assets are shown at book value (cost less accumulated depreciation or amortization). Land is a fixed asset that is not depreciated.
Attribution Rules	Rules under the *Income Tax Act* provide that, where property is transferred, directly or through a trust, for the benefit of a spouse or certain minor children, the income (and in some cases, capital gains) on that property may be deemed to be income or gains of the transferor and not the transferee. This guarantees that the tax burden for the property is retained by the transferor rather than being passed to the transferee.

Balance Sheet	A balance sheet is part of the financial statements. The balance sheet reports the amounts of assets, liabilities, and owners' equity at a specific date. The total of all assets is always equal to the total of liabilities plus owners' equity. This is a function of the double-entry accounting system.
Benefit Period	The time during which benefits are paid under an insurance contract. The benefit period may be a fixed term, for example five years, or to a specific age like 65.
Book Value (of an asset)	The book value of fixed assets is original cost less accumulated depreciation.
Capital Cost Allowance (CCA)	This is the depreciation that is allowed to be expensed for tax purposes. Different types of assets are allocated to different CCA classes, and each class has its own rate for capital cost allowance. For instance, most automobiles would be class 10, which is allowed to be expensed at 30% per year on a declining balance basis. In most cases, the CCA allowed in the year an asset is purchased is only 50% of the normal amount. Thus, the class 10 CCA would be 15% in the first year.
Capital Dividend Account	A notional account where untaxed gains are deposited within a private company. These untaxed gains are usually distributed to shareholders or owners without additional tax liability. Capital dividends can arise as a result of the tax-free portion of a capital gain, or the proceeds of a life insurance policy minus its adjusted cost base.
Capital Gain or Loss	Gain or loss resulting from the sale of a capital asset, such as stocks, bonds, art, stamp collections, and real estate (other than a principal residence).
Cash Basis Accounting	Under the cash basis for preparing accounting records, the revenues and expenses are recorded when the revenues are received and the expenses are paid. Using the accrual basis, revenues and costs are recorded in the accounting period in which they occur, even if the revenue has not been received or the costs have not been paid.
Cash Flow Statement	The cash flow statement is a financial statement that reports the reasons for changes in cash balances for a period of time. It provides details of changes in cash balances resulting from operating activities, financing activities, and investing activities.

CCPC (Canadian Controlled Private Corporation)	A CCPC is a corporation that is private (i.e., it does not have shares listed on a stock exchange). The corporation must also be controlled by Canadian resident shareholders. For this purpose, control is generally meant to mean possession of a majority of the votes to elect the board of directors. Other concepts do come into play, so it is not as simple as it seems.
CRA	Canada Revenue Agency formerly Revenue Canada
CNIL (Cumulative Net Investment Loss)	CNIL is a concept that applies only to individuals. When an individual realizes a capital gain on shares of a qualified small business corporation, that gain may qualify for the $750,000 enhanced capital gains deduction. Not only do the shares that are sold have to meet the very strict definition of a qualified small business corporation, the amount is reduced by a CNIL balance. The CNIL balance is the sum of an individual's investment expenses claimed from 1988 onward and is reduced by the sum of an individual's investment income from 1988 onward. Investment expenses include deductions claimed for interest expenses and investment counsel fees, rental losses and limited partnership losses. Investment income includes interest income, dividend income, limited partnership income and net rental income.
Common Shares	When a company is formed, common shares are purchased by investors who then become shareholders in the corporation, and usually hold voting privileges. Common shareholders elect directors and vote on matters that require the approval of the owners of the company. If a corporation is liquidated, the common shareholders have the right to a share of the assets of the corporation, after any prior claims on the corporation have been settled. A corporation may authorize an unlimited number of common shares to be issued, so that they may raise funds in the future by issuing more shares.
Cost Basis (stocks)	The cost basis is calculated separately for each security owned. It is the total cost of all shares owned and is divided by the total number of shares owned to get the cost basis per share, or weighted average cost per share. This cost per share is used in calculating any capital gains or losses when some or all of the shares are sold.

Current Assets	These are assets that are expected to be either consumed or converted to cash within one year, or are able to be readily converted to cash. Examples are accounts receivable, inventories, short-term investments, and prepaid expenses such as insurance.
Current Liabilities	These are debts that are due to be paid within one year, such as accounts payable, accrued liabilities, and the portion of long term debt that is due within one year.
Deemed Disposition	A capital gain or loss normally occurs when a property is actually sold. However, there are instances where a property may be deemed to be sold, that is, you must treat the situation as if you have actually sold the asset. Types of deemed dispositions: • Securities are transferred from a non-registered investment account into an RRSP. In this case, the deemed proceeds will be the market value of the securities at the time of transfer to the RRSP. Note that if a loss has occurred in the transfer to an RRSP, it will be considered a superficial loss and will not be deductible for tax purposes. • Property is gifted to a third party. In this case, the property is deemed to have been sold at its fair market value at that time. • Use of property changes from personal use to business or investment use, or vice versa. Again, the property is deemed to have been sold at its fair market value. An example is a personal residence converted to a rental property, or a rental property converted to a personal residence. • A taxpayer ceases to be a resident of Canada for tax purposes. Certain properties are excluded, and in some cases where capital gains occur, a tax payment can be delayed until the property is sold. • When an individual dies, all of their capital property is deemed to have been sold immediately prior to death.
Defined Benefit Pension Plan	A retirement plan that uses a specific predetermined formula to calculate the amount of an employee's future benefit. The amount contributed to the plan depends on the amount required to meet the future obligation.

Defined Contribution Pension Plan	A registered pension plan that does not promise an employee a specific benefit upon retirement. Benefits depend on the performance of investments made to the plan. The contributions are set, not the benefit.
Depreciation	Depreciation is the expensing, over a period of years, of the cost of fixed assets; usually based on the estimated useful life of the fixed asset. There are various methods of depreciation, with two of the most common being straight line and declining balance.

Straight-line depreciation – the original cost of the asset is written off in equal amounts over the estimated useful life. Example: equipment with an estimated useful life of five years, original cost $50,000. Straight-line depreciation amount = $50,000/5 or $10,000 per year.

Declining balance depreciation – a fixed percentage is applied to the remaining book value each year to determine the deprecation amount. Example: equipment with an estimated useful life of five years, original cost $50,000 assuming depreciation rate of 40%

Year	Depreciation expense	Accumulated depreciation	Book value
1	50,000 x 40% = 20,000	20,000	30,000
2	30,000 x 40% = 12,000	32,000	18,000
3	18,000 x 40% = 7,200	39,200	10,800
4	10,800 x 40% = 4,320	43,520	6,480
5	6,480 x 40% = 2,592	46,112	3,888

This continues each year, and of course the book value never gets to zero. When fixed assets are depreciated for tax purposes, the depreciation is called a capital cost allowance (CCA), and the method of depreciation is usually declining balance, using a rate designated by the *Income Tax Act* and regulations.

Dividend	An amount distributed out of a company's retained earnings (accumulated profits) to shareholders. Dividends on preferred shares will usually be for a fixed amount. Dividends on common shares may fluctuate depending on the profits of the company. Some companies pay dividends on common shares, and some do not.
Dividend Tax Credit	An income tax credit available to investors who earn dividend income through investments in the shares of Canadian corporations.
Effective Tax Rate	The amount of tax you pay as a percentage of your taxable income. A single person earning $40,000 who pays $9,369 in income tax has an effective tax rate of 23.42% ($9,369 divided by $40,000 times 100).
Elimination Period	A type of deductible; the length of time the individual must pay for covered services before the insurance company will begin to make payments. The longer the elimination period, the lower the premium.
Eligible Dividend	An eligible dividend is any taxable dividend paid, after 2005, to a resident of Canada by a Canadian corporation that is designated by that corporation to be an eligible dividend. A corporation's capacity to pay eligible dividends depends mostly on its status.
Family Trust	A trust that has family members as its beneficiaries. However, non-family members can also be in the trust.
Financial Statements	These usually consist of a balance sheet, income statement, cash flow statement, and notes to the financial statements.
Fiscal Year	An accounting period of 365 days (366 in leap years), but not necessary starting on January 1.
Fixed Assets	Also called property, plant and equipment. These are assets that have a long life and can include land, buildings, machinery and equipment.

Freeze	A freeze is a process by which a client takes steps to stop or limit the future growth of their assets and provides for future growth to accrue to the benefit of their spouse or children. An estate freeze is normally accomplished by the transfer of capital assets into a company in exchange for preferred shares in the company and a promissory note, or by the exchange of common shares in a company for preferred shares having a redemption value equal to the fair market value of the common shares. When holding shares of an existing company, a freeze can be accomplished by reorganizing the capital or stock dividends.
General Rate Income Pool (GRIP)	A balance, generally reflecting taxable income that has not benefited from the small business deduction or any other special tax rate - without incurring Part III.1 tax.
Goodwill	When one corporation acquires another, goodwill (an intangible asset) will be shown on the purchaser's balance sheet if the purchaser pays more than the agreed-upon value of the fixed assets acquired. Goodwill is calculated as the total cost of the acquired corporation minus the agreed-upon value of the assets acquired minus liabilities assumed. Beginning in 2002, the value of goodwill on the balance sheet need not be written down unless it is determined that there has been an impairment in the value of the goodwill.
Gross Up	Eligible dividends - to add 45% to the amount of dividends received, and show the total income from dividends on your tax return ($1,000 of actual eligible dividends receive would be reported on your tax return as $1,450). Other than eligible dividends - to add 25% to the amount of dividends received, and show the total income from dividends on your tax return ($1,000 of actual eligible dividends received would be reported on your tax return as $1,250).
Income Statement	An income statement is part of the financial statement of a business. The income statement reports the net income of the business for a period of time, showing the total income, operating expenses, general and administrative expenses, interest expense, income tax expense, and extraordinary expenses. The financial statements of a business are normally prepared monthly, although they may be prepared less often.

Intangible Assets	An asset having no physical substance, such as goodwill. Intangible assets are recorded at cost on the balance sheet. That cost must be reviewed annually to determine if its current value is less than the cost in which case the value would be written down on the balance sheet. Due to this change in accounting rules, corporate net earnings will likely be increased over prior years, as will earnings per share.
Interest Offset	An individual is entitled to interest offset on deficient tax instalment payments if they prepay subsequent payments or overpay the amount they were required to pay. However, early payment of instalments will not generate refundable interest. Therefore, if you underpay, you can either pay subsequent instalments early or over pay them and get interest on those payments, that can be used to offset interest charged by the CRA on the underpaid amount.
Intestate	A person who dies without a valid will is said to die intestate or in intestacy.
Liabilities	Amounts owed. These may be current, which means due to be paid within one year, or they may be long term, which means not due for at least one year.
Locked-in RRSP	RRSP set up to receive funds transferred from a registered pension plan on the condition that it is used solely for retirement income purposes.
Marginal Tax Rate	The ratio of the increase in tax to the increase in the tax base (i.e., the tax rate on each additional dollar of income). A single individual earning $40,000 who experiences a $1,000 increase in income and has to pay an additional $452 in income tax has a marginal tax rate of 45.2 per cent ($452 divided by $1,000).
Net Income	The part of income remaining after all expenses and taxes have been paid; also called net profit.
Outstanding Shares	Shares that a company has sold and issued to shareholders; also called "issued" shares.
Periodic Payments	Regular payments, usually monthly, quarterly, semi-annual or annual.
Preferred Shares	Preferred shares are a class of corporate capital stock that normally holds priority over common shares in dividend payments and in distribution of the corporate assets in a liquidation.

Prepaid Expenses	A prepaid expense occurs when services or supplies are purchased but not used by the end of the accounting period.
	For example, the term of insurance is normally one year or longer. Thus, if the term is one year but the insurance payment date is not at the end of the fiscal year, then a portion of the insurance cost applies to the next fiscal year. At the end of the year this portion will show on the balance sheet as a prepaid expense.
Prescribed Interest Rate	The prescribed interest rate is set by the Bank of Canada every three months and is used primarily for three tasks.
	1. The prescribed interest rate is used to calculate interest on taxes owing to the CRA. Currently the actual amount of interest to make this calculation is 5%.
	2. The prescribed rate is used to calculate interest on overpayments of tax. This is the amount that the CRA will pay you if they owe you money. Currently the actual amount of interest to make this calculation is 3%.
	3. The prescribed rate is used to calculate taxable benefits to employees and to ensure that related parties are acting on a third-party basis to determine interest rates.
	The actual rate is based on the average yield of 90-day T-bills sold at auction during the first month of every quarter and is currently 1%.
Private Corporation	Shares of a private corporation are not publicly traded on a stock exchange. This includes shares of a professional corporation.
Retained Earnings/ Accumulated Deficit	The net income, or net profit, generated by a company each year is transferred to retained earnings, which is a part of shareholders' equity on the balance sheet. Retained earnings are the accumulated profits of the company, and show as a positive amount on the balance sheet. If the company has accumulated losses instead of profits, this is called an accumulated deficit, and shows up as a negative amount on the balance sheet.

Revenue	The amount of sales, rental, interest and other income earned by a business. The revenue of a business is reported on the income statement.
Rollover	Rollover is a tax expression and is not defined in the *Income Tax Act*. A rollover is any transaction that takes place on a tax-deferred basis.
	For example, when an individual dies, all of their assets are disposed of at fair market value for tax purposes, leading to a potentially significant tax liability. If the deceased's assets pass to their spouse on death, there is no fair market value deemed disposition. Instead, the assets pass to the surviving spouse at their tax cost, and no tax consequences result at death. The tax consequences are deferred and will only occur when the surviving spouse dies or the assets are actually sold. This would be an example of a spousal rollover at death.
	There are certain provisions of the *Income Tax Act* that allow assets to be transferred at their tax cost. Let's say you personally own your practice that you bought for $300,000, but it is now worth $400,000. Section 85 of the *Income Tax Act* would allow you to transfer these assets to a Canadian corporation (professional corporation) at their tax cost, allowing the shares to be disposed of without triggering a capital gain in your hands. The corporation would inherit your $300,000 ACB (adjusted cost base), and it would be the corporation that would realize the capital gain if the practice is sold for $400,000.
RRIF (Registered Retirement Income Fund)	RRIFs are funds for individuals, established at financial institutions and registered under the *Income Tax Act*, that provide income in retirement. RRIFs are established by directly transferring monies from RRSPs or from lump-sum payments from registered pension plans. Amounts withdrawn from RRIFs are taxable. A minimum amount must be withdrawn from a RRIF each year; beginning in the year after the RRIF is established.
	RRIF's can be set up at any time prior to age 72. Minimum withdrawal requirements are based on age.
Shareholder	A shareholder owns shares in a corporation. The shareholders are the owners of a corporation.
Tax Credit	A tax credit reduces the actual amount of tax that must be paid.

Tax Deduction	A deduction, such as an RRSP deposit or interest expense, is used to reduce taxable income.
Tax Spouse	A tax spouse can be someone who an individual is legally married to, or is living with, of either the same or opposite gender and for whom at least one of the following applies. • is the natural or adoptive parent (legal or in fact) of the individual's child • has been living with and having a relationship with the individual for at least 12 continuous months; or • lived with the individual as the individual's spouse or common-law partner for at least 12 continuous months.
Vesting	Vesting is the non-forfeitable ownership (or partial ownership) rights by an employee of the retirement account balances, or benefits, contributed on the employees' behalf by an employer.

Appendix A

2011 Corporate Tax Rates

This table shows the different rates for various incomes inside a professional corporation. Interest and net rental are subject to the highest corporate tax rates. Active business income (active income) is taxed at the lowest corporate rate.

	Interest	Net Rental Income	Capital Gains	Active Business Income
British Columbia	44.67%	45.7%	22.33%	13.5%
Alberta	44.67	44.7	22.33	14.0
Saskatchewan	46.67	46.7	23.33	15.5
Manitoba	46.67	47.2	23.33	11.0*
Ontario	46.42	48.7	23.21	15.5
Quebec	46.57	46.6	23.28	19.0
New Brunswick	45.17	47.2	22.58	16.0
Nova Scotia	50.67	50.7	25.33	16.0*
Newfoundland	48.67	48.7	24.33	15.0
Yukon	49.67	49.7	24.83	15.0*
Northwest Territories	46.17	46.2	23.08	15.0
Nunavut	46.67	46.7	23.33	15.0
Prince Edward Island	50.67	50.7	25.33	12.0

* Rate applicable to the small business deduction limit of $400,000

Consider the following example using a personal top tax rate of 45 per cent and a corporate tax rate of 20 per cent. As a professional, you earn $200,000 per year. After reviewing your cash flow requirements you determine that you need $8,000 per month, net after tax. As a sole proprietor you would pay tax personally on the entire $200,000 leaving you with $132,000. If you subtract your living requirement of $96,000 ($8,000 x 12) you would have $36,000 left to invest.

If that same $200,000 was earned inside your professional corporation, you could take wages of $140,000 leaving you with $96,000 net for personal use and the balance of $60,000 could be left inside the professional corporation to be taxed at the lower corporate rate.

The after-tax difference of $48,000, inside the professional corporation, allows for an increased amount of funds available for investments.

Appendix B

2011 Individual (Combined Federal and Provincial) Marginal Tax Rates for Wages, Salary, Interest and Net Rental Income

The following chart shows the various federal, provincial and territorial tax brackets. The federal tax brackets are shown on the top line. At the bottom of the chart you will see the different provincial and territorial tax brackets. Because the two don't always match, it creates a number of different tax rates as shown. For example the three rates shown in British Columbia's second bracket (29.7 per cent, 32.5 per cent, 34.29 per cent). This is a result of the second federal tax bracket being $41,545 - $83,088 and British Columbia's brackets being slightly different.

	1st Bracket	2nd Bracket	3rd Bracket	Top Bracket
Federal	First $41,544	$41,545 - $83,088	$83,089 - $128,800	Over $128,800
	15%	22%	26%	29%
British Columbia	20.06/22.07%	29.7/32.5/34.29%	38.29/40.7%	43.7%
Alberta	25%	32%	36%	39%
Saskatchewan	26/28%	35%	39/41%	44%
Manitoba	28.8/27.75%	34.75/39.4%	43.4%	46.4%
Ontario	20.05/24.15%	31.15/32.98/ 35.39/39.41%	43.41%	46.41%
Quebec	28.53/32.53%	38.37/42.37%	45.71%	48.22%
New Brunswick	24.1/27.1%	34.1/34.4%	38.4/38.7%	41.7%
Nova Scotia	23.79/29.95%	36.95/38.67%	42.67/43.5%	46.5/50%
Prince Edward Island	24.8/28.8%	35.8/38.7%	42.7/44.37%	47.37%
Newfoundland	22.7/27.5%	34.5/35.3%	39.3%	42.3%
Yukon	22.04%	31.68/32.16%	38.01%	42.4%
Northwest Territories	20.9/23.6%	30.6/34.2%	38.2/40.05%	43.05%
Nunavut	19/22%	29/31%	35%	40.5%

Federal Brackets

$0 - $41,544 (first bracket)

$41,545 - $83,088 (second bracket)

$83,089 - $128,800 (third bracket)

Over $128,800 (top bracket)

British Columbia

$0 - $36,146 (first bracket)

$35,147 - $41,544 (second bracket)

$41,545 - $72,293 (third bracket)

$72,294 - $83,001 (fourth bracket)

$83,002 - $83,088 (fifth bracket)

$83,089 - $100,787 (sixth bracket)

$100,789 - $128,800 (seventh bracket)

Over $128,800 (top bracket)

Alberta

$0 - $41,544 (first bracket)

$41,545 - $83,088 (second bracket)

$83,089 - $128,800 (third bracket)

Over $128,800 (top bracket)

Saskatchewan

$0 - $40,919 (first bracket)

$40,920 - $41,544 (second bracket)

$41,545 - $83,088 (third bracket)

$83,089 - $116,911 (fourth bracket)

$116,912 - $128,800 (fifth bracket)

Over $128,800 (top bracket)

Manitoba

$0 - $31,000 (first bracket)

$31,001 - $41,544 (second bracket)

$41,545 - $67,000 (third bracket)

$67,011 - $83,088 (fourth bracket)

$83,089 - $128,800 (fifth bracket)

Over $128,800 (top bracket)

Ontario

$0 - $37,774 (first bracket)

$37,775 - $41,544 (second bracket)

$41,545 - $66,514 (third bracket)

$66,515 - $75,550 (fourth bracket)

$75,551 - $78,361 (fifth bracket)

$78,362 - $83,088 (sixth bracket)

$83,089 - $128,800 (seventh bracket)

Over $128,800 (top bracket)

Quebec

$0 - $39,060 (first bracket)

$39,061 - $41,544 (second bracket)

$41,545 - $78,120 (third bracket)

$78,121 - $83,088 (fourth bracket)

$83,089 - $128,800 (fifth bracket)

Over $128,800 (top bracket)

New Brunswick

$0 - $37,150 (first bracket)

$37,151 - $41,544 (second bracket)

$41,545 - $74,300 (third bracket)

$74,301 - $83,088 (fourth bracket)

$83,089 - $120,796 (fifth bracket)

$120,797 - $128,800 (sixth bracket)

Over $128,800 (top bracket)

Nova Scotia

$0 - $29,590 (first bracket)

$29,591 - $41,544 (second bracket)

$41,545 - $59,180 (third bracket)

$59,181 - $83,088 (fourth bracket)

$83,089 - $93,000 (fifth bracket)

$93,001 - $128,800 (sixth bracket)

$128,801 - $150,000 (seventh bracket)

Over $150,000 (top bracket)

Prince Edward Island

$0 - $31,984 (first bracket)

$31,985 - $41,544 (second bracket)

$41,545 – 63,969 (third bracket)

$63,970 - $83,088 (fourth bracket)

$83,089 - $98,145 (fifth bracket)

$98,146 - $128,800 (sixth bracket)

Over $128,800 (top bracket)

Newfoundland

$0 - $31,904 (first bracket)

$31,905 - $41,544 (second bracket)

$41,545 - $63,807 (third bracket)

$63,808 - $83,088 (fourth bracket)

$83,089 - $128,800 (fifth bracket)

Over $128,800 (top bracket)

Yukon

$0 - $41,544 (first bracket)

$41,545 - $80,966 (second bracket)

$80,967 - $83,088 (third bracket)

$83,089 - $128,800 (fourth bracket)

Over $128,800 (top bracket)

Northwest Territories

$0 – 37,626 (first bracket)

$37,627 - $41,544 (second bracket)

$41,545 – $75,253 (third bracket)

$75,254 - $83,088 (fourth bracket)

$83,089 - $122,345 (fifth bracket)

$122,346 - $128,800 (sixth bracket)

Over $128,800 (top bracket)

Nunavut

$0 - $39,612 (first bracket)

$39,613 - $41,544 (second bracket)

$41,545 - $79,224 (third bracket)

$79,225 - $83,088 (fourth bracket)

$83,089 - $128,800 (fifth bracket)

Over $128,800 (top bracket)

Appendix C

2011 Individual Marginal Tax Rates for Capital Gains

The following table shows the different tax rates for capital gains reported personally. Capital gains are taxed preferred because only 50 per cent of the gain has to be reported as income.

	1st Bracket	2nd Bracket	3rd Bracket	Top Bracket
Federal	First $41,544	$41,545 to $83,088	$83,089 to $128,800	$128,801 and over
British Columbia	10.03/11.04%	14.85/16.31/17.3%	19.3/20.4%	21.9%
Alberta	12.5%	16%	18%	19.5%
Saskatchewan	13/14%	17.5%	19.5/20.5%	22%
Manitoba	14.4/13.9%	17.4%	21.7%	23.2%
Ontario	10.1/12.2%	15.6/16.5/17.7/19.7%	21.7%	23.2%
Quebec	14.3/16.3%	21.2%	22.9%	24.1%
New Brunswick	12.1/13.6%	17.1/17.2%	19.2/19.4%	20.9%
Nova Scotia	11.9/15%	18.5.19.4%	21.34/21.8%	23.3/25%
P. E. I.	12.4/14.4%	17.9/19.4%	21.4/22.2%	23.7%
Newfoundland	11.4/13.8%	17.3/17.7%	16.7%	21.2%
Yukon	11.2%	15.9/16.0%	19%	21.2%
Northwest Territories	10.5/11.8%	15.3/17.1%	19.1/20%	21.5%
Nunavut	9.5/11%	14.5/16.5%	17.5%	20.2%

Appendix D

2011 Individual Marginal Tax Rates for Other Than Eligible Dividends

The following table shows the different tax rates for dividend income reported personally. Dividends are also tax preferred as a result of the dividend tax credit.

	1st Bracket	2nd Bracket	3rd Bracket	Top Bracket
Federal	First $41,544	$41,545 to $83,088	$83,089 to $128,800	$128,801 and over
British Columbia	4.2/7.5%	16.2/19.7%	22/27/30%	33.7%
Alberta	10.2%	19%	24%	27.7%
Saskatchewan	8.3/10.9%	19.6%	24.6/27%	30.8%
Manitoba	13.4/15.8%	24.6/30.4%	35.4%	39.2%
Ontario	2.8/7.9%	16.7/17.8/20.9%	23.8/28.8%	32.6%
Quebec	11.7/16.7%	24/29%	33.2%	36.4%
New Brunswick	6.8/10.6%	19.3/19.7%	24.7/25%	28.9%
Nova Scotia	3.5/11.2%	19.9/22%	27/28%	31.8%
P. E. I.	13/18%	26.9/30.5%	35.5/37.4%	41.2%
Newfoundland	5.5/11.5%	20.2/21.2%	26.2%	30%
Yukon	5.3%	17.4/17.7%	25%	30.5%
Northwest Territories	2/5.4%	14.1/18.6%	23.6/25.9%	29.7%
Nunavut	2.1/5.9%	14.6/17.1%	22.1%	29%

Appendix E

2011 Individual Marginal Tax Rates for Eligible Dividends

The following table shows the different tax rates for dividend income reported personally. Dividends are also tax preferred as a result of the dividend tax credit.

	1st Bracket	2nd Bracket	3rd Bracket	Top Bracket
Federal	First $41,544	$41,545 to $83,088	$83,089 to $128,800	$128,801 and over
British Columbia	-9.4/-5.7%	4.2/8.1/10.7%	16.3/19.7%	23.9%
Alberta	-2%	7.9%	13.5%	17.8%
Saskatchewan	-2/.8%	10.7%	16.3/19.2%	23.4%
Manitoba	-2.3/.5%	10.3/16.9%	22.5%	26.8%
Ontario	-4/1.9%	11.8/12.5/ 15.9/18.3%	24%	28.2%
Quebec	4.1/9.8%	18/23.6%	28.3%	31.9%
New Brunswick	-6.1/-1.9%	8/8.4%	14.1/14.5%	18.7%
Nova Scotia	-1.3/7.4%	17.3/19.7%	25.3/26.5%	30.7/35.63%*
P. E. I.	-3/2.7%	12.5/16.6%	22.3/23.1%	27.4%
Newfoundland	-6.7/.1%	10/11.1%	16.8%	21%
Yukon	-6.7/7%	7%	15.2%	21.4%
Northwest Territories	-8.9/-5.1%	4.8/9.9%	15.5/18.1%	22.4%
Nunavut	-4.6/-.4%	9.5/12.4%	18%	25.8%

* Over $150,000

Appendix F

Provincial and Territorial Divisions of the Canadian Medical Association

British Columbia Medical Association

115 – 1665 Broadway West
Vancouver, BC V6J 5A4
Telephone: 604 736-5551
Fax: 604 736-4566
www.bcma.org

Alberta Medical Association

400 – 12230 106 Avenue NW
Edmonton, AB T5N 3Z1
Telephone: 780 482-2626
Fax: 780 482-5445
Email: amamial@albertadoctors.org
www.albertadoctors.org

Saskatchewan Medical Association

402 – 321A 21st Street East
Hong Kong Bank Building
Saskatoon, SK S7K 0C1
Telephone: 306 244-2196
Fax: 306 653-1631
Email: sma@sma.sk.ca
www.sma.sk.ca

Manitoba Medical Association

20 Desjardins Drive
Winnipeg, Manitoba R3X 0E8
Telephone: 204-985-5888
Toll-Free: 1-888-322-4242
Fax: 204-985-5844
www.docsmb.org

Ontario Medical Association

300 – 525 University Avenue
Toronto ON M5G 2K7
Telephone: 416 599-2580
Fax: 416 599-9309
Web Site: www.oma.org

Quebec Medical Association

660 – 1000, rue de la Gauchetiere ouest
Montreal QC H3B 4W5
Telephone: 514 866-0660
Fax: 514 866-0670
Email: admin@amq.ca
Web site: www.amq.ca

New Brunswick Medical Society

176 York Street
Fredericton NB E3B 3N7
Telephone: 506 458-8860
Fax: 506 458-9853
Email: nbms@nbnet.nb.ca
Web site: www.nbms.nb.ca

Medical Society of Nova Scotia

5 Spectacle Lake Drive
City of Lakes Business Park
Dartmouth NS B3B 1X7
Telephone: 902 468-1866
Fax: 902 468-6578
Web site: www.doctorsns.com

Medical Society of Prince Edward Island

3 Myrtle Street
Stratford PE C1B 1P4
Telephone: 902 368-7303
Fax: 902 566-3934
Email: mspei@mspei.pe.ca
Web site: www.mspei.pe.ca

Newfoundland and Labrador Medical Association

164 MacDonald Drive
St. John's NF A1A 4B3
Telephone: 709 726-7424
Fax: 709 726-7525
Email: nima@nlma.nf.ca
Web site: www.nima.nf.ca

Yukon Medical Association

#5 Hospital Road
Whitehorse YT Y1A 3H7
Telephone: 867 633-3294
Fax: 867 633-3294
Email: yma@yukondoctors.ca
Web site: www.yukondoctors.ca

Northwest Territories Medical Association

PO Box 1732
Yellowknife NT X1A 2P3
Telephone and Fax: 867 920-4575
Web site: www.nwtma.ca

Canadian Dental Association – Provincial Dental Regulatory Authority

College of Dental Surgeons of British Columbia
Registrar
500 – 1765 West 8th Avenue
Vancouver BC V6J 5C6
Telephone: 604 736-3621
Fax: 604 734-9448
Web Site: www.cdsbc.org

Alberta Dental Association and College

Registrar
101 – 8230 105th Street
Edmonton, AB T6E 5H9
Telephone: 780 432-1012
Fax: 780 433-4864
Web Site: wwwabda.ab.ca

College of Dental Surgeons of Saskatchewan

Registrar
202 – 728 Spadina Crescent East
Saskatoon SK S7K 4H7
Telephone: 306 244-5072
Fax: 306 244-2476
Web Site: www.saskdentists.com

Manitoba Dental Association

Registrar
103 – 698 Corydon Avenue
Winnipeg MB R3M 0X9
Telephone: 204 988-5300
Fax: 204 988-5310
Web Site: www.manitobadentist.ca

Royal College of Dental Surgeons of Ontario

Registrar
6 Crescent Road
Toronto ON M4W 1T1
Telephone: 416 961-6555
Fax: 416 961-5814
Email: info@rcdso.org
Web Site: www.rcdso.org

Order of Dentists of Quebec

15e etage, 625 boulevard Réné Lévesque Ouest
Montreal QC H3B 1R2
Telephone: 514 875-8511
Fax: 514 393-9248
Web Site: www.ordredesdentistesduquebec.qc.ca

New Brunswick Dental Society

Registrar
#820 – 520 King Street – Carleton Place
PO Box 488 – Station 'A'
Fredericton, NB E3B 4Z9
Telephone: 506 452-8575
Fax: 506 452-1872
Web Site: nbdental.com

Provincial Dental Board of Nova Scotia

Registrar
102 – 1559 Brunswick Street
Halifax NS B3J 2G1
Telephone: 902 420-0083
Fax: 902 492-0301
Email: admins@pdbns.ca
Web Site: www.pdbns.ca

Dental Council of Prince Edward Island

Registrar
184 Belvedere Avenue
Charlottetown PEI C1A 2Z1
Telephone: 902 892-4470
Web Site: www.dapei.ca

Newfoundland Dental Board

Registrar
6th Floor, The Fortis Building
139 Water Street
St. John's NL A1C 1B2
Telephone: 709 579-2391
Fax: 709 579-2392
Web Site: www.nlda.net

Government of Yukon

Department of Community Services
Yukon Consumer Services
Box 2703 C-5
Whitehorse, YT Y1A 2C6
Telephone: 867 667-5111
Fax: 867 667 – 3609
Email: consumer@gov.yk.ca
Web Site: www.gov.yk.ca

Government of Northwest Territories

Safety and Public Services
Registrar, Dental Profession
Yellowknife NWT X1A 2L9
Telephone: 867 920-8058
Fax: 867 873-0272
Web Site: www.gov.nt.ca

Nunavut Registrar's Office

P.O. Box 390
Kuglukpuk, NU X0B 0E0
Telephone: 867 982-7668
Fax: 867 982-3256
Email: kharvey@gov.nu.ca

Appendix G

Resources for Hiring Employees

Provincial Employment Standards web sites

British Columbia
Web Site: www.labour.gov.bc.ca/esb/esaguide/

Alberta
Web Site: www.employment.alberta.ca

Saskatchewan
Web Site: www.labour.gov.sk.ca/standards/index.htm

Manitoba
Web Site: www.gov.mb.ca/labour/standards/

Ontario
Web Site: www.labour.gov.on.ca/english/es/

Quebec
Web Site: www.publicationsduquebec.gouv.qc.ca/home.php#

New Brunswick
Web Site: www.gnb.ca/0062/acts/acts/e-07-2.htm

Nova Scotia
Web Site: www.gov.ns.ca/legislature/legc/statutes/labourst.htm

Prince Edward Island
Web Site: www.gov.pe.ca/commcul/lair-info/index.php3

Newfoundland

Web Site: www.nlimmigration.ca/media/2839/employmentstandards.pdf

Yukon

Web Site: www.gov.yk.ca/legislation/acts/emst.pdf

Northwest Territories

Web Site: www.justice.gov.nt.ca/pdf/acts/employment%20standards.pdf

Government of Canada

Business Start-up information:

Web Site: www.canadabusiness.ca/eng/125/

Human Resource **Management inform**ation:
www.hrmanagement.gc.ca/gol/hrmanagement/site.nsf/eng/index.html

Human Rights

Human Rights in British Columbia. British Columbia Ministry of Attorney General, Policy, Planning and Legislation Branch. April, 2003

www.llbc.leg.bc.ca/public/pubdocs/bcdocs/361555/protectdiscrimination.pdf

Other Resources

Butteriss, Margaret. *Help Wanted: The Complete Guide to Human Resources for Canadian Entrepreneurs*. Wiley, Toronto. 1999

Gomex-Meija, Luis, with David B. Balkin, Robert L Cardy, and David E. Dimick. *Managing Human Resources*. Prentice Hall. Scarborough, Ontario. 2000.

Association of Dental Surgeons of British Columbia (ADSBC)
400 – 1765 West 8th Ave., Vancouver, BC, V6J 5C6
www.bcdental.com

Index

D

deemed disposition 279, 325
Deferred Profit Sharing Plan
    (DPSP) 265
defined benefit pension Plan 325
defined contribution pension plan 326
dependent life insurance 126
depreciation 326
disability benefits 215
disability insurance 134
discretionary trust 228
discrimination in hiring and
    employment practices 114
dividend 327
dividend resolutions 170
dividends 180
dividend tax credit 327
divorce and separation 242

E

education amount 52
effective tax rate 327
eligible dividend 327
eligible dividends 180
elimination period 327
employee profit sharing plans 263
employment agreements 117
Employment Insurance (EI) 100
employment standards 103
excluded employment 99

F

family education 257
family trust 233, 327
financial coordinator 308
financial planner 307
financial statements 172, 327
fiscal year 64, 327
fixed assets 327
freeze 328
Future Insurance Guarantee
    (FIG) 138

G

general rate income pool 181
General Rate Income Pool
    (GRIP) 328
Goods and Services Tax (GST) 96
goodwill 82, 328
gross up 328
group benefits 152

H

harassment in the workplace 115
Harmonized Sales Tax (HST) 96
health and welfare trusts 186
health care profession rider 142
hiring employees 116
holding companies 221
home offices 199
human resources 97
Human Rights Legislation 114

I

income beneficiary 226
income-splitting 181, 289
income statement 328
independent contractor 98
individual pension plans 204
instalments 167
intangible assets 329
interest deductibility 86
interest offset 329
inter vivos trust 227
intestate 329
irrevocable trust 228

J

joint life insurance 132
jury duty or court leave 113

K

kiddie tax 228

Professional Corporations:
The Secret to Success (new edition 2011)

To order additional copies of this book please call us at the toll free number below or mail or fax the following information to:

TPC Financial Group Limited
760 Hillside Ave.
Victoria, BC, V8T 1Z6

Toll Free: 888.315.0058
Fax: 886-822-0078
Email: info@tpcfinancial.com
www.tpcfinancial.com

Contact Information

Name: _____

Company Name:_____

Telephone: _____

Email: _____

Pricing

	Unit Price
Professional Corporations	$49.95
GST/HST 5%	$2.50
Sub-total	$52.45
Shipping & Handling	$22.55
Total per book inc. shipping	$75.00

Order Form

No. of Copies*	Unit Price (inc. taxes and shipping)	Total
	$75.00	

For more than 3 copies please call for a quote.

Payment Method

❏ Visa   ❏ MasterCard   ❏ Cheque*

For more than 3 copies please call for a quote.

Account Number _____

Expiry Date_____ 3-digit security code_____

Name on Card _____

Signature_____

Let Us Keep You Up To Date!

Professional Corporations: The Secret to Success (new edition 2011)

If you would like to receive regular updates on the information contained in Professional Corporations please email us at info@tpcfinancial.com and put in the subject line: PC-2011 Free Update Service.

Reserve Your Signed Copy of Tim's New Book

The Financial Navigator: The Professional's Guide to Keeping More of What You Earn

If you would like a signed copy of Tim's new book due to be published summer 2011, please provide the following information by email, telephone or snail mail to:

TPC Financial Group Limited
760 Hillside Ave.
Victoria, BC, V8T 1Z6

Toll Free: 888.315.0058
Email: info@tpcfinancial.com
www.tpcfinancial.com

Contact Information

Name: _____

Company Name: _____

Telephone: _____

Email: _____

A Sneak Peek
At The Financial Navigator by Tim Paziuk

Here are a few pages from chapter one of my new book, The Financial Navigator: A Professional's Guide to Keeping More of What You Earn, which will be published early summer 2011.

Money is a funny thing. Everyone has it and everyone assumes they know how to handle it. But when you look real close it's frightening how the odds of successfully managing it are stacked against you. Banks, insurance companies or investment firms are not working totally altruistically for you; they are working for, or responsible to their shareholders, and themselves.

It's really simple to get lost in the financial jungle. I hope with this book I can help navigate you past some of the raging rapids and dangerous detours so you have a safer, smoother journey on the road to financial independence.

Chapter One – Trading and Collecting Marbles

Before I made the decision to add this chapter I was contemplating writing a whole new book called Trading Marbles. But at the end of the day I decided that it was important, in terms of context, to start The Financial Navigator with some background about our neighbor to the south's financial situation.

The United States is over $12 trillion in debt. At the present time they are paying about $52 million a day in interest. I haven't read or heard one thing about how they're going to pay this off. I'm very concerned about how this is going to play out, and you should be too.

Conservative estimates put the real US National Debt at $56.4 trillion (according to Peter G. Peterson Foundation[1]). It's important to understand how this number is calculated because, believe it or not, it's going to affect you.

So, let's look at how they came up with $56.4 trillion. First, there are the federal government's known liabilities, which it is legally obligated to fulfill. These include publically held debt, military and civil pensions and retiree health benefits. As of September 30, 2008, these liabilities added up to $13.5 trillion.

Then there are various commitments and contingencies – i.e. contractual requirements that government is expected to fulfill, when and if specified conditions are met. These include federal insurance payouts, loan guarantees and leases. As of September 30, 2008, these liabilities added up to $1.4 trillion.

So, you may be asking, where does the remaining $43 trillion or so come from? It's what the government of the United States has promised to pay in Social Security and Medicare benefits in excess of projected revenues. As of January 1, 2008, current and promised future Social Security benefits amounted to $6.6 trillion. And between Medicare's three programs (hospital insurance, outpatient, and prescription drugs), current and future promised Medicare benefits amount to $36.3 trillion. You can now see why current and future health care reform in the United States is so important.

To further expand your awareness of the problem let's look at a fundamental difference between Canada and the United States, specifically the Canada Pension Plan (CPP) and U.S. Social Security.

Prior to 1997, all excess CPP contributions were invested in federal government bonds. Government bonds of course are a type of I.O.U. You give me money today (principal) so I can spend it and I'll give it back to you in the future (maturity date) with interest (yield).

Since 1997 excess contributions are invested similar to the way the Ontario Teachers Pension invests their funds. As of March 31, 2008 the CPP "fund" was invested 62.7% in equities (23.5% Canadian and 39.2% Foreign), 24.3% Fixed Income, 1.3% Absolute Return Strategies and 11.7% Inflation-Sensitive Assets (5.6% Real Estate, 3.9% Inflation-Linked Bonds and 2.2%

---

1   If you've never heard of "The Peter G. Foundation" you should take a few minutes and look them up on the Internet. They're trying to educate both the public and politicians about the actual fiscal problems in the United States.

Infrastructure). As of 30 September 2009 the CPP fund was valued at $123.8 Billion.

Contrast this with the U.S. Social Security Trust Fund. The total amount of "real" assets invested in the Social Security Trust Fund is zero. All surplus Social Security premiums are being replaced by I.O.U.'s from the United States government. If you haven't seen it yet you should take the time to rent the movie I.O.U.S.A. It really is an eye opener.

Many people believe that the bulk of U.S. debt is owed to foreigners. This is not the case; according to the U.S. Department of the Treasury about a quarter of the total national debt is held by foreigners. The majority is owed to Americans.

As an example: an estimated 100 federal and state pension plans are unfunded. This means that the government has effectively issued I.O.U.'s to employees and retired workers. These obligations can only be funded by future revenue.

As if this problem isn't bad enough, think about this. For the last number of years the average American has been a net spender not a net saver. Savings rates in the United States have been negative. That means that the average American was spending more than they made. However, over the last couple of years the savings rate in the US has been increasing. The reason quite simply, is fear. At the same time the American people are starting to clean up their act, the US government is on a spending spree. To raise money to spend, the US government either issues debt (bonds and T-bills) or prints money. At a time when stock markets are swinging crazily up and down, where do you think Americans are putting their money? Well, a lot of it is going into US bonds and T-bills (directly, or through money market and bond funds). Can you see where this is going? In order to pay back the money they borrow, the US government is going to have to raise taxes or print money. If they increase taxes who's paying the bill? The answer is easy, the very people who lent them the money in the first place. If on the other hand they print more money, they'll be paying back the public with devalued dollars. Ironic isn't it?

Before I go any further I should tell you why I'm spending all this time talking about what's going on in the United States. It's about self-preservation; if they collapse under the weight of their debt it's going to affect us here in Canada.

Now, I'm no economist but it's pretty obvious to me that you can't keep borrowing from yourself. It simply doesn't make sense. And, even if I could borrow from myself then obviously I'd at some point have to pay myself back. It doesn't take an economics degree to see that, that is just crazy.

Now, let's extrapolate this thinking a little. Imagine your parents spend all their money and die in debt. Is it your responsibility to pay off their debts? Is it your children's responsibility to pay off their grandparent's debts? Of course it's not. Neither you, nor your children, have legal responsibility to pay for your parent's debts. That's the law in both Canada and the United States.

So, why is it that when a government goes into debt using the money to benefit today's population, you and your children, and your children's children become legally responsible for those debts? I'm sorry but this just isn't morally, or ethically right. I certainly don't want to leave my children and grandchildren in financial ruin. Today, especially in this current economic environment, we have to protect ourselves, because we sure as heck can't rely on the government to do it for us.

I feel this rant isn't quite over, so let me throw another example of the "harvest now, and ignore the future" mentality that exists in government today. How many people would agree that it's morally acceptable to give birth to a child so that you can eventually harvest its' organs to help you survive? It's unthinkable isn't it?

So, why is it that we think nothing of having children only to enslave them in debt so that we may live a healthier and more prosperous life? Future generations, including young people alive today, have no say in the liabilities we are creating for them. Yet we as responsible adults seem to have no concern for their future suffering. We don't want our taxes raised by 10 or 20 per cent, but we don't seem to care that they'll end up paying for it. Isn't the definition of a successful life, leaving things better for our children and grand children?

Okay, the detour's over, let's get back to the United States debt problems.

We are constantly reminded that the problem isn't "that" bad because the national debt only represents a portion of the GDP (Gross Domestic Product). At the end of 2009 the U.S. national debt was estimated to be 83.41% of GDP. Interest on the debt uses up about 13% of all federal revenue.

The question is, is owing 83.41% of GDP a big or small problem? Personally, I think it's a big problem, because if you look at what makes up the GDP you will see that you are comparing real debt owing with imaginary productivity.

So let's define what GDP really is.

GDP is the monetary value of all the finished goods and services produced within a country's borders within a specific time period (GDP is usually calculated on an annual basis). It includes all private and public consumption, government outlays, investments and exports, less imports, that occur within a defined territory.

That sounds impressive, but what's included in finished goods and services? If General Electric manufactures a new jet engine at its factory in Batesville, Mississippi and sells it to Airbus of France the resulting transaction will show up in the GDP figures. This to me represents a finished good. So what about a "finished" service?

In 2009, the U.S. government bailed out Chrysler. The estimated legal fees in the entire restructuring process were $200 million. This figure would show up in the GDP figures as a finished service.

Look at Fannie Mae (which few Canadians had heard of until recently); they put out a bunch of sub-prime mortgages and in turn package them up and sell them to Bear Sterns. That financial transaction shows up in the GDP. Bear Sterns changes the wrapping and sells them to some unsuspecting pension manager and that financial transaction shows up in the GDP. It doesn't matter that the whole thing is smoke and mirrors. As money passes hands it all adds to the GDP. But aren't those all the same dollars? I'm being a little simplistic again here, but the point is that the government can twist any and all indicators to project whatever spin they want. Here's a big statement: In my opinion, debt as a percentage of GDP is a useless comparison.

Back to the United States being in big trouble; it's been said before that if the U.S. catches a cold we sneeze. It may be a cliché but it's true. It is vital that we start positioning ourselves, so we are at least somewhat insulated if they go down; the truth of the matter is that we need to start building our own personal arks well before the flood occurs.

In 2009, the U.S. unemployment rate went above 10 per cent. In Canada it stayed below that figure. Some people might look at this positively and say that means about 90 per cent of eligible workers are working. And that even in a "recession" the vast majority of people are working. But, what happens when a depression hits, or a country goes bankrupt? Does that put the majority of people out of work? The simple answer is no, during the Great Depression in the U.S. unemployment rose to about 25 per cent. In other countries it went as high as 33 per cent. That still means that the majority of people were working. Countries go on and citizens continue with their lives.

The last time I was in the United States I didn't see people on mass moving out of their homes and moving into tents. Yes, some people are losing their houses but the thing is, many of these people should never have been incentivized to buy property in the first place.

Last year (2009) saw Iceland go bankrupt. In 476 A.D. the Roman Empire went "bankrupt". But, there are still people working and living in Iceland and Italy. Just because a country goes bankrupt doesn't mean that everyone is out of work and homeless. Arguably a country can't go bankrupt, because the government can just print more money to pay off its debtors. Unfortunately though, this results in the value of money decreasing, which leads us back to the root of the problem. The United States is going to have to increase revenue and decrease expenses, in the same way we manage a basic household budget. In order to increase revenue the government is going to have to increase taxes. How high I don't know, but in the past they have been as high as 94 per cent. No, that's not a misprint – it happened in 1944-1945. More recently, in 1963, the top marginal rate was 91 per cent.

What's happened over the last 50 years is that the top marginal rates have come down and the tax base has widened. In 1963, the top marginal rate of 91 per cent was applied on income in excess of $400,000. In 2009, the top US federal tax rate was 35 per cent on income above $372,950. As we move into the future I can see the U.S. government increasing the top rate and decreasing the top bracket threshold. I'm sure that the American people are not going to be too thrilled with this, but it has to happen. At the same time the government is going to have to decrease expenses, primarily Medicare and Social Security benefits. This is very dangerous financial triple play, if you're a politician.

...to be continued in The Financial Navigator by Tim Paziuk